A Cultural History

Crypto-Jews
The Long Journey

Frontispiece
Ibn Sushan Synagogue
Confiscated by the Catholic Church
Renamed Santa Maria La Blanca
Toledo, Spain

Ron Duncan Hart

Crypto-Jews
The Long Journey

Institute for Tolerance Studies
Tolerance and Diversity Series

Institute for Tolerance Studies
www.tolerancestudies.org

Crypto-Jews: The Long Journey. Ron Duncan Hart. Copyright 2020. All rights reserved. This publication is in copyright. Subject to statutory exception and to the provisions of relevant collective licensing agreements, no reproduction of any part may be made without the written permission of the Institute for Tolerance Studies, except for brief quotations included in analytical articles, chapters, and reviews. For permissions, group pricing, and other information contact Gaon Books, P.O. Box 23924, Santa Fe, NM 87502 or write (admin@tolerancestudies.org). www.tolerancestudies.org

Manufactured in the United States of America.

The paper used in this publication is acid free and meets all ANSI (American National Standards for Information Sciences) standards for archival quality paper. All wood product components used in this book are Sustainable Forest Initiative (SFI) certified.

First edition

Library of Congress Cataloging-in-Publication Data

Names: Duncan Hart, Ron, author.
Title: Crypto-Jews : the Long Journey / Ron Duncan Hart.
Description: Santa Fe, NM : Institute for Tolerance Studies/Gaon Books, 2020. | Includes bibliographical references and index. |
Identifiers: LCCN 2020002186 (print) | LCCN 2020002187 (ebook) | ISBN 9781935604839 (paperback) | ISBN 9781935604846 (cloth) | ISBN 9781935604853 (ebook)
Subjects: LCSH: Marranos--United States--History. | Crypto-Jews--Latin America--History | Marranos--Religious life. | Jews--Identity.
Classification: LCC E184.36.E84 D86 2020 (print) | LCC E184.36.E84 (ebook) | DDC 305.892/4073--dc23
LC record available at https://lccn.loc.gov/2020002186
LC ebook record available at https://lccn.loc.gov/2020002187

Table of Contents

An Introduction	9
Part I Being Jewish	13
1. Somos Judios (We are Jews)	15
Part II Jewish Conversos in Spain and Portugal	35
2. Origins of Jewish Conversos	37
3. Forced Conversions and Crypto-Jews	51
4. Inquisition and Expulsion	69
Part III From Spain to the Americas	87
5. Sephardic Diaspora	89
6. The Grand Conspiracy: Fear of Jews and Protestants	103
Part IV United States and Mexico	121
7. Crypto-Jews in New Spain 1520-1650	123
8. Secret Santa Fe: Jewish Conversos in New Mexico	137
9. Oral Tradition, Folklore, and the Arts	149
Part V The Jewish Identity Movement	163
10. Reframing Jewish Identity	165
11. Jewish Identity Movement	179
12. Hidden Traditions	191
Notes	203
Acknowledgments	217
About the Author	219
Glossary	221
Recommended Readings and Films	223
List of Figures	225
Bibliography	227
Index	245

Dedicated
to those who stand against
intolerance, anti-Semitism, racism and bigotry

An Introduction

What did the medieval Spanish have against the Jews? Religion and Otherness? In that Catholic world Jews were heretics, and they had customs and language that became foreign as Spain redefined itself as Christian only. Jews no longer fit in New Christian Spain, and the Spanish reacted by expelling them. Those who wanted to stay became a pariah class of people who were Spanish in language and culture but tainted by Jewishness. Even converting to Catholicism could not cleanse the mark from them. They were still suspected of being Jews, crypto-Jews.

Why did crypto-Jews defy the Inquisition and the threat of death to continue Jewish lives in Catholic only Spain? Was it the inescapability of being chosen? Was it the bond of spirit that overcame the collective enmity? Why do descendants 500 years later still carry the mark? Is it family, collective mind, DNA, primal gestalt, history, culture? Can we know?

In Spanish the phrase "La Ley de Moises", the Law of Moses, means the Torah, the five books of Moses. The Inquisition arrested conversos and crypto-Jews for practicing the teachings of "La Ley de Moises" or the Torah.

The crypto-Jewish experience has been shrouded in mystery for a past that might have been and the imagined future that could be. In the American Southwest and in parts of Latin America there is a movement to reclaim Jewish identity, and people are describing remnants of Jewish life in their families even though their ancestors renounced Jewishness long ago. People want to learn about the Sepharad of their ancestors, the Spain of the Jews. Many ask, "What is our place in that heritage." Others simply say, "Somos Judios." We are Jews.

Inquisition records are often the only information we have about crypto-Jews. We lack information about what they thought about their religious identity and what their Jewishness meant. Investigating their past is more like archaeology than history because conversos left few traces of their lives as Jews. Invisibility was the shell that protected them. We have cultural fragments in the memories of families and in the residue of practices, bits and pieces here and there. With rare exception the only written records are from the Inquisition, which is a suspect source because of its anti-Jewish bias.

Crypto-Jews

When I read cases of people arrested by the *Santo Oficio de la Inquisición* (Holy Office of the Inquisition) for Judaizing, I am always struck by the resoluteness of some to not cooperate in the face of torture in contrast to the readiness of others to talk, perhaps because of fear and pain. Scribes recorded the most minute details down to the long strings of "Ay, ay, ay, ay, ay" of the pain of the prisoner as the Inquisitors ordered another turn of the rack to force the accused Judaizer to answer questions. The Inquisitors were trained prosecutors, and they built cases based on testimony from fellow Judaizers and interviews with the accused themselves.

Twenty-five years ago, I sat in the Archivo Histórico Nacional (National History Archives) in Madrid awaiting the first Inquisition trial transcript that I would read. It was of a midwife in her 80s who was arrested because she had been accused of washing the baptismal water off new babies. When they brought the inches thick stack of parchment bound with a ribbon from a case 500 years old, I sat in silence contemplating what was on the table before me, a life in parchment, bound in ribbon. I saw the vulnerability of an eighty-year-old woman whose years had been dedicated to bringing life into this world, and now the power of life or death over her rested in the hands of these Inquisitors, who were the gatekeepers of Catholic conformity in this land.

It was her third arrest for the same offense, and normally, that would have meant a strong sentence and a prohibition against acting as a midwife for life. But she pleaded age and infirmity, and after a stern rebuke, her case was left in abeyance, not acquitted, but left open like a wound, a threat, a reminder of the power that could be re-activated at any moment. In the thousands of cases against accused Judaizers in Spain and the Americas over the centuries mothers and fathers were arrested because they did not eat pork or maybe they took baths on Friday. Maybe they did not work on Saturday. It was all to erase the taint of Judaism from Christian lands.

In New Mexico I have found that local oral traditions about Jewish family identity or reclaimed Jewish identity can be rich, and there are multiple tracks of inherited beliefs in addition to historical documentation. This book, *Crypto-Jews,* is an attempt to provide a historical baseline of information about those times and draw an outline of what the experience of the descendants of hidden Jews might have been.

An Introduction

I will use the terms *converso*, crypto-Jew, and New Christian to refer to differences of behavior and identity of Jews who converted to Catholicism. New Christian and *converso* are generic terms used to refer to anyone who converted without our knowing how they understood their Jewishness. New Christians were set apart from Old Christians, also called Natural Christians, suggesting that Jewish conversos were unnatural in having accepted Christianity. The term "crypto-Jew" refers to people who converted but continued to think of themselves as Jews and to practice Jewish rituals in private. The term *anusim* (the forced ones) refers to the tens of thousands of people who were coerced into baptism under threat in Spain and Portugal, and many of them continued to identify and practice as Jews. The term Sephardic Jew refers to those who left Spain to live as Jews.

For various reasons information about crypto-Jews largely disappeared from Inquisition records in Spain after 1600 and from Portugal and the Americas after 1650. But elements of Jewish identity did survive, and that is the subject of this book.

In the 1490s Spain tried to rid itself of Jews, and in the 1940s Germany tried to rid itself and Europe of Jews. The Enlightenment and a gap of 450 years separate the two, but the morality was all too familiar. In both instances they destroyed the richest European centers of Jewish life, but the survivors did rebuild. Out of the social wreckage of the Expulsion of Jews and the fires of the Inquisition, Jews of Spanish descent did survive, sometimes in hiding. We will explore this history of their clinging to life and legacy.

In recent decades hundreds and thousands of people have begun searching for the Jewish heritage of their families. This wave of Jewish renewal across the Spanish and Portuguese-speaking Americas is largely in places where there had been Jewish converso populations in the colonial era. Many identify as Jews, and some have returned to Jewish lifestyles, keeping kosher, observing Shabbat, doing Torah study, and living in Jewish communities. This is the Jewish identity movement.

Crypto-Jews: The Long Journey is written to provide information about Jewish conversos and crypto-Jews and the evolution of their experience from Spain and Portugal to what has survived of their heritage among their descendants in the Americas. As an anthropologist, I can write the history and give the background, but the real telling is in the voices of the people. It is their story.

Part 1

Being Jewish

The lives of Jewish conversos and crypto-Jews in the Spanish and Portuguese worlds have been fraught with dissent from the beginning. When a Jew converted to Christianity in Spain, their families and friends would probably have disapproved. If they were suspected of continuing Jewish practices, the Spanish Inquisition would have disapproved. When Spanish-speaking people identify as being Jewish today, they frequently find that family and community members disapprove.

To take on Jewish identity and adopt a Jewish lifestyle requires a commitment. Then, to speak out publicly about that decision to become a Jew is an act of courage. Not all families are opposed, but many are. Descendants of conversos (those who converted) or crypto-Jews (hidden Jews), who reverse the decisions of their ancestors 500 years ago and choose to identify as Jewish today, can find it challenging living in families and communities that are predominantly Christian.

Some descendants of those who suffered pogroms at the hands of the Russians and the Holocaust at the hands of the Germans have asked, "Why would you want to be Jewish?" For those reclaiming Jewish identity from the converso/crypto-Jewish background, the reasons cannot always be easily articulated, but the commitment is there.

Crypto-Jews

Isabelle Medina Sandoval

Marginal Threads

On the fringe I wander
Boundary of periphery
Wondering just where I belong

Trailing Tarshish tzitzit translate
Oye Israel! El Eterno es Nuestro
Dios El Eterno uno es

On the border I ponder
bound by jaded Jews judging my
Judaism juggling their own justice

Rachel's reaching rebozo renders
Hear O Israel Hashem is our God
Hashem the One and Only

Inside the tallit I have rights
Outside the rebozo
I have a right to return

On the outside looking in
On the inside looking out
To other Jews my soul is
in constant state of doubt

Insidious inside
Let me in
Outrageous outside
Let me out

On the edge I stand
Now knowing why
I do not understand

Chapter 1

Somos Judios

SOMOS JUDIOS IS A STATEMENT THAT I HEAR REPEATEDLY from those on the path of Jewish identity in the American Southwest and Latin America. It is an affirmation. "We are Jews." Each one is on their own long journey of return to claim what their ancestors feared to claim, to relearn the life of a Jew, the prayers, the customs that had faded to memories generations before. These are stories of triumph and disappointment, stories of joy and pain, stories of compelling passion and doubt. Each one, who tells their story here, represents thousands more who are on this path or beginning it. The voices heard in these pages give voice to so many more.

It can only be explained in their own words. Here are the voices of a few who publicly say, *Somos Judios*. They have reclaimed this legacy. Each story is unique and personal.

Rabbi Juan Mejia

Rabbi Mejia was born in Colombia and educated in the United States and Israel. He is the coordinator for *Be'chol Lashon* for the American Southwest and lives in Oklahoma City with his wife, who is a rabbi, and their children.

My name is Juan Mejía. I was born to a middle-class Catholic family in Bogotá, Colombia. I was privileged enough to be accepted in an elite Catholic school for boys run by American Benedictine monks, where I learned English and developed a strong sense of vocation and religiosity.

Crypto-Jews

When I was 15, while celebrating Christmas with my family, my grandfather revealed that we had Jewish origins, much to the astonishment of all. He didn't know much, just that in his childhood hacienda the men met twice a day in a special room and prayed with "towels" on their heads from tiny books in a strange language. Later in life when he confronted his relatives concerning the strange traditions of his family, they confessed to him openly that they were, indeed, Jews.

This revelation started me on a journey that would end in Jerusalem many years later. While studying philosophy in the National University of Colombia, I became fascinated with Medieval thought and started to read the works of Maimonides and to find out more about the Jews of Spain and what became of them. The knowledge that the blood in my veins had somehow participated in the splendorous Golden Age of Sefarad made me incredibly proud, although at that time I did not consider the option of conversion.

Only many years later, while taking a backpacking trip across Europe, did I find my way back to the land of my ancestors: I decided to take a detour and visit Israel. There, in the Western Wall, I realized the incredible injustice that had been perpetrated against my family and my heritage. I decided to correct the historical mistake and cheat the Inquisition by converting back to Judaism.

The trip back was not easy. Colombia, unlike America, does not have a thriving and learned community that is willing, albeit sometimes reluctant, to receive converts. One cannot go into a bookstore and buy a siddur as easily as one can do in America. And most important of all, the doors of all the synagogues - Orthodox and liberal alike - are closed to those who come from the outside, either to learn Torah or to worship. Only through the indefatigable efforts of a wonderful member of the Conservative synagogue in Bogota, a ger tzedek himself, was I able after a couple of years to see the inside of a synagogue. Meanwhile I studied on my own and read voraciously. With the help of my Ancient Greek teacher I started to teach myself Biblical Hebrew. I had a friend in America buy me a tallit, and I started to pray regularly on my own. I started to keep kashrut and got more and more involved in my observance of Shabbat.

Fortunately, Hashem was very gracious to me. As soon as I finished my undergraduate studies, I earned a scholarship to study for a Master's Degree in Jewish Philosophy in Hebrew University in Jerusalem. Back in Israel, I studied voraciously - both in and out of the classroom. Having been denied access to synagogues back home, I shul-hopped and learned in as many yeshivot *as I could, while at the same time studying for my degree. After one year of intense studies, plus my many years of reading on my own, I was ready to finish my conversion, which I did under the auspices of the Conservative Movement.*

During my last year at the University, I began studying Talmud intensely at the Conservative Yeshiva in Jerusalem, where, I met my wife Abby, an American student, who is now, like myself, a rabbi. We decided to go together to New York to study at the Jewish Theological Seminary, and there we were married. We decided the best way to spend our first year as a married couple was to return to Jerusalem, where we met, for a full year of intensive study in the Conservative Yeshiva, two young Jews in love studying Torah in Jerusalem-what could top that?

At that time, I never thought that the rabbinate was for me. But I became aware that there were many people in Latin America who were interested in learning more about Judaism, either as a way of connecting to their roots or embracing a deep and meaningful millennial wisdom. I wanted to be the resource that I was lacking when I started on my journey and had no place that could teach me robust, clear Judaism in my own language. My wife persuaded me using the wise words of Hillel the Elder: "In a place where there is no one, you be that someone." We both enrolled in the Rabbinical School of the Jewish Theological Seminary in New York.

After our ordination, she accepted a position as rabbi in Oklahoma, where we have been for the last decade and now have three beautiful children. I am the co-ordinator for Be'chol Lashon *for the American Southwest. I have published a* siddur *in Spanish and a number of articles on Jewish experience, and I teach about Judaism to Spanish-speaking Jews and seekers throughout the Americas and around the world.*

Sonya Loya

Sonya Loya has been active in recognizing the converso roots in her family, as she talks about her own return to active Jewish life. She organized the Bat Zion Learning Center in Ruidoso, New Mexico and regularly invited speakers for talks about Judaism. She has been active in regional, national, and international conferences on crypto-Jewish life.

After being an activist for the b'nai anousim since 1999, it was an honor and privilege to be invited to attend the first caucus in Jerusalem to welcome back b'nai anusim. This was a great historical moment many have been working towards for years. Being recognized by the Israeli government as part of the Jewish diaspora was emotional and profound. The round table held the day after the caucus in Jerusalem, at the Academic College of Netanya was also another moment of achievement for the b'nai anusim movement.

After the caucus seven of us were invited to a private meeting with a well-known Sephardic rabbi. As he asked what our surnames were, when he got to me, he said, "Ah you must be of the family of Rabbi Izak de Loya who was the chief rabbi in Marrakesh Morocco." As I shared the information found by Dr. Roger Martínez-Dávila in his research in Plascencia Spain on Rabbi Abraham de Loya during 1430, he nodded with a smile of approval. The rabbi then autographed his book for me and gave it as a gift. He asked about both my parents, and asked what my mother's surnames were, when I told him my maternal grandmother was a Lopez-Robles. The rabbi also asked about family traditions; when I shared the practices of my maternal grandmother praying three times a day facing the east with her head covered. Checking eggs for blood, and draining meat from blood with salt, as well as my maternal great grandmother asking to have her feet facing the east before she passed away. Another piece of family information he found interesting was that before my maternal great grandmother passed my grandmother and her sisters made sure the family priest was present, his name was Father Jose Gabriel Lopez, so they could say special prayers all night before her burial the next day.

My paternal great grandmother also wanted my grandfather Loya to marry my grandmother Lopez. My parents grew up knowing each other their entire lives and married within their own community. Both family traditions were not to marry outside of their faith or ethnicity. Discovering family traditions after my conversion to Judaism in 2005, have been filled with ah-ha moments and finally understanding why I never seemed to feel connected to Christianity and have always felt a strong connection to Judaism. A year after my conversion my daughter went through her conversion and now my three granddaughters are the third generation to be recognized as Jewish.

Rabbi Dr. Jordan Gendra-Molina

Rabbi Dr. Jordan Gendra-Molina was the first native born rabbi from Spain since the Expulsion of Jews 500 years ago. He is the Director, of Casa Sefarad New Mexico, an organization in Albuquerque that celebrates the Spanish Jewish heritage. He was the lead genealogist in the Sephardic Certificate Program of the Jewish Federation of New Mexico. He has a Ph.D. in medieval Jewish history from University of Girona and an M.A. in Semitic languages, (Hebrew and Aramaic) from the University of Barcelona.

Le dor va dor – *From generation to generation. Judaism is a religion that relies on the previous generation. We rely on the wisdom and experience of the generations that preceded us. My coming back to Judaism was a gradual process of connection with past generations and the discovery of my own religious life. Growing up I did not question the traditions we had regarding food. As a kid, I just assumed they were "normal" until one day my grandfather told me that we had Jewish ancestry. The "great revelation" was far from dramatic. It happened in an everyday conversation. However, I was the chosen one to carry that knowledge maybe because I was the firstborn, maybe because of my curious mind and constant questioning. Now, I realize that the revelation gave me a sense of place. I was part of a long chain of tradition, and I wanted to learn more.*

At age fifteen I began to attend services at the only synagogue in Barcelona, and I had no knowledge of Hebrew or how the service works. Those were the days of the young Spanish democracy, and the Jewish community still kept a very low profile. I still remember the day when the shamash *[rabbi's assistant] put the siddur [prayer book] in my hands. Printed in Morocco in the 1940s with a page overflowing with old Hebrew types, no translation into Spanish. This was the beginning of a passionate journey into the Hebrew language, history, religion, and spirituality. I kept attending services, and I began to learn Hebrew and to understand the siddur. I began to memorize the prayers as well as the tunes. When I went to the university, there were no Jewish studies departments in Spain, so I studied Hebrew and Aramaic.*

In the meantime, I was becoming active in the Jewish community. When I was twenty-two years old, I decided to start my process of "conversion." I fought with the rabbi about the concept of "conversion." "Why do I need to convert when I am already part of the Jewish people?" I protested. Today I know that this a common argument between those who descend from old Jewish families forcefully converted into Christianity. Inside me, I was already Jewish. I just wanted to come back to the community that was mine and take my place. It took several months for me to adjust to that idea, but I did. The conversion process lasted three years. Then, in September 1995, I was one of the forty people who came back into Judaism in Spain. The Beit Din *[Rabbinical court] took place in Barcelona.*

The tevilah [total immersion in water] took place in the magnificent mikveh of the Mediterranean Sea. Five hundred years later the very same waves that took the lives and bodies of Jews who tried to escape that land of oppression, now were bringing them back under the eyes of three rabbis and an anonymous crowd who could not grasp the historical importance of what they were seeing.

This was not an easy process. While certainly, I experienced the perplexity and the opposition of some, I was fortunate to count with the support of family and friends, and along this journey I have encountered many people who have nourished me. I became the first native born rabbi in Spain after 500 years. I could return to Judaism and become a rabbi because of those who supported me and because of all those who will come after me, who will be able to take their places as Jews who have returned.

Maria Apodaca

Maria Apodaca is a family historian, Road Scholar lecturer, and active in the Jewish identity movement. She is a board member of the Society for Crypto-Judaic Studies and a leader of Casa Sefarad New Mexico.

I am going to talk about the last crypto-Jew in my family. The one person who did influence me the most was my father, Solomon Chavez Luna Apodaca. He gave me information, but I got it in bits and pieces. I would always ask him about the family and what he did when he was growing up. He told me that his Dad taught him animal husbandry, and he told me in a secret way. He was very cautious. What I had to do was connect all the dots by myself after he was gone.

So, the information that he gave me and after reading and studying Judaism, I put it all together. He gave me a lot of informa-

tion. I was a very curious child, and I would ask a lot of questions about where we came from and our history. He told me the history about all the different people that were in Spain, and he loved history very much.

He told me that when a person died, they would cover the mirrors and mourn for seven days. When an animal was to be slaughtered, it was to be done humanely and have the blood drained and buried. And, Jews were not permitted to consume blood, as part of keeping kashrut. You will sweep to the center of the room and avoid putting dust on the mezuzah, even though we did not have a mezuzah, it was symbolic of having one. While making tortillas, we would burn the first one. It was always a custom of throwing a piece of dough into the hot oil. This represents the first burnt offering.

I learned the custom of the dieta that is the practice following the birth of a child, the new mother would not go out into public for forty days and would abstain from the normal life of a woman. In the Old Testament a new mother would go to the Temple after forty days for purification.

There are many other customs. When my grandmother Sofia Chavez Luna Apodaca was getting ready for her bath, she would put water on the top of her head three times as if she were doing a Mikvah. She did know what it meant. It was also done when the children would go swimming. I would ask her, "Grandma, why do you do this?" She would never tell me. Finally, when I was around fourteen years old, I asked again, and she told me, "Para que tu alma no se escape." She meant, so that my soul would not escape. I didn't ask her anymore, and I was satisfied with that. My grandmother Sofia also refused to have a priest at her bed side when she died.

My parents bought a Bible for me from a traveling book salesman when I was about ten years old. The first thing that my Dad did was to place my name on the front page. It was my Bible. I think he felt that the questions that I was always asking might be answered in this book. In the tenth grade we were studying the five great religions of the world, and of course I chose to write about the Jews. When I finished writing my paper, I showed it to him, and he read it quietly and put the paper down and said to me in a whisper that we were Jews. "Somos Judios." And, I thought he meant that there was a Jew in the family, and there were many of us.

I believe that he felt that I was the one to pass the history down to. It was the custom to give the information to the young teens in the family, but everyone always knew that it was a secret. In some families, not everyone was told. I think the elders would choose the one who showed the most interest and asked the questions…Now I am the one in the family to pass this history to others, since my siblings' families do not wish to hear or understand our past. I have a responsibility to continue the stories that my Dad told me…I know that he guides me on this path that I have chosen. He had to keep a secret. I don't. I can live my life completely as a Jew.

John Garcia

John Garcia is an attorney in El Paso, who made his return to Judaism in 2000, and since then he has been an active member of the Congregation B'nei Zion where he frequently leads services. He is fluent in Hebrew, and in this interview, he gives the basic story of his life and return to Judaism.

Luis Carvajal had trouble with the Inquisition, but of course, the one that was burned at the stake was Luis Carvajal, el Mozo [the younger]. I don't think the uncle was burned. He died under mysterious circumstances. We were all related. My ancestor was related to the Carvajal family. My ancestor's mother was one of the Rodriguez sisters. Inez Rodriguez was my ancestor's mother, and his father was Balthasar de Sosa, and we think that Sosa was the city he came from, and we think he was probably Mendez. So, we think we might even be connected to Gracia Mendez. That family. We have been studying that for years. And for me it was just a yearning. It was a yearning all the time.

I was brought up Roman Catholic, and I learned Roman Catholicism. I was taught by the Jesuits. I went to Jesuit high school, and I graduated in 1969. And, I had this yearning, and I wanted to reconnect, and Rabbi Leon is the one who opened the door. If I had known there was an open door, I would have opened it a long time ago. I have been studying it [Hebrew], *I am drawn to it because I am a linguist.*

I learned English a lot better than many Americans. I know English and Spanish. I was a top student in Spanish. I learned Latin, and I was a top student in Latin, and when I came here [B'nai Zion], *I connected with the Hebrew. I feel it in my heart, and it is a phonetic language just like Spanish, so it is something I can adapt to very easily...*

I would go to church, and I would hear them saying what Jesus said, and I didn't believe it. I did not believe he said those things; I did not connect with it. I started to lose it very fast. And, when I started listening to Rabbi Leon...I tell you, if I had known that there was a door that I could have opened, I would have opened it...I agree with him that we are the future. Here in this community, there is a dichotomy. There are a lot of people who are hesitant about us, but they are learning to accept us.

Blanca Garza Enriquez Carrasco

Blanca Garza Enriquez Carrasco is from El Paso. Blanca did not grow up with teachings about Judaism, and she made her return as an adult, very similar to the experience of many other people. She was guided on her return by Rabbi Stephen Leon of the Congregation B'nai Zion in El Paso. Blanca is an active member and leader of that congregation.

My name is Blanca Garza Enriquez from El Paso, Texas. I've been practicing Judaism for over 25 years, not knowing about my family's Jewish roots but longing to find out about my passion to embrace Judaism, a religion that seemed to be distant from my family's experience.

Somos Judios

In 2018 I went on a trip to find out who my father was, knowing only his name - Israel Garza Salinas, and that he used to live in Monterrey, Mexico. To my amazement, I found out that my father was a descendant of Marco Alonso de La Garza y del Arcón, co-founder of Monterrey, Nuevo Leon, an important center for conversos and crypto-Jews in Mexico since the time of Luis Carvajal and Diego de Montemayor. That information certainly changed my life from that moment! I used to say that I had nothing "in writing" to show that I had Jewish ancestry, and I remember the words of a friend who said, 'What matters is what you do right now with what you have chosen to become.' Even though I wasn't aware of my family's ancestry, I embraced my conversion to Judaism and became very involved with the Jewish community in El Paso. I volunteered with the El Paso Jewish Federation and became a member of the Board. I was awarded with the Young Leadership Award in 2012 and the Volunteer of the Year Award in 2014. I was also invited to be the editor and graphic designer of the Jewish newspaper, which I did for over four years. My husband and I are members of B'nai Zion Synagogue. I have served as President of Sisterhood for two years, and I have served in the board in different capacities until now. Overall, the Jewish community of El Paso has been good to me and my family. My husband, César Carrasco, is also a convert, and he became the President of B'nai Zion's Board of Directors.

Although the community has been receptive and have welcomed me and my family, there is still some sense of mistrust toward crypto-Jews. I believe there is important work to be done, educating other Jews about the Spanish Inquisition and how the descendants of crypto-Jews from Mexico, Latin American, and other places are struggling to be accepted by them.

What keeps me going are the people who understand what we yearn for, and they embrace and support us. I believe there is a lot more that needs to be done, and I know the time for action is now. I am happy to be living in this time in history where more people are interested in finding out if they have Jewish roots. It took me twenty years to find out that I had Jewish ancestors, but it came at the right time for me and my family. We are Jews.

Jewish Conversos

Jewish conversos and crypto-Jews are a legacy of the intolerance of medieval Catholicism, shaping the lives of hundreds of thousands of descendants, a legacy still unfolding in our contemporary world. The six voices heard here give an indication of the many threads of experiences, desires, and paths that people are following in this movement of return to Judaism across the Americas from New Mexico, Colorado, and Texas to Brazil, Bolivia, Peru, Ecuador, Colombia, Costa Rica, and Mexico. As descendants of Jewish conversos seek to re-connect with Judaism, they come with a hybrid religious culture build over centuries of having lived in Catholic societies. From their links to Judaism in medieval Sepharad, each is learning how to connect with the reality of Jewish life in the twenty-first century.

Some of the original Jewish conversos in Spain and Portugal 500 years ago became sincere Catholics and assimilated into Catholic society. Others feigned conversion, identifying as Catholics in public but continuing Jewish practice and identity in the privacy of their homes. They created a hybrid religious practice, blending Jewish practices with a public face of Catholicism. How people balanced the public and private spheres of their lives was gender specific with men unable to continue the synagogue based male practice of Judaism. Women were able to retain more of their Jewish practice which was home based and less visible to public scrutiny.

According to historian David Graizbord, the concept of "Judaism" is a Christian concept formulated by the medieval Catholic Church to define Jewishness as an institutionalized religion like the Church.[1] In contrast, Jews thought of themselves as a community, a tribe, descendants of Abraham, Jacob, and Moses. They were a people with a religious legacy, not an organized religion comparable to Catholicism. The Hebrew word for "religion" (דת) rarely appears in the Bible, and it when it does, it refers to laws or commandments.

The Inquisition defined people as Judaizers, or crypto-Jews, if they practiced rituals that seemed to be Jewish. After 1492 the Jewish conversos, who stayed in Spain as Christians, were cut off from contact with practicing Jews, and the next few decades led to a winnowing of the true converts to Christianity and crypto-Jews. The former stayed in Spain and assimilated, while the latter tended to leave for kingdoms that accepted Jews, such as the Netherlands, Poland, Morocco, and the Ottoman Empire. Some Jewish conversos or crypto-Jews migrated to Spanish colonies in the Americas.

The term "crypto-Jew" is problematic and is even considered to be a misnomer by some. The person who recently converted in Spain or Portugal in 1500 might still think of himself or herself as a Jew although a hidden one because of the force of circumstances. This person who had grown up in a Jewish family practicing as a Jew could be defined as a Jew in hiding, but the experience of his or her descendant 300 years later would not be the same. The descendant in 1800 would be culturally Catholic, perhaps retaining elements of Jewish practice, but they would not be Jewish in the same way their ancestors were 300 years earlier.

Is a Jewish converso or a crypto-Jew still a Jew? What is the standard of Jewishness? Is it public or private identification? Is it living in a Jewish community? How Jewish is a Jew with no Jewish group? Is it doing Jewish practices, such as lighting candles on Friday night? Is it observing Shabbat? Is it keeping kosher? Is it observing the holidays and Yom Kippur? Is it marrying someone who is Jewish and having a Jewish family? Is it attending synagogue for the daily prayers? How many elements mentioned here can you subtract and still be Jewish?

I will use the terms "Jewish converso" and "descendants of Jewish conversos" as the default term referring to anyone who converted and only use "crypto-Jew" when it describes a person who retained their Jewish identity and lived as a Jew in hiding. Of course, this is not a black and white division. There are many variations on practice and identity in the Jewishness of the millions of people who have been descendants of Jewish conversos over the last twenty-five generations.

Theories of Jewish Conversion and Its Aftermath

Different lines of thought have developed about the contemporary Jewish identity movement and its linkage to historical Jewish converso experiences in Spain, Portugal, and their American colonies. One group of scholars interpret Jewish linked practices as being historically continuous and cultural markers of Jewish heritage. Others have emphasized identity and intention in the use of cultural practices, rather than legacy, as the indication of Jewishness. While some question whether these practices are Jewish at all.

The Heritage Theory

Stanley Hordes, David Gitlitz, Haim Beinart and Janet Liebman Jacobs among others have written about cultural practices as survivals that represent heritage from Jewish ritual in Spain and Portugal and as indications of crypto-Jewish lives. Former New Mexico State Historian Stanley Hordes says these practices had been part of life in New Mexico from the initial exploration by the Spanish until the mid-twentieth century.[2]

Based on records from the Inquisition, Hordes began doing research on crypto-Jewish life in the Spanish colonial period of Mexico, as a graduate student in history at Tulane University. Later, he did research in New Mexico on memory and rituals of Jewish significance among people who identified as descendants of conversos. Hordes argues that these memories of people about practices of their grandparents could well be an indication of crypto-Jewish practices that survived in New Mexico into the twentieth century.

Hordes points out that crypto-Jewish practices have been lost by the newer generations because of assimilation to Anglo-American culture. The core of his argument is that after the documentation of Jewish practices by the Inquisition was eclipsed in Mexico during the late 1600s, crypto-Jewish families continued these ethnic and religious practices in New Mexico, and that their vestiges were still being reported in recent decades.

Identity Theory

Anthropologist Seth Kunin has done research with people who identify as having Jewish heritage, and he suggests that there are frequently three stages on the path to claiming Jewish ancestry, starting as a Catholic, then converting to Protestantism, and finally identifying as Jewish. He has studied contemporary identity and does not assume that it has a continuous history back to Spain although memory is an element for some people. He says that individuals improvise as they negotiate identity, and their practices change and develop as people shift their identity.

Kunin gives four levels or stages of people identifying as crypto-Jews or descendants of crypto-Jews:[3]

- **Strong Crypto-Jews.** This group has identity as being Jews even through their ritual practice has Catholic elements.
- **Weak Crypto-Jews.** These are people who are aware of having a Jewish background, but it is not their primary identity.
- **Strong Catholics with Jewish Awareness.** These are people with clear Catholic identity, and they are aware of the converso history of the family, but they consider it not relevant to their current lives.
- **Adventist and Messianic.** These are Christians who add Jewish elements to their practice of Christianity.

Kunin emphasizes the complex nature of crypto-Jewish practice and the fact that it is not a singular phenomenon. He says, "Crypto-Judaism is also particularly complex due…to the absence of a community with shared identity, practices, and culture. Indeed, rather than speaking of crypto-Judaism, it would be more proper to speak of it in the plural, crypto-Judaisms—a diverse set of individual identities and histories, which only today are beginning to reunite, or to create a sense of shared community and destiny." [4]

A person's search for a new religious identity frequently has begun as dissatisfaction with Catholic traditions, practices, or clergy. As Protestant churches were established in New Mexico after the American occupation of the territory in 1846, Spanish-speakers began joining them in a move away from the Catholic Church. Was this conversion to Protestantism evidence of a latent cultural anti-clericalism inherited from those who converted under pressure in the fourteenth and fifteenth centuries, or was it simply part of an exploration to find a new religious path? Kunin goes on to describe the markers of those who clearly identified as crypto-Jews, which included self-identification as a Jew and observance of Jewish practices.

Fusion Theory

In New Mexico, Tomás Atencio has agreed that there are cultural practices that parallel Jewish rituals, but he has argued that these practices were fused into the local *manito* culture[5] of northern New Mexico in recent centuries and took on Catholic meanings, losing the Jewish ones.

Atencio was the first social scientist to give major attention to the converso legacy in New Mexico. As Director of the Southwest Hispanic Research Institute at the University of New Mexico, he focused on the social realities of Hispanic life in the state. Atencio argued that crypto-Judaism had existed in New Mexico in the past, but that it had not been documented in recent history. He argued further that crypto-Jewish influences had been incorporated into the Catholic-based *manito* culture and language, inherited from the Spanish colonial period and still alive in northern New Mexico.

Atencio[6] mentioned the example of death rituals and candle lighting practices shared with Jews were incorporated into the larger *manito* culture and were no longer distinctively Jewish. He argued that lighting candles on Friday night while reciting the rosary was a Catholic practice, not a Jewish one. Atencio also addressed the question of whether the Spanish dialect spoken in northern New Mexico had Jewish influences, and he agreed that it has sixteenth century Spanish linguistic survivals but no Hebrew or Judeo-Spanish elements.

Atencio said that crypto-Jewish practice in New Mexico is undocumented, covered by the veil of the past, and that the history of hiding and purposeful distortion has obscured what might have been known about it. For crypto-Jews, the centuries of hiding identity have meant that their culture became one of privacy and secrecy. Atencio says that the hidden nature of this experience has led to forgotten meanings and changes in practices that could have been Jewish in the beginning, but they are no longer. According to Atencio's argument, the Jewish ethnic markers that have been documented in the American Southwest would seem to be fragments of cultural practices from the past incorporated into the *manito* culture, rather than being the distinct cultural whole of an active crypto-Jewish life.

Crypto-Jews as a Creation of the Catholic Church

Benzion Netanyahu argues that fifteenth century conversos in Spain were assimilated Christians and not crypto-Jews. He goes further to say that the Inquisition fabricated the idea of crypto-Jewish practice as a pseudo-heresy to give a basis for arresting converted Jews and eliminating them from Spain. For Netanyahu there was an anti-Jewish, conspiracy between the Church and the Crown to rid Spain of Jews, even converted Jews. The implication is that both secular and religious authorities used the Inquisition in unison to control the society and force it to be more Christian. He is correct that the goal of the Inquisition was to rid Spanish society of "unchristian" behaviors from heresy to witchcraft, Protestantism, and bigamy among things. He says, "the aim of the Inquisition...was not to eradicate a Jewish heresy from the midst of the Marrano group, but to eradicate the Marrano group from the midst of the Spanish..."[7]

Netanyahu points out that the accusation of Judaizing was used in cases in which people were not crypto-Jews, and he also notes the paucity of documentation about crypto-Jewish practice outside of Inquisition records. Based on that, he argues that crypto-Jewish practice either did not exist or was not a historical factor in Spain.

David Graizbord agrees with Netanyahu that the concept of crypto-Judaism was a formulation of Catholic Church authorities, and that it was used to label Jewish conversos as still being Jews. Graizbord understands it differently. He says that it was a way to categorize conversos as Jews, because Church officials thought they were inherently Jewish. In fact, conversos were required to pay the special tax on Jews because they were still seen as Jews even though they had converted. From the Jewish perspective, Graizbord suggests that "crypto-Jews" were not really Jews because they had "no public and communal setting within which New Christians could have learned the culture of the Jews..."[8]

Crypto-Jews: A Mistaken Identity

In 2000 Barbara Ferry and Debbie Nathan published a critique of the crypto-Jewish identity movement in New Mexico in *The Atlantic*,[9] questioning its validity. They asked, "Has it all been a mistake? Historically, perhaps. But faith, of course, is always about more than history. Religions are built on collective wishes and hopes. And with southwestern crypto-Judaism the wishes and hopes may, in the end, prevail."

They question the work of Hordes as "speculation" and quote Tomas Atencio as saying, "Such references to a Jewish past may have been factual, or they may have been the usual anti-Semitic village rumor-mongering." They also question whether the Jewish references in the work of writer Isabelle Medina Sandoval and folk artist Juan Sandoval are authentic or advantageous commercializing. Some people in academic and Jewish circles follow this line of doubting the validity of Jewish identity among descendants of conversos, which creates a tension between them and those who identify with an ancestral Jewish legacy.

Conclusion

Questioning of the existence of the crypto-Jewish experience seemed to peak with the work of Netanyahu (1999) and Ferry and Nathan (2000). Since then, a body of research on self-identified Jewish-related experiences has been accumulating, as reported by Jacobs (2002), Hordes (2005), Kunin (2009), Levine (2016), *Fractured Faiths* (2016), and Martínez-Dávila (2018) among others. We will explore some of the many branches of this experience and how it is being manifest in the Jewish identity movement among the Spanish and Portuguese-speaking peoples of the Americas.

Part II

Jewish Conversos in Spain and Portugal

The Jewish converso experience exists in lands that were historically subject to either the Spanish or Portuguese Inquisitions. It began in medieval Spain and has left its traces in people's lives until the present. Some Jewish *conversos* became crypto-Jews, and the experience of their descendants evolved over time to a culture of hiding and even deception about their identity to protect themselves. To study the life experiences of the descendants of the Jewish conversos from 500 years ago is sometimes like smoke and mirrors. We get glimpses of that life from memory and rare documents.

What was the reality of that experience for the generations of descendants of Jewish conversos who lived out their lives in fear of being identified and persecuted? The religious or spiritual self in the interior of a person is private and largely unknowable to others. The paucity of documention about the spiritual life of descendants of Jewish conversos or crypto-Jews in Peru, Colombia, Brazil, Mexico, or New Mexico during the Spanish Colonial period limits what we can know.

As in Plato's Allegory of the Cave, we see mostly shadows of what that reality was, but fortunately with the Jewish converso experience we have a few glimpses of it in the light of day. Those of us who are not descendants of converso families may never be able to know its full reality, but the shadows on the wall can give us an idea of what it might have been.

Figure 7
View of the Medieval Jewish Quarter across the Bridge
Besalu, Spain

Chapter 2

Origins of Jewish Conversos

TENS OF THOUSANDS OF JEWISH CONVERSOS

were accused by the Inquisition of being crypto-Jews and practicing Jewish rituals in secret in Spain, Portugal, and the Americas. Starting in Spain in the late 1300s, Jews were pressured to convert, sometimes with direct threats to their lives. Converso families in Spain would have been different from those of Portugal, and both were different from their descendants who lived later in the colonial territories in the Americas. In the 1500s and 1600s many tens of thousands of conversos in Spain and Portugal eventually fled to other countries that welcomed Jews. In contrast, there was a core that chose to continue juggling the two identities living in Spain and Portugal, their public face as Christians and their private lives as Jews.

Stages of Memory and Practice

In the history of Jewish conversos from Spain and Portugal to the Americas we can identify four stages of Jewish memory and practice. The phenomena loosely lumped together under the label of crypto-Jews has evolved over the years from its original manifestation in Spain and Portugal in the 1500s to the Spanish colonial version in the Americas, to the twilight of the Jewish converso experience in the 1700s and 1800s, and finally to the Jewish identity movements of the twentieth and twenty-first centuries.[10]

Stage One: Jewish Conversos in Spain and Portugal

Myths about Sepharad (Jewish Spain) have obscured the realities of what it was. There was a "golden age" for Jews in Spain during the early Muslim period, but as the reconquest heated up and Christian rule replaced that of Muslims, the Jewish experience turned dark until the last light of the Jews was put out by Catholic Spain.

By the mid-1300s, the Catholic Church was increasing its proselytizing pressure on Jews, sometimes using forceful tactics. Over the next 150 years 200,000 Jews or more did convert, and a large number assimilated into Spanish Catholic society, losing and often rejecting their Jewish background. In contrast, some families accepted conversion under pressure but continued a semblance of their Jewish lives.

Hidden Jewish life became different from the Jewish community life they had known. With no synagogues the public practice of assembly and prayer was lost, but women continued home-based practices. Secrecy was key to survival for these families, as identity hiding or dissembling evolved into a cultural practice.

Stage Two: The Mosaic Period in Colonial Americas

A hybrid version of Jewish identity survived in the American colonies from Mexico into South America until the mid to late 1600s. Conversos from Spain and Portugal migrated to the Americas by the thousands in the 1500s and early 1600s, some in search of economic opportunities, especially in mining and the sugar industry.[11] For most of the 1500s, the Inquisition was not active in the Americas, but that was to change, and by the mid-1600s the offices of the Inquisition in Mexico, Cartagena, and Lima seem to have eliminated those who retained some knowledge of their Jewish heritage or intimidated them to the point of going underground so effectively that little is recorded about them after that.[12]

By that time their Jewish practices would have been severely degraded. Jewish converso families had retained elements of normative Judaism in the 1500s, but as the decades passed in the 1600s the successive generations would have become less Jewish and more Catholic.

Memory is a combination of recollection and re-creation of the past. Memory is not exact, and the greater distance from the historical events, memory becomes more re-creation than recollection. As generation after generation became more distant from the original Jewish practice, the knowledge of that practice declined.

Stage Three: Period of Cultural Remnants

The period from 1650 to 1950 was the twilight of Jewishness among the descendants of conversos; it was an interlude in which information about their lives becomes increasingly scarce. This was a critical stage for the descendants of conversos, now largely limited to the Americas. It was during this period that people in Brazil, Mexico, and Colombia, either left those countries for English and Dutch territories, or migrated to more remote, safer areas in the hinterlands to avoid persecution by the Inquisition. In Colombia, that meant migrating to the mining areas in the mountainous regions of Antioquia, and in Mexico it meant migrating to the far northern frontier in present day New Mexico, Colorado, and Texas.

Many families could have secretly retained their Jewish identity, but knowledge and practice of Judaism was increasingly assimilated with Catholic practices. For some, only the identity remained, and for others their frugal Jewish rituals of lighting candles on Friday night or covering mirrors at the passing of a family member morphed into memories and family practices of vague origins.

Stage Four: Jewish Identity Reclaimed: Epilogue, 1950 to present

From the 1950s to the present, Spanish-speaking people from New Mexico to Mexico, Colombia, Brazil, Bolivia, and Peru have initiated a Jewish identity movement that continues to grow. As the Jewishness of their ancestors was slipping away into memory, this resurgence of interest has launched a new wave of reclaiming the ancestral identity. Although it is only a memory for some descendants of conversos, for others it has meant re-initiating Jewish practice, a time of rejudaizing. It is a new era, no longer of hidden Jewishness but now of Jewish identity revealed.

In these pages we will follow conversos and their descendants from fifteenth century Spain to the twenty-first century in the Americas. Jewish practice does not occur in a continuous line in this narrative. There are gaps, and we have to assume that Inquisition records were skewed by the beliefs and biases of the Dominicans who asked the questions and recorded the answers. Furthermore, the use of torture or the threat of it could produce questionable information.

Yet, the repetition of accounts of Jewish conversos hiding their ancestral identity from the Catholic Church can be found from the 1400s to the twenty-first century. Ignoring the persistence of that voice would put the understanding of historic events in peril.

Christian Spain versus Muslim Spain

Jews lived in two different Spains between 711 (the Muslim conquest of the Iberian Peninsula) and 1492 (the Christian conquest of the last Muslim kingdom). The Jewish experience was different in language, culture, religious life, and social acceptance between the Muslim and Christian periods. Under Muslim rule Spain became the center of Jewish life in Europe. It had the largest Jewish population, and it was a center of Jewish scholarship, especially in the "Golden Age" period from 900 to 1100. Jews in Spain prospered, and it was a time of *convivencia* when Christians, Jews, and Muslims lived together with relative harmony.

Jews were active in commerce and politics and frequently had important positions in government in Muslim Spain. Jewish works of theology, poetry, philosophy, and science reached a high point in this environment with Judah Halevi, Ibn Gabirol, and others. Ultimately, that experiment was a failure, as Christians drove the Muslims to the last corner of Spain, then out of the country altogether.

By the twelfth century, as the Christian forces were becoming stronger in the Iberian Peninsula, the Muslim kingdoms became weaker and less tolerant of Jews. With that shift to Muslim intolerance, Jewish families began migrating northward into the new Catholic kingdoms.

Initially the Christian kings welcomed Jews, who brought literacy skills, advanced technology, and commerce from the Muslim south. Jews were accepted in the courts and frequently lived next to the castle for protection. As scholars, merchants, and tax collectors, Jews had important roles in society.

During the 1100s and 1200s the Catholic Church began turning against the Jews, bringing the Church into conflict with civil authorities. The monarchs and secular leaders initially defended Jews, but as clerical forces continued to build their arguments against Jewish heresy, the support of secular authorities began to fade. By the 1400s the Church had won their campaign against the Jews, and kings turned from defending them to enacting discriminatory laws against them.[13]

As the Catholic Church hardened its position against Jews, anti-Semitism and discrimination grew among the common people. Dominicans and others used their dominance to proselytize Jews, increasingly using pressure and even force to oblige them to convert. Even though Jews had lived in Spain for 1,500 years or more, they were no longer guaranteed tolerance, either in the Muslim or Christian worlds. Eventually, Christian intolerance, attacks, forced conversions, and expulsions eliminated the possibility of productive Jewish life.

Medieval Catholicism snuffed out the Jewish presence in Spain , leaving only the flickering flames of Jews in hiding. Eventually, even these Jewish conversos left Spain and Portugal for fear of their lives, and their descendants survived, still hiding, in remote colonies in the Americas. The Inquisition had achieved its purpose of eliminating Jews in Spain.

Pope Innocent III and Anti-Judaism

Between 1100 and 1200 the Catholic Church was consolidating its power in Europe and increasingly focused on eliminating heretical movements, especially Judaism, Islam, and the Albigensian "heresy". When Pope Urban II called for the first Crusade to drive the Muslims out of the Holy Land in 1095, it morphed into an early campaign against Jews in Europe. As Crusaders began marching to the Holy Land, along the way they attacked Jewish communities in the Rhineland, killing thousands with the argument that they were also infidels. This call for a Crusade strengthened the fervor of Spanish Christians to drive Muslims out of their country.

In 1215 Pope Innocent III convened the Fourth Lateran Council in Toledo which began to formalize restrictions on Jewish life in Europe.

Pope Innocent was a strong influence over the Catholic kings, and his reign marks the beginning of the social and political decline of Jews in Spain and the rest of Western Europe. The restrictions imposed by the Council with the approval of the Pope included:

On Loaning Money
The more the Christian religion is restrained from usurious practices, so much the more does the perfidy of the Jews grow in these matters, so that within a short time they are exhausting the resources of Christians. Wishing therefore to see that Christians are not savagely oppressed by Jews in this matter, we ordain by this synodal decree that if Jews in future, on any pretext, extort oppressive and excessive interest from Christians, then they are to be removed from contact with Christians until they have made adequate satisfaction for the immoderate burden...

On Jews and Dress
A difference of dress distinguishes Jews or Saracens from Christians in some provinces, but in others a certain confusion has developed so that they are indistinguishable. Whence it sometimes happens that by mistake Christians join with Jewish or Saracen women, and Jews or Saracens with Christian women. In order that the offence of such a damnable mixing may not spread further, under the excuse of a mistake of this kind, we decree that such persons of either sex, in every Christian province and at all times, are to be distinguished in public from other people by the character of their dress.

The Fourth Lateran Council also denounced crypto-Judaism with a call to control it.[14] This is one of the earliest mentions of hidden Jewish practice. The campaign of Pope Innocent III against the Jews led to their expulsions from France (1182, 1306, and 1394), England in 1290, and Spain in 1492. The 277 years (1215-1492) between the Fourth Lateran Council and the Expulsion of Jews from Spain, mark the growth of virulent anti-Semitism in Europe. It eventually led to Jews being virtually eliminated in Western Europe and pushed into Eastern Europe and the Muslim world, the outer borders of the influence of the Roman Catholic Church.

The fourteenth and fifteenth centuries were difficult for Jewish communities in Europe, starting with the expulsions from England and France, then the Black Death in 1348. At its peak the epidemic killed one-third of Europe's population, and Jews were accused of causing the epidemic by poisoning the drinking water of Christians. In revenge, Christians attacked Jewish communities, killing tens of thousands.[15] Easter was a particularly threatening time because Christians would attack Jews based on the belief that they had killed Jesus.

The Growing Pressure on Jews to Convert

The Christian re-conquest (*reconquista*) of Spain from the Muslims was a centuries long crusade to drive the "infidels" out of the Iberian Peninsula. During this time, Christians and Muslims sometimes collaborated with each other against common enemies, but both began to discriminate against Jews.[16]

Robert Chazan says that the intense atmosphere of Christian Europe in the 1240s led to the growth of anti-Semitism.[17] In medieval Europe, war and religion were two important forces in the society, and in Spain they were fused into one long religious war. The passion and loyalty to Catholicism reached a height in Spanish society that was not matched in any other European country. To be Spanish was to be Catholic, and that passionate identity of Spain with the Church was ultimately the undoing of the Jews.

Dominican preachers actively toured the towns and cities of Spain giving sermons denouncing Jewish beliefs and practices. Obtaining the support of local authorities, they forced Jews to attend sermons to confront them with Christian teachings and pressure them to convert to Catholicism.

Figure 8
Queen Isabella's Castle
Segovia

In the 1300s and 1400s, Spain was firmly entrenched in the medieval world of castles, knights in armor, and soaring cathedrals. Castile and Aragon were among the most zealous kingdoms in Europe, and Christian devotion had been shaped by the passions of battle in the successful re-conquest against the Muslims. The Christian monarchs, Ferdinand and Isabella benefited from the glories of war and conquest. When they accepted the surrender of the last Muslim kingdom in Granada in 1492, they were on the verge of launching a new stage in history. Although the Iberian Peninsula was still fractured into four different Christian kingdoms (Castile, Aragon, Navarre, and Portugal), that was to change, and the first three kingdoms were soon unified in to one country, Spain.

Defeating the last Muslim kingdom changed Spanish history, and it freed the Christian monarchs to approve two monumental decisions. The first was to expel the Jews, and the second was to approve the voyage by Christopher Columbus to explore a route to Asia across the great sea. In these watershed decisions the King and Queen launched their kingdoms in a new direction that would change the world.

Origins

The Disputation: The Intellectual Attack on Jews

After Pope Innocent III, the Catholic hierarchy continued to ramp up pressure on Jews to convert, one of the tools they used was debate, the disputation. The first major one in Spain was in 1263 when Church officials in Catalunya challenged the Jewish community to a debate about Jesus being the Messiah. Nahmanides, the most prominent rabbi in Catalunya, was selected to speak for the Jews. Pablo Cristiani, a Jewish convert, was chosen to lead the debate for the Christian side because of his knowledge of Hebrew, the Torah, and the Talmud. King James I oversaw the event.

Nahmanides (1194-1270) was known for his adherence to traditional religious teachings, as well as his scholarship. His conservative respect of rabbinical law distinguished his work throughout his life.[18]

Figure 9
Jew in Disputation with Christians
Codex Manesse

The Disputation of Barcelona marked a turning point in Jewish thought, reflecting the increased role of Talmudic reasoning and the growing influence of Rashi, Rabbi Shomo Yitzchaki. The unique mixture of poetry, science, philosophy, and rabbinical thought that had characterized Jewish thought in the Muslim Golden Age had lost its dominance, and the up and coming practice of Talmudic logic and debate was taking its place. Jews had moved from the intellectual influences of the Muslim south to those of the Christian north.

Nahmanides challenged Christian beliefs and openly stated that he did not accept them, arguing that Jesus was not divine. His arguments generated such hostility that the King ended the debate after four days and urged Nahmanides to leave the kingdom because he could no longer guarantee his safety. Under that threat Nahmanides left Spain for Israel and lived the remainder of his life there. Maimonides had already left Spain a hundred years earlier after his family was forced to feign conversion and hide their Jewish identity under the dogmatic Almohad regime in southern Spain. Now, dogmatic Catholics forced Nahmanides to leave, marking the end of the era of great Jewish scholars in the country.

Mysticism and Messianic Dreams

In the 1200s Jews in Spain turned inward toward mysticism in the religiously constricting world of the Christian north, and that was to become a prominent feature of Sephardic and crypto-Jewish life. As anti-Semitism grew in Europe, so did Jewish mystical thought and messianic dreams. The latter would become more prominent in the Sephardic Diaspora after the Expulsion from Spain.

Mysticism and Kabbalah

Rabbi Isaac the Blind in Provence (1160-1235) was a leader in exploring kabbalistic mysticism in understanding the Torah and Jewish practice itself. He was followed by the Gerona circle of Kabbalists, Rabbis Ezra ben Solomon, Azriel, and Moses ben Nahman (Nahmanides) and their disciples. For mystical thinkers their understanding of God and spirituality is rooted in metaphysical, mystical experience.

Talmudic debate and detailed reasoning are important in Jewish thought, but mysticism, the spiritual quality of experiencing God directly, has a long history in Jewish practice. The important kabbalistic work,

Origins

The Zohar, by Moses de León, was produced in Spain in the 1270s and 1280s, shortly after Nahmanides' death.[19] It is essentially a kabbalistic midrash on the Torah, arranged according to the weekly portions of Torah study. More than a book, it is a collection of writings giving mystical interpretations of the Torah and of spiritual life. Jews have turned to mysticism in times of stress, and in the climate of growing anti-Jewishness in Catholic Spain, *The Zohar* became a popular source of study and understanding of the spiritual life.

Today, we find a mystical connection to God and Judaism expressed by many in the Jewish identity movement. Through how many generations can the structures of the culture of a people survive? How does that pattern of mystical thinking among those claiming Jewish identity today connect to the mysticism from Jewish Spain? Is mysticism itself a primal link that connects people to Jewishness, the feeling or yearning to be Jewish?

Rabbi Martin Levy explains mysticism as,

God is both transcendent and imminent, and thus the average person will not achieve/perceive the highest levels of spiritual understanding, or atzilut. *Only a few personalities, such as Moses, reach that level. Hence the divine is both understandable on some levels, and beyond us in many others. Mysticism embraces a personal belief in G-d and allows the believer to bridge the gap between divine revelation and concealment in our material world. Thus, we strive to elevate ourselves past the mundane to seek the divine presence in all of creation.*[20]

Mysticism is the spiritual within, a faith in Godliness as the essence of religious experience. Mysticism and law might seem to be contradictory, one ethereal and the other concrete, but on the contrary, they are inextricably linked. Jewish mysticism interprets the Scriptures by finding truths intuitively, lifting the formal meanings of the text to reach the true meaning hidden beneath. Allegorical and esoteric interpretations of Biblical texts search for the true meanings of texts implied or occulted in the formal meanings of the words.

How did the mystical practice of normative Judaism, as in Kabbalah, carry over into the hidden practices of Jewish converts and their descendants? You might ask, "How did the Jewish identity survive among the descendants of conversos with ancestry 500 years ago in Spain and Portugal?" How is it that after twenty-five generations of Catholic practice, descendants of crypto-Jews still think of themselves as Jews? In my interviews with people reclaiming their Jewish identity, they have repeatedly mentioned the "feeling" of being Jewish, the "longing", or "yearning" for something that they found in Jewish identity. This mystical connection with Judaism is not unlike the kabbalistic direct experience of God that goes beyond rational thought.

Millennial Dreams and Messianism [21]

Millennial dreams are one expression of the mysticism in Jewish thought. The dream that a far-off figure will arrive and fix the evils of the world and create a utopia is a mystical solution for a troubled time. As the anti-Jewishness and persecution grew in Christian Spain, it provided fertile ground for the growth of messianic dreams, which continued in the Sephardic Diaspora and among crypto-Jews into the 1500s and 1600s.

There is a long line of declared messiahs in Jewish history, but the Shabbetai Zvi episode from 1648 to 1666 is the most dramatic example. In the mid-1600s messianism spread widely throughout the Sephardic Diaspora from the Ottoman Empire to Israel, Amsterdam, and beyond. Menasseh ben Israel and Isaac Aboab da Fonseca, the former crypto-Jewish rabbinical leaders of the community in Amsterdam, were among those caught up in the millennial dreams of the moment.

In Mexico some crypto-Jews believed that the Messiah would be born of a Mexican Jewish mother, and the Messiah would deliver them from their situation. Expectant mothers prayed to St. Moses that their child might be the Messiah. See pages 154-155. Among Sephardic Jews and crypto-Jews in the 1600s millennialism and messianism were the dreams of a mystical solution for the problems of their world.

Chapter 3

Forced Conversions and Crypto-Jews

Figure 10
Auto-da-Fé
Portugal 1685

IN THE EARLY 1300S, THERE HAD BEEN SEVERAL HUNDRED thousand Jews in Spain, perhaps as much as 5 to 6 percent of the population. No other country in Europe had so many Jews, but the history of persecution and massacres began decimating the Jewish community.

As mentioned earlier, anti-Jewish sentiments had been growing in Spain from the time of Pope Innocent III in the early 1200s, and in the mid-1300s it broke out in violent attacks on Jewish communities. The combination of the Black Death (1348), the Dominican campaign against Jews led by Vicente Ferrer (1391-1420), the Expulsion of Jews (1492), and the Inquisition campaign against Jewish conversos (1480-1530) devastated the Jewish community.

In the late 1340s, the Jews were blamed for being the source of the Black Death, leading to Jewish communities being attacked in an uprising resulting in part from Church led propaganda.[22] Thousands were killed, and many converted to save their lives. Jewish conversos became a significant issue in the Spanish population in the process. Jonathan Israel points out that the catastrophic loss of population and contraction of economic activity in Europe in the century 1350-1450, led to the persecution of the Jews in virtually every European country except Italy during this time.[23]

The Dominican Campaign against Jews Led by Vicente Ferrer 1391-1420

The Dominican Order (known as the Order of the Preachers) was founded by a Spanish priest, Dominic, and approved by Pope Innocent III in 1216. They were also called "the hounds of the Lord," and the mission of the Order was to preach and stamp out heresy. Starting in the 1200s through the 1400s, their focus was on eradicating Jews. Dominican preachers were the leaders in carrying out evangelical campaigns against Jews, which led to repeated attacks on *juderias* (Jewish quarters), the destruction of synagogues, and the killings of untold numbers of Jews. The Dominican Order, as anti-Jewish preachers and leaders of the Inquisition, was the spear point of the Catholic Church in its attack on Jewish life in Spain.

Dominican Preaching to Jews

From 1390 to 1419 the Dominican Friar Vicente Ferrer was a central figure in the attack on Jews. Ferrer, who had wide popular appeal, was overtly anti-Jewish, reflecting a position that had been growing in Christian thought since the 1200s. Ferrer was known for his long evangelical campaigns visiting hundreds of towns. When he would arrive to a town, the local Jews were rounded up and forced to hear his sermons, denouncing them as infidels and appealing directly to them to convert to Catholicism. His strident denunciations led Christian throngs to attack Jewish neighborhoods and businesses with chains, clubs, and other weapons, turning his followers into mobs.[24] An element to his success as an evangelist was the atmosphere created by the mob behavior of those who followed him.[25] Thousands of Jews did convert under the threat of being attacked and beaten or even killed after his visits.[26]

Ferrer's first campaign against Jews was in 1390 when he encouraged the wave of anti-Semitism that was sweeping Spain at the time.

He went on an evangelizing mission to Castile that year accompanied by Cardinal Pedro de Luna, who was later elected Pope Benedict XIII. The two were to lead the anti-Jewish forces in Spain over the next three decades, each re-enforcing the other.

The smoldering anti-Semitism burst into full view the next year, 1391, in Seville, the richest and most important Jewish community in the country. The King and the Archbishop died within months of each other, leaving a power vacuum. Ferrán Martínez, Vicar General to the Archbishop and long-time anti-Jewish advocate, took advantage of that moment to order the destruction of all synagogues in the city.[27] As he fanned anti-Semitic sentiments over the next few months, mobs not only destroyed the synagogues, but they also pillaged Jewish neighborhoods and killed thousands of Jews.

Vicente Ferrer was a leader of this campaign in the rest of Spain, and the attacks quickly spread from Seville to Toledo, Burgos, Valencia, and Barcelona. In some cities the entire Jewish quarter was destroyed including houses, businesses, and synagogues.

After the threat of the riots subsided, many of the Jews who converted under threat seem to have regretted their conversion and wanted to return to Jewish life and practice, but once they were baptized, they were considered Christians by both the Church and the Crown. The converts who wanted to return to Jewish life were perceived as turncoats by Church officials, and they were derided with the offensive term, marranos (i.e. pigs). Jane Gerber estimates that after the year of rioting in 1391, 100,000 Jews converted, 100,000 had been murdered, and another 100,000 survived by going into hiding or fleeing the country.[28]

When the Jewish community of Toledo was attacked by Christian forces in 1391, it was largely destroyed. When Toledo had been taken by the Christians in 1085, it had been a wealthy community of merchants, financiers, and diplomats. The lives of Jews initially remained unchanged, but that was to change by laws discriminating against Jews and banning them from public positions. After the attacks of 1391, the community was impoverished and could no longer pay the annual taxes levied on them by the king.

When Vicente Ferrer came to Toledo in 1411, he entered the Jewish quarter under armed guard and confiscated the Ibn Shushan Synagogue in the name of the Church. The seizure of this synagogue was symbolically important because it was the oldest synagogue in Spain built in 1180. The Jewish community seems to have been so weakened that they could not block the loss of their synagogue. After the synagogue was taken by the Church, it was renamed Santa Maria la Blanca (The White [Pure] Saint Mary), and it is still owned by the Catholic Church. It is shown as the Frontispiece of this book.

This cultural and religious genocide of 1391 occurred during the reign of King Henry III of Castile and Leon (1390-1406). It was condoned by the Crown and encouraged by Dominican friars as part of the emerging policy of the Catholic Church to erase Jewish life in the Iberian Peninsula. Jewish communities were devastated, never to recover, and the 100,000 converts were unprepared for life as Christians. These attacks starting in 1391 left the Jewish world in Spain fatally crippled and on an irreversible downward slope.

Ferrer's preaching in this crusade through Castile was a part of the environment of anti-Semitism that led to the 1391 assaults on Jews. As entire Jewish populations were wiped out in various cities, the experience seems to have honed his vision that it was in fact possible to eradicate Jews from Spain. In the week of August 30, 1411, Ferrer preached in Segovia, the capital of King Henry III, and in surrounding towns where there were Jews. In one sermon he said,

> *Now, good people, listen that this goes against the Jews, because they say, "Cursed is the man who believes in a man [i.e. Jesus]." Here, I will catch them! Listen, you Jews, trust in the king Messiah and don't say that the king Messiah cannot be man and god...They say 'That the king Messiah is not God, and that is the reason that they are the corrupt and hated of all people.*[29]
>
> -- Translation by author

Ferrer's impact on Jews in Spain during the 1390's and early 1400's was immeasurable. Spanish Jews were demoralized, and their communities destroyed. In his denunciation of Jews as the "corrupt and hated of all people," and building on the environment of hatred and fear, he was credited with the conversion of 25,000 Jews, including Jewish leaders and rabbis. Their conversions caused a crisis, weakening the solidarity of communities and leading to further conversions, a descending spiral that would end with the Expulsion in 1492.

Ferrer had established his credentials as an evangelist, but he had done so in the environment of anti-Jewish pogroms. In the early 1400's he began elaborating a plan to crush the *aljamas*, or Jewish communities, that had survived the genocidal attacks of 1391. His plan was to ghettoize the remaining Jews and remove them completely from contact with Christians.

As Vicente Ferrer's influence grew, he worked with the rulers of various kingdoms in Spain to enact restrictive laws against Jews,[30] limiting their access to education and to professions. Jewish councils that had made decisions about their own communities were abolished, and Jews were no longer allowed to provide services to Christians as doctors, pharmacists, surgeons, barbers, blacksmiths, carpenters, tailors, shoemakers, butchers, leather workers, or other occupations.[31]

These economic restrictions blocked Jews from most of their traditional jobs, eliminating the Jewish educated elite from working in the administrative, financial, and judicial branches of government and Jewish commoners from working in the crafts. These laws reduced Jews to poverty. Ferrer's plan set the Jews apart as exile communities within their own towns, isolating them from Christians. It was a precursor to the Expulsion of Jews from Spain itself.

In subsequent years, Jewish ghettos were set up throughout Castile and Aragón, and Jews lived as a separate people. They could no longer dress in fine attire and were limited to the most modest clothes of the poor. Men were required to grow their beards and hair long, and no one could use Christian names, hire Christians to work for them, attend Christian weddings or funerals, or carry arms.

These restrictive measures continued to push Jews toward conversion or emigration, and throughout the 1400s the Jewish population steadily declined. In the long slow bleed from 1348 to 1492, two-thirds of the Jewish population had been killed, left Spain or converted. Spain was no longer the center of Jewish life in Europe.

As the number of converted Jews grew steadily, their presence led to another crisis. Converso families were aware of Shabbat and when the Jewish holidays were coming. If converso families were actually preserving Jewish observance, they could consult with family members about Jewish law or even the dates of holidays and fasts. That was one of the problems that the Edict of Expulsion was intended to solve. By expelling openly practicing Jews, it would be easier to supervise and control the converted Jews, the so-called "New Christians", and this divide and conquer strategy worked.

During 1411 and 1412 Ferrer traveled throughout the kingdoms of Castile and Aragón in evangelistic crusades and joined forces with his old friend Pedro de Luna, who was now Pope Benedict XIII, having been elected by the Avignon court during the schism with Rome. The Pope had established his court in Aragon, and his personal doctor was a Jewish physician, Joshua Lorkí, who had been a student of Rabbi Solomon Halevi in Burgos. Lorkí already had doubts about his faith, and Ferrer persuaded him to become a Christian. After converting he took the Christian name of Geronimo de Santa Fé and became an advocate of the Christian campaign to convert Jews.

Disputation of Tortosa

In 1413, the collaboration between Ferrer and the schismatic Pope Benedict XIII led to a confrontation with Jews when the Pope ordered each of the Jewish communities of Aragón and Cataluña to send their rabbis to the papal court at Tortosa to receive instruction in Christian beliefs. Geronimo de Santa Fé (Joshua Lorkí) became a key figure in the Disputation of Tortosa, trying to proselytize the Jewish leaders.

One hundred and fifty years after the Disputation of Barcelona between Nahmanides and Church officials about the divinity of Jesus, Pope Benedict XIII made the Disputation of Tortosa a proselytizing event directed against Jewish leaders. In contrast to Barcelona where one rabbi, Nahmanides, represented the Jewish community, in a Disputation that lasted four days, in Tortosa the Church sequestered twenty-two rabbis and Jewish scholars for most of two years. This was a show trial of

Catholic power and Jewish vulnerability in the presence of the court of cardinals loyal to the Pope.[32] The Pope had called the Disputation of Tortosa in a gamble that if he could put enough pressure on Jewish leaders they would convert, and in turn they would lead the Jews of Aragón and Catalunya to convert. The conversion of so many would have supported his claim to be the legitimate pope.

When all seemed to be lost, there was a turning point, a reprieve for the Jewish communities. The rabbis resisted. Benedict XIII lost his gamble, and after two years the rabbis were allowed to go home. In 1416 Benedict's primary supporter, King Fernand of Aragon, died. Months later Benedict was declared schismatic; his authority as Pope was revoked; and, he was excommunicated from the Catholic Church. Without those two powerful supporters, Ferrer lost his political influence. After that his projection as a preacher and religious activist declined. Ferrer died three years later in 1419, and the anti-Jewish forces lost their most forceful protagonist.

The Matter of New Christians

The Church and Spanish society were unprepared for 100,000 converts in 1391 and the flood of converts that ebbed and flowed for the next century. In spite of the fact that apparently no preparations had been made to provide education or orientation for these families after conversion, many were successful in their transition to becoming New Christians. The Halevi/Santa Maria family is an example.

One of the famous cases of conversion was that of Rabbi Solomon Halevi, a scholar of the Talmud and rabbinical literature in Burgos, who converted on July 21, 1391 during the attacks on Jews in his city.[33] He took the Christian name of Pablo de Santa Maria. His two brothers, sister, and his five children all converted at the same time. Only his wife did not convert, but it seems that she must have converted later because at her death, she was buried in the church that her former husband, now priest, had built.

Pablo de Santa Maria and his family are examples of conversos being successful as New Christians; they survived and prospered. Because of their education, many conversos went directly into important positions reserved only for Christians. Joining the Church hierarchy was a successful strategy for many. Pablo de Santa Maria became a priest, studied in Paris and received a doctorate in theology, and returned to Burgos, where he was named Archbishop.[34] He was later named Lord Chancellor of Castile, and when the old king died, he served as Regent until the young king came of age. Santa Maria acquired such power in the Church in Spain that he became a king maker and might have had aspirations to the papacy itself. He remained an ally of Ferrer, and as Chancellor, they collaborated in formulating restrictive laws against Jewish communities.

The Carvajal-Santa Maria Family

Historian Roger Martínez-Dávila's research on the Old Christian family, the Carvajal, and the successful converso family, the Santa Maria has shown how people integrated their lives first in Spain and then later in the Americas. His book *Creating Conversos: the Carvajal-Santa Maria Family in Early Modern Spain* gives the details of marriages and family arrangements in an integrated historical narrative.

Martínez-Dávila[35] has complied a detailed history of the Solomon Halevi family, and this is arguably the most detailed history of a family of conversos and how they assimilated into the Catholic life. As the Santa Maria family intermarried with the Carvajal family, their descendants had significant impact both in Church positions, as well as in secular life. Three sons of Rabbi Solomon Halevi, now priest Pablo de Santa Maria, followed their father into the priesthood, which was not uncommon in converso families. They were located in Plasencia and the nearby region of Spain.

Relatives of the Carvajal and Santa Maria families migrated to the Americas and became major figures in Mexico. They were even involved in the Inquisition, and in at least one instance, they oversaw the trial and executions of conversos in their own extended family. Martínez-Dávila has shown how this family covered up converso elements in their background to preserve their identity as devout adherents to the Catholic Church. Referring to his own branch of that family, he says,

Forced Conversions

My Carvajal family settled in San Antonio de Bejar, Texas, in 1703. Although our oral family history imparted that we were related to Luis de Carvajal "the Younger"...we had no tangible historical record to connect us to this Sephardic Jewish lineage. Furthermore, as intensely devoted Roman Catholics with a carefully documented genealogy leading back to Mateo de Carvajal from Santiago de la Monclova, Mexico, in the late 1600s, we did not know how to reconcile our disparate Christian and Jewish histories.[36]

Based on years of archival research, he has reconstructed the history of this family, its involvement in the Church, and the navigation of the troubled waters between a Jewish converso background, the Inquisition, and a predominantly Catholic society.

The Aftermath of Conversion

Although there were restrictions on Jewish converso families, they could be employed in the government if they had the right credentials, and they were allowed to open businesses unavailable to Jews, improving their economic situation. As New Christians with the right documentation, they could now marry into Old Christian families, and many did.

As the pressure increased on Jews to convert during the fourteenth century, conversos became an increasing reality and an important presence in Spain in the affairs of state and the economy. The success in converting Jews created problems because these New Christians did not have the same cultural practices as Old Christians. For example, they were not inclined toward the mortification of the flesh, such as self-flagellation, which was a Christian practice, and they might not have understood the centrality of belief over practice in Catholicism.

The success of New Christians created envy among Old Christians who saw these converts a threat to Catholicism because they did not always behave like Christians. Jews were equally offended at seeing the collusion of these New Christian converts with the Christian establishment.[37] Although many of the conversos achieved success as Christians and adapted to their new lives, others did not adapt to Catholic life and eventually left Spain to migrate elsewhere.

Crypto-Jews

Jews who nominally converted but continued Jewish observance, emerged as a major preoccupation for the Church. Priests were aware of New Christians who did not attend mass or confession and were negligent in Christian practice. As the number of converts grew, the Church became focused on the issues of heresy and apostasy among the tens of thousands who had converted. From our distance of several centuries, it is difficult to know to what extent the Church used the image of crypto-Jews as a straw man threat to enhance their control over New Christians and other potential heretics.

As the number of Jewish converts living in Spain grew into the tens of thousands and then to 100,000 and more, no doubt there were many thousands who were not loyal Catholics. Since heresy was intolerable to the Church, it was a real problem. Even while this matter of false conversions was becoming more and more apparent, Dominican preachers continued their pressure on Jews to convert.

Thousands of conversos became hidden or crypto-Jews, continuing to practice their Jewish tradition in secret. The psychological turmoil must have been profound for these New Christians. They converted to save their lives and their families, but how many felt the emotional backlash of their actions later?

Jane Gerber asks at what point does a converso stop thinking of himself or herself as a Jew? Since the Church did not teach them how to be Catholics, a converso might continue thinking of themselves as a Jew and observing traditional practices for years.[38] After the Expulsion of the Jews in 1492, there could have been 100,000 to 200,000 conversos in Spain, and we can only imagine the number that would have been crypto-Jews.

The Church saw these false converts as a threat that had to be eradicated. Working together with the Spanish Crown to solve the problem, the Spanish Inquisition was established to police converso behavior, and then came the drastic decision of expelling the Jews.

The Demography of Jewish Conversion in Spain 1300-1492

The Jewish population of Spain fell dramatically between 1350 and 1492. The overall population of Spain dropped from eight million at the beginning of the millennium to six million after the Black Death and the continuing warfare between the Christian kingdoms and the Muslims. By 1500 it is estimated to have risen again to eight million people.

Jewish Population Trend in Spain 1300-1492

Years	1300	1350	1400	1450	1492	1500
400,000	■					
350,000	■	■				
300,000	■	■				
250,000	■	■	■			
200,000	■	■	■	■		
150,000	■	■	■	■	■	
0	■	■	■	■	■	

Chart 3.1

Chart 2.1 shows the dramatic decline of the Jewish population in Christian Spain from the largest in Europe to zero in a period of 150 years. Spain was trying to eliminate its Jewish population, and it did. The cultural genocide or annihilation of large concentrations of Jews has happened three times in the modern era, first in Spain (1350-1500), secondly in Russia and Eastern Europe by the Russian Czars and the German Nazis (1880-1945), and thirdly in the Arab world (1948-1975). In these three instances major Jewish populations were eliminated after having lived for centuries in the land.

Crypto-Jews

As the Church and Crown became more involved in eradicating Jews from Spain and the Jewish community became smaller and weaker, the rates of conversion became steadily higher.

Pattern of Conversion Rates of Jews in Spain 1300-1492 by Percentage of Jewish Population					
Percent	6.25	10	33	20.0	50.0
60.00					
55.00					
50.00					■
45.00					■
40.00					■
35.00					■
30.00			■		■
25.00			■		■
20.00			■		■
15.00			■		■
10.00		■	■		■
5.0	■	■	■		■
Years	1300	1350	1391	1450	1492

Chart 3.2

When the population of Jews in Spain was still large in the early 1300s, the rates of conversion were small, only 5 or 6 percent, but that increased to 15 percent following the persecutions of the Black Death and 30 percent following the 1391 massacres. The climax came with a conversion rate that was 35 to 50 percent at the time of the Expulsion. The pressure on the Jews to convert grew as the community became smaller and more vulnerable, leading to an increased percentage of conversions, and the community becoming smaller and weaker, a repeating cycle.

The more than 200,000 Jewish converts to Catholicism between 1350 and 1492 represent an average of more than 1,000 converts per year. Half of those (100,000) occurred between 1450 and 1492. Anthropologist Seth Kunin points out that the number of people who converted and became crypto-Jews was minuscule in the context of the total Spanish population.[39]

The conversion of 50,000 to 75,000 Jews in one year, 1492, was huge, but it represented less than one percent of the larger Spanish population of eight million. This was the largest concentration of conversos in the history of Spain, and some percentage of these conversos would have maintained Jewish identity as crypto-Jews.[40]

Over the next few decades, they were persecuted by the forces of the Inquisition, producing a series of emigrations from Spain throughout the 1500s. In the two hundred years from 1300 to 1500 Jewish populations were persecuted and exiled across much of Western Europe, but Spain was the most prominent example.

True Believers and Feigned Conversions

Many Jews converted to Catholicism as true believers and practitioners, and as we have seen, some even became leaders in the Church. Others must have been more casual about the conversion and while attending mass and observing Christian holidays, probably also observed their traditional Jewish holidays, maybe having Shabbat dinner with family members.

The Maimonides Principle

After the Almohad invasion of Spain in 1148, the invaders brought pressure on Jews to convert to Islam. Maimonides and his family left Spain at that point, perhaps feigning conversion to Islam to save their lives. In 1164-65 he wrote the "Epistle on Martyrdom"[41] providing the theological support for false conversions when he advocated that rather than die, a Jew should feign conversion to save his or her life and then move as soon as possible to a safer place to resume life as a practicing Jew. This was a letter to the Jews of Spain who were confronting forced conversions. When Jews in Christian and Muslim lands have come under pressure historically, some have converted, but the false conversion, as a massive social phenomenon occurs for the first time in Spain.

For the feigned conversion principle to work, Jewish conversos would have had to leave Spain and Portugal soon and move to a place where they could resume living as Jews, or their children would assimilate, and Jewish practice would be degraded or lost. In the decades subsequent to 1492, tens of thousands of Jewish conversos from Spain and Portugal did migrate to lands accepting Jews. Those who stayed and chose to migrate to the Americas violated the reasoning of the Maimonides principle. By staying in lands of the Inquisition, they did not give their descendants the opportunity to return to the practice of Judaism.

Crypto-Jews and Assimilation

Maintaining a crypto-Jewish life in the hostile environment of the Church-controlled Spanish and Portuguese societies would have been difficult. With no synagogues, rabbis, or Torah scrolls Jewish life would have inevitably faded to more memory than practice.

David Graizbord writes about the crisis of identity among Jews who converted to Catholicism.[42] Among Jewish scholars, conversos were initially considered to be *anusim,* the ones forced to convert, but with time they came to be considered as *meshummadim,* the ones destroyed by conversion. In parallel manner, Christians also began to see conversos in a less favorable light, and the term "converso" began to be conflated with the idea of someone who was still essentially a Jew.[43]

In cultural terms, memory of family history normally does not endure for more than three or four generations unless there is an institutionalized oral tradition in stories or songs to preserve that memory. Studies of contemporary American society show high rates of assimilation by the second or third generations and total assimilation by the fourth generation, a period of 80 to 100 years.

If that applied in Spain and Portugal, the normal process of assimilation would have absorbed most descendants of Jewish conversos by 1600. Although the Inquisition continued to prosecute people in Spain for Judaizing throughout the 1600s, the numbers of those convicted dropped dramatically. On one hand, this suggests that there were few crypto-Jews left in Spain to prosecute, and on the other the focus of the Inquisition was shifting toward other heresies. By the late 1500s the Protestant movement was more of a threat to the Catholic Church than were Jews.

Although cultural and religious practices tend to be lost through assimilation after four or five generations, there are exceptions. There are documented cases of survival of Jewish rituals or customs for generations or even centuries when the origins of the practice have been forgotten. University of Cambridge researcher Vanessa Paloma Elbaz has documented the singing of *Ein Kelohenu* in Judeo-Spanish in the city of Taroudant, where the Jewish community speaks Arabic, not Spanish. It is sung once a year during *Simchat Torah,* and people sing the words from memory without knowing their meaning. The singing of this song is a survival from the migration of a Sephardic family or families to the city at some unknown point in the past, and the song continues to be performed in memory of those distant Sephardic ancestors.[44]

Jewish conversos did survive in Portugal until later, but they were also leaving by the early 1600s in two migrations, one to the Americas and the other to the Netherlands. Those who migrated to the Americas risked continuing their lives as crypto-Jews even though the Inquisition was not as daunting there as in Spain. The group migrating to The Netherlands did so to return to living as Jews. Amsterdam was the most important location, and that city grew to 5,000 Portuguese Jews and became one of the richest Jewish communities in the Europe.

1492
A Year that Changed Jewish Life in Europe

- January 2. Muhammad XII surrendered the Emirate of Granada the last Muslim kingdom on the Iberian Peninsula to the Christian monarchs, Ferdinand and Isabella. Muslims left for Morocco.
- March 31. The Alhambra Decree (Edict of Expulsion). Ferdinand and Isabella issued the Edict expelling all Jews from their kingdoms of Castile and Aragon.
- April 17. Christopher Columbus received authorization from Ferdinand and Isabella for a voyage to the west. The voyage was not funded by the Crown but by Jews and conversos.
- July 31. The deadline for Jews to leave Spain or convert. An estimated 50,000 to 100,000 converted and stayed, but the majority left Spain. Thousands migrated to Portugal.
- August 2. *Tisha B'Av.* Because of the short notice on selling properties and preparing to leave, Isaac Abarbanel gained a concession of two days for Jews to leave. It fell on Tisha B'Av, the remembrance of tragedy in Jewish life, including the Fall of the two temples and the 1306 expulsion of Jews from France.
- August 3. Columbus and crew set sail for the lands to the west. Four crew members were conversos.
- October 12. Columbus made landfall in the Americas, claiming the new lands in the name of the King of Spain. The Jewish converso, Luis Torres, a translator, was one of the first on shore.
- October 24. Twenty-four Jews burned at the stake in Mecklenburg, Germany.
- November 15. In La Guardia, Spain, 6 Jews and 5 conversos were accused of ritual murder
- December 31. 100,000 Jews were expelled from Sicily.

Chapter 4

Inquisition and Expulsion

Figure 12
National Theater Maria II
Rossio Square, Lisbon
Formerly Estaus Palace
Tribunal of the Inquisition

THE CATHOLIC MONARCHS, Queen Isabella and King Ferdinand were the ultimate power couple of the late fifteenth century. They started the Spanish Inquisition, drove out the Muslims,[45] expelled Jews, launched the discovery of the Americas, and transformed their small, fragmented kingdoms into the modern nation state of Spain, which became a superpower of its day.

Ferdinand and Isabella had a history of making restrictions on Jewish life. In 1480 they had re-instituted the order that all Jews be separated into *juderias* or ghettos and not have contact with Christians. They accused the Jews of continuing to teach Judaism to the conversos, making it difficult for them to be good Catholics.

Tomás de Torquemada, a Dominican priest and architect of the Expulsion of Jews, was the personal confessor to Queen Isabella and an important presence at court. He argued that as long as practicing Jews lived in Spain, it was impossible for conversos to be good New Christians. After initially consulting with the Pope on the question, he appealed to King Ferdinand and Queen Isabella, and they agreed to expel the Jews.

Torquemada had been named the director of the Spanish Inquisition in 1483, and he led it until his death in 1498,[46] persecuting Jewish conversos thought to be crypto-Jews. Although he came from an observant Christian family, one of his grandmothers was from a family of conversos. As happened with many Jewish families that converted, they were assimilated New Christians and had a history of dedicated service to the Church, and his becoming a priest, personal confessor to the queen, and Chief Inquisitor was a continuation of that service.

The Spanish Inquisition

The Spanish Inquisition (1478-1834) was authorized by the Vatican and established by the Spanish Crown to combat heresy in Spain. In actual fact the Inquisition helped the monarchy to consolidate its power over a unified Spain, which had been divided into four kingdoms when the Inquisition was established. Previously, there had been many Inquisitions in Europe, but they were normally under the direction of the Church and for short periods of time.

The Spanish Inquisition was unusual because it was an institution under the Spanish Crown, not under the Pope, and it existed for more than 300 years.[46] The Inquisitors or Judges were Church officials, working for the Spanish Crown. A person being judged was held in an Inquisitional prison. If they were convicted of a religious crime by the Inquisitors, Crown officials transferred the person to a Crown prison to carry out the sentence.

The Spanish Inquisition, also known to as the Holy Inquisition or the Holy Office of the Inquisition, was led by members of the Dominican Order. They acted as the judges, jury, prosecutors, and defenders for people arrested on the suspicion of Judaizing or observing the Law of Moses, the Torah. In some aspects the Inquisition was ahead of its time with trained judges and defenders assigned to the accused person. But the Inquisition was also an institution of its time, focused on belief and religious practice. The Enlightenment era emphasizing rationalism and human rights was still centuries in the future.

Queen Isabella, who was deeply religious, seemed to have believed that political institutions must have a religious foundation. In the early decades the focus was on policing Jewish converts, but that evolved over the centuries. Later, the Inquisition was more focused on Protestants, witchcraft, bigamy, blasphemy, the solicitation of women in the confessional by priests, and Enlightenment thought among other religious crimes.

Torture

The Inquisition was the religious police force to identify, arrest, and punish people who did not accept official Catholic creed. The purpose of the Spanish Inquisition was to stamp out heretical movements, among both Old and New Christians. The historian Cecil Roth describes the torture techniques used to elicit confessions and to obtain the names of other followers of the "Law of Moses". He describes a broad range of torture from scourging to burning the feet, the rack, a version of waterboarding, and hanging a person from their bound arms behind their back. Prisoners, men, women, teen-age boys and girls, and pregnant women alike, would be stripped as the torture would begin. They would be badgered to confess the crimes for which they were accused, such as not eating pork or putting on fresh clothes for Saturday. The torture would be increased in increments to force the confessions. The management of torture varied over time and from office to office of the Inquisition.[47]

Punishment and the Auto-de-Fé

Although the Office of the Inquisition persecuted other heretics, a major focus of its efforts in the late 1400s and early 1500s was on Judaizing. Convicted Judaizers were sentenced in grand public events, referred to as an *auto-de-fé* (act of faith), which were stadium sized events in large plazas of cities. People who confessed their Judaizing and repented could be reconciled with the Church and allowed to live. It was a celebration of the combined power of the Church and the Crown.

Punishment for crimes against the Church included being publicly sentenced in an *auto-de-fé* and wearing the *sanbenito*, a cape-like penitential garment whenever in public as a punishment of shame. The sentence of wearing the *sanbenito* could be for several years. After the sentence was completed, the *sanbenito* of each punished person was then hung in the local Church to continue shaming the person for life. A conical hat completed the display of their wrongdoing. Since this was a Church event, a Mass was said with prayer in addition to the procession of religious convicts.

After their sentences were read, the prisoners were turned over to Crown authorities. For those condemned to death, they were burned at the stake in a separate event.[48] In the Americas, burning people at the stake was rare, and people convicted of Judaizing were more commonly expelled from Spanish territories without the right of return.

According to historian Henry Kamen, the period of most intense activity by the Inquisition in Spain was 1480 to 1530, and his review of Inquisition records indicates that more than 10,000 conversos were arrested during those fifty years, and 2,000 were burned at the stake in a death foretelling the hell to which their souls were being committed.[49] Some estimates put the number of people arrested and executed much higher. The period of most intense activity in the American colonies came a century later the 1630-1650 time frame.

The Alhambra Decree: the Edict of Expulsion

After defeating and driving out the last Muslim kingdom in January of 1492, Ferdinand and Isabella issued the Alhambra Decree, the Edict of Expulsion of Jews, on March 31, 1492 in a move to create an all Christian Spain.[50] Muslims were defeated and driven out, and Jews were ordered to leave by July 31, 1492.

They were not allowed to take gold with them. Those who were leaving had to sell properties and businesses or abandon them. The Crown confiscated the public buildings of Jewish communities, such as hospitals and schools, giving synagogues to the Church, which converted most into churches. Synagogue buildings were given Christian names, such as Sangre de Cristo or "Blood of Christ", in keeping with the old accusation that Jews had been responsible for the death of Jesus.

The decision by a Jewish family to leave meant financial losses. A year after the Expulsion the monarchs issued a call to the Jews who had left, offering them the possibility of returning and recovering their properties if they would convert. Most ignored the message.

According to the Edict of Expulsion,

> *This proved by many statements and confessions, both from these same Jews and from those who have been perverted and enticed by them, which has redounded to the great injury, detriment, and opprobrium of our holy Catholic faith.*

Because the Jews were believed to be a danger to the faith of New Christians, they were expelled from all the territories of Spain. In the Decree Ferdinand and Isabella specifically stated,

Inquisition and Expulsion

Therefore, we, with the counsel and advice of prelates, great noblemen of our kingdoms, and other persons of learning and wisdom of our Council, having taken deliberation about this matter, resolve to order the said Jews and Jewesses of our kingdoms to depart and never to return or come back to them or to any of them.

The Exodus

One of the stories of the drama of the Expulsion occurred with Isaac Abarbanel and Abraham Senior, who had been important advisers to Isabella. They advocated with the King and Queen to rescind the Edict of Expulsion,[51] offering them a large amount of money gathered from the Jewish community. As we know, the monarchs did not revoke the Edict, and Torquemada is said to have intervened and denounced the plan as evidence of the unchristian influence of the Jews in Spain. The Jews were expelled.

Isaac Abarbanel and his family left for Italy with 10,000 other Jews, but Abraham Senior and his family stayed and converted.

Those Who Left

Perhaps the more observant Jews were those who chose to leave Spain rather than convert, but what did being more observant mean? Were they more identified with Judaism? Was the synagogue more a part of their lives? Were they more identified with the traditions of food, the holidays, the stories, the bonds of family and community? In Sephardic communities today the sacred and the profane spheres of life are fused and inseparable. We can only imagine that observant Jews in Spain in 1492 would have found it intolerable to have the sacred part of their public lives taken away from them. They would have left Spain to preserve the synagogue prayers, Torah study, and the *derasha* or teachings of the rabbis.

Crypto-Jews Who Converted and Stayed

As citizens of the twenty-first century, we might ask, "Why would Jews chose to stay in Spain with the threat of arrest, torture, and being burned at the stake?" What would have been the motivations for crypto-Jews to choose Spanish and Portuguese territories over migration to freedom in countries where Jewish practice was legal?

Who decided to convert and stay in Spain? Were they more assimilated as Spaniards? Were they more secular and loosely connected to the Jewish community and their identity as Jews? Did they identify more with Spanish traditions, holidays, and foods? Did they have sons and daughters or other family members who had converted, so they converted to be able to stay with them? We know that at least one of the members of Columbus crew in 1492 converted days before leaving just to be able to go on the voyage. So, there were many personal reasons for converting and staying.

Did they convert to protect property and businesses and avoid catastrophic economic losses? Did some think that the Expulsion would be short term, as happened in France, and they could convert and wait it out? Many of them like Jews in Germany in the 1930s must have miscalculated what was to come. Did the more pessimistic leave because they thought the worst could happen, and the more optimistic stay because they never believed it could get as bad as it did? Were some poor and simply could not afford the expense of moving to another country?

Even though they might have converted to Catholicism, they were still culturally Jews. Culture is deeply rooted; it is the comfort zone of life. Identification with language and homeland is strong and could have commanded the loyalty that was motivation to stay. Some wanted to continue being Spanish and Jewish at the same time, even after it was clearly illegal to do so. From our historical distance, how can we understand the diverse motivations that might have led Jews to convert and stay in Spain?

For others not leaving Spain might have been inertia, or the fear of leaving what was familiar to them. People heard about the difficulties of traveling over unknown roads to new lands they did not know. People were attacked along the way. Although Jews were not legally allowed to take gold with them as they left, some tried. Historian David Gitlitz mentions that people could have seen "the bodies of Jews eviscerated for the gold they had allegedly swallowed trying to smuggle it out of Spain."[52] These and other considerations might have made the decision to stay more compelling than leaving.

Abraham Senior was the most important Jew who decided to convert and stay in Spain in 1492. He and his son-in-law Rabbi Meir Melamed were baptized on June 15, 1492 in the presence of the King Ferdinand and Queen Isabella and other members of the Court. For the King and Queen his conversion and that of his family was especially important. He was a major tax official in the Kingdom of Castile for Queen Isabella which guaranteed the collection of taxes would continue uninterrupted. He was also one of the leaders in the Jewish community in Spain, which gave validation to the tens of thousands of Jews who were converting to stay.[53]

After 1492 anyone in Spain was considered to be a Christian, but Jewish businessmen, who escaped to nearby countries, especially France, Italy, and Morocco, continued to enter and leave Spain over the next few decades and for more than a century. They would do so with different sets of identity papers and different dress, one Christian to travel in Spain and the other Jewish for regular life in their home country.

How Many Left in 1492?

How many Jews were still living in Spain at the time of the Expulsion? We do not know the exact numbers, but the estimates range between 100,000 and 200,000.[54] At the lower end historian Henry Kamen's analysis of tax returns gave a population of 80,000 Jews in Spain at the time of the Expulsion.[55] His estimate is that fewer than 40,000 converted and stayed. Most scholars agree that one-third to one-half chose to stay and convert (35,000 to 100,000) while half to two-thirds left (50,000 to 125,000).[56] Given the pre-existing Jewish converso population, this could have pushed their numbers up to 100,000 or more, as the fifteenth century ended.

Linajudos and Limpieza de Sangre

By the 1450s blood purity or *limpieza de sangre* statues were being put in place by the Catholic Church, the Spanish Crown, and other institutions. Roger Martínez-Dávila notes that blood purity laws were based on the merging of the religious self and genealogy. Jewishness and Muslimness were considered to be conditions inherent in "blood" descent, and both groups were thought to be spiritually flawed. Acceptance into good society in Spain meant not having any Jewish or Muslim family background.[57]

Crypto-Jews

Historian Ruth Pike describes how the insistence on *limpieza de sangre* as a qualification for offices and honors gave rise to the *linajudo*, essentially a genealogist who examined lineages to identify traces of Jewish or Muslim ancestry. Since New Christians were not allowed to go to the Americas, the scrutiny was most intense in Seville, which was the port for leaving. After the religious and ethnic cleansing in Spain was more or less complete by the 1600s, it was assumed that only Christians lived in the motherland, but the American colonies were less secure for Catholicism because of the Indians, Africans, crypto-Jews, and non-Catholics from other countries.

The Inquisitions in the Americas were weak compared to the one in Spain, so there was fear that New Christians going to the Americas might relapse and return to Jewish practice. Since the American territories were in the process of being Christianized, only Old Christians were legally allowed to travel there, but it was a rule impossible to enforce.

Migrants to the American colonies had to provide certification that none of their ancestors were of Jewish or Muslim descent, and that no one had been convicted by the Inquisition. A *linajudo* did the necessary genealogical research, but the system was noted for corruption, and with the right payment the necessary certification could be arranged.[58] Enforcing *limpieza de sangre* was difficult, and it was probably more observed in the breach than in practice.

Since everyone in Spain was a Christian by definition after 1492, one way to block a person from a position, an award, or travel to the Americas was to accuse them of being a New Christian. The Spanish focus on lineage and family ancestry gave genealogists a key role in society, but the *linajudo* was a new phenomenon that ran parallel to the Inquisition.[59]

Seville and other cities had thriving businesses of people creating identity papers. The *linajudos* produced genealogical booklets or passports for people, and even if a person had Jewish descent, some *linajudos* could "prune" the family tree to prove that the person was from an Old Christian family with no Jewish blood. Conversos changed their names to Christian names, frequently adopting family names that were very Catholic, such as Santa Maria or Cristiani.

The descendants of wealthy Jews, who converted at the time of the Expulsion, were able to get blood purity certificates, which enabled them to get certain jobs, receive awards and honors, and marry into wealthy Old Christian families. In Seville these families dominated the transatlantic trade and governed the city in the sixteenth and seventeenth centuries. The descendants of conversos in these families were the principal victims of the accusations of having Jewish blood, and they became an important source of income for the *linajudos*.

Although a descendant of conversos was not Judaizing, the person still could be defamed by being publicly denounced as having Jewish blood. Christian groups kept records of Jews who converted to identify people in the future who might deny their Jewish ancestry. This was an attempt to avoid descendants of conversos marrying into Old Christian families or gaining important positions in society. The *Libro Verde* (Green Book) of Aragon was one such document. It cataloged the descendants of converso families and could be consulted if an individual's legacy came into question. These documents were an attempt to block Jewish conversos from circumventing the norms and laws controlling their behavior.[60]

The Portuguese Ruse

In 1492, as many as 50,000 Jews leaving Spain went to Portugal. The Portuguese King John granted permanent residence to a few hundred wealthy families and craftsmen with skills, such as navigation and making armaments. Tens of thousands of others were granted temporary permits to stay in exchange for payment to the royal coffers. Not long afterwards, King John died and was succeeded by the younger King Manuel, who wanted to marry Isabella, the daughter of Ferdinand and Isabella of Spain. The King and Queen agreed to the marriage, but with the pre-condition that Manuel expel the Jews first. The young king wanted to marry Isabella, but he was not eager to lose the Jews, so he conspired to make an Edict of Expulsion that would be effective one year after it was issued in 1496. That gave the Jews one year to convert, and it gave him a year to develop a strategy to avoid their leaving.

Increasing the pressure on the Portuguese Jews, in March 1497 Jewish parents were ordered to convert or surrender their children to

Christian families. An unknown number did convert under that pressure, but those who stood firm saw their children taken from them. During this time Jews were leaving Portugal in significant numbers.

Seeing the undesired emigration, King Manuel ordered Jews who wanted to leave to assemble in Lisbon, and some 20,000 gathered, expecting to leave, only to hear that he had issued a second decree declaring all Jews to be Christians. Later, Jews were denied the rights of either disposing of property or leaving the country. King Manuel could then report to his prospective in-laws, Queen Isabella and King Ferdinand that there were no more Jews in Portugal. With that he could marry their daughter.

That day in Lisbon created tens of thousands of Jewish conversos without their consent. To give these forcibly converted Jews time to become Catholic, King Manuel ordered that the Inquisition would not be established in Portugal for another forty years, allowing a period of two generations for Jews to make the transition to becoming Catholic.

Soon the anti-Semitism in Portugal would lead to conflict with these thousands of forced converts, *anusim*. During Easter week in 1506, 2,000 conversos being killed by mobs in Lisbon, led by two Dominican friars, who called on people to avenge the death of Jesus. Although the violence did not reach the level that it did on multiple occasions in Spain, it left a scar on Jewish life in Portugal that has never been erased.

Although these forcibly baptized Jews were not initially allowed to leave Portugal, they were allowed important positions in the Court and other prominent institutions. For example, Abraham Zacuto became court astronomer and mathematician, and he encouraged and trained Vasco da Gama for his historic voyage to India in 1497. Christopher Columbus had already used Zacuto's calculations for his voyage in 1492. Portuguese conversos and crypto-Jews were at the forefront of international commerce and helped project that country into a major role in the exploration of the African coast.

The Portuguese captured a number of existing port cities along the coast of Morocco and built their own forts from Tangier to Rabat, El Jadida, and Essaouira. They extended their presence to the West Coast of Africa, building other forts along the way. Their political ambitions in Morocco ultimately failed, but they did successfully take sugar cane from Africa to the Americas and developed the slave trade along with it.[61]

Crypto-Jews continued to live in Portugal until the early 1600s, but after the Inquisition was established in 1536, they began leaving in large numbers. So many fled to the Americas that any one of Portuguese origin in the Spanish colonies was suspected of having a Jewish background.

Jewish conversos in Portugal were discriminated against and killed like Jews in Spain, but they were also incorporated into national life to a greater extent. In one town, Belmonte, in the mountains between Portugal and Spain, the descendants of Jewish families were openly recognized in the community until the twentieth century when they did make a return to Jewish practice, including the formation of a synagogue.

In the poem below João Pinto Delgado writes about the children of Israel leaving Egypt as a parallel to his family leaving Portugal for Amsterdam and their new life of living openly as Jews.

> João Pinto Delgado (1580-1653)
> La Salida de Egipto (Leaving Egypt)
>
> In this fierce Egypt
> of my sin, where my soul
> suffers the tyrannical servitude,
> of the infinite treasure
> of your divine flame,
> may you send, Master, a ray,
> may your holy inspiration be my guide;
> so that the light of your loving fire
> may call upon me in the desert, not coursed
> in mundane memory:
> therein naked, for your cause, in the blind
> veil of error, the past habit,
> may I ascend in joy to contemplate your glory,
> where my being by miraculous effect
> may become in itself a sovereign object.
> -- Translation Ilan Stavans

Emerging Crypto-Jewish Practice

Crypto-Jewish practice began to develop in the adaptations that conversos made to the Inquisition and the Expulsion. The crypto-Jews living in Spain in the early 1500s might still have lived in their hometowns where people knew that they were conversos, and where they were still fairly knowledgeable of Jewish practices. As they and their descendants moved to other locations in Portugal or the Americas, they would have had more anonymity, but they would also have had increasingly fading memories of what Jewish practice was. Gitlitz points out that:

> No single crypto-Jew ever observed the full gamut of crypto-Jewish customs. Individual religious practice varied in accord with conversos' family traditions, the habits of the crypto-Jewish local community of which they were a part, the degree of vigilance over conversos in their community, and their personal predilections.[62]

One of the windows into classic crypto-Jewish practice in Spain comes from research by Maria Antonia Bel Bravo on the convictions for Judaizing in the city of Granada in 1593. The Inquisition condemned eighty-six people for committing the following acts of Judaizing:

- Fasting (93 percent of the men and 89 percent of the women)
- Jewish dietary laws (47 percent men and 58 percent of the women)
- Observing Shabbat (33 percent men and 48 percent women)
- Observing Yom Kippur (33 percent men and 28 percent women)
- Observing Fast of Esther (20 percent men and 25 percent women) [63]

Crypto-Jews were arrested for specific observable practices, which focused on dietary laws and fasting and observing Shabbat or holidays. By 1593, it had been a century (or five generations) since the Expulsion, and most people would not have remembered the prayers in Hebrew. No Jewish books existed, so they could not study, so their Jewish lives were becoming a shadow of what they had been, but Bel Bravo's study indicates that crypto-Jews were maintaining a version of Jewish life. True to Jewish thought, crypto-Jews continued to believe that the Messiah was yet to come. Either the observance of Jewish practices or not believing Jesus was the Messiah would trigger an arrest if known by the Inquisition.

The Spectrum of Jewishness

Jewish conversos in the fifteenth and sixteenth centuries in Spain did not form a unified group. They varied in their retention of Jewish practices and adaptation to the Christian world. Renée Levine Melammed points out that there were differences in converso identity and practice between those who assimilated to Christianity, those who returned to Judaism leaving Spain and Portugal, and the Portuguese Anusim who were forced converts retaining their Jewish ethnic and religious identity, and what she calls the "fuzzy Jews" or those who would shift between identities.[64]

Converso behavior would have been spread along a spectrum of Jewishness from almost 0 to almost 100 percent. The conversos at the almost 0 end have been fully identified as Christians with only remnants of Jewish values or attitudes in their behavior. At the almost 100 percent end of the spectrum would have been those crypto-Jews who were fully committed to preserving their Jewish heritage. This group would have been those who later left Spain and Portugal for lands where they could return to living openly as Jews. Between these two ends of the spectrum a wide range of behaviors and identities would have been interwoven in the tens of thousands of lives of conversos with people negotiating with their surroundings for survival and integrity.

The voluntary converts to Catholicism had higher rates of loyalty to the Church, and their descendants assimilated more quickly. In contrast, many of those who were forced to convert (the *anusim*) continued to think of themselves as Jews and privately practice as crypto-Jews for a longer period of time.

By the 1530s the converso families in Spain must have realized that the Edict of Expulsion was a long-term feature of life. The mass arrests and burning of people at the stake, as staged public events by the Inquisition, threatened the very lives of anyone who was a converso. Life under the continued threat of arrest, torture, and death sentences must have been intolerable. As the 1500s progressed, the crypto-Jewish interest in leaving Spain and Portugal to escape the Inquisition grew. But it was illegal for New Christians to leave the country, even to travel to the Americas and being caught trying to leave could be considered as evidence of Judaizing.

A New Era of Jewish Conversos

In the 400 years of the Christian reconquest of Spain from the taking of Toledo in 1085 to the taking of Granada in 1492, Jewish life in Spain was slowly transformed from its Golden Age to the Expulsion and total elimination of Jews. Under Muslim rule, Jews had flourished, but under Christian rulers Jews were gradually impoverished, enclosed in *juderias* (Jewish ghettos), and expelled as undesirables.[65]

As Jews were pushed out of Spain, the resulting Diaspora transformed countries from the Ottoman Empire in the east to the Netherlands and England in the west. Portugal, with its Jewish navigators and mapmakers, changed the world making voyages to the East Indies and demonstrating the possibility of water routes to the sources of luxury goods in Asia. Jews and crypto-Jews led the way as spice traders with India, bringing new luxuries to Europe and creating the wealth of great Jewish merchant families. With Europe controlling the Americas and the sea routes to Asia, it was launched suddenly into the first era of global commerce with the resulting power and wealth, and Jews and their crypto-Jewish relatives were active in this new international trade.[66]

The century between 1450 and 1550 marked a profound change in European society, as it shifted from the medieval feudal, land-based system dominated by the Catholic Church to a pre-modern economy in which the centrality of the Church was broken. Commerce and international trade began to replace land as the basis of wealth with the development of shipping and ocean routes to distant lands.[67] Jews and crypto-Jews had roles in shipping, navigation, and the resulting international commerce in luxury items from sugar to gold and silver, spices, silks and porcelains.[68]

Was Columbus a Jew?

Existing evidence does not prove that Columbus was a Jew, but he did have close associations with Jews and conversos. He was from Genoa, but his ancestors might have been Spanish, and there are some indications that they had been Jewish.[69] As mapmakers, navigators, sailors, and people in maritime trade, Jews were his colleagues, an integral part of the ocean-going world of his day.

Isaac Abarbanel, who was an important Jewish presence at court before the Expulsion, had supported the idea of his voyage of discovery, and Abarbanel collaborated with two conversos Luis de Santangel and Gabriel Sanchez to loan Columbus the money to pay for the voyage. The family in the port of Palos that aided him with ships and supplies for the trip were conversos, and he had four conversos among the crew that sailed with him to the West. One of those was Luis de Torres, the translator, who Columbus referred to as a man who had been Jewish and knew Hebrew and Arabic. Others included Alonso de la Calle, the bursar, Rodrigo Sanchez, a physician, and Bernal of Tortosa, also a physician.

So, was Columbus of a Jewish converso family? Maybe. He lived and worked in a world ever present with Jews and conversos. His friends and colleagues were Jews, and he knew enough Hebrew to write cryptic notes in the language. He had an interest in Jewish matters, but he lived in a Catholic environment that did not permit being Jewish. If he had been known to be a Jew, he would never have received the support of King Ferdinand and Queen Isabella to make his famous voyage of 1492. If Columbus were a Jew, he was successful in hiding it like a crypto-Jew.

Jews and Crypto-Jews
in the Century that Changed the World 1450-1550

- 1450 - Anti-Semitism put Jews under pressure to convert to Catholicism. Jews are being driven out of Western Europe.
- 1453 - Turkish armies took Constantinople/Byzantium converting the Christian city into a Muslim one, Istanbul. Jews were welcomed.
- 1460-1470 - Printing revolutionizes Jewish life with the printed Torah, Talmud, *siddurim, haggadot*. Oldest surviving printed Hebrew book with a date is Rashi's commentary on the Torah from 1475.
- 1478 - Establishment of the Spanish Inquisition. From 1480 to 1530, 10,000 arrested for Judaizing, and 2,000 burned at the stake.
- 1492 - Jews were expelled from Spain. Sephardic Diaspora begins. Conversos sail with Columbus.[70]
- 1498 - Abraham Zacuto was a Jewish astronomer and mathematician who made astronomical tables and maps, and he trained Vasco de Gama, who reached India by the Cape of Good Hope. Levi ben Gerson invented the sea-quadrant or astrolabe for ocean navigation.
- 1500-1520 was the High Renaissance in Italy where Jews had freedom of religious practice.[71]
- 1517 - With Martin Luther's challenge to the Roman Church, Protestantism became a larger challenge to the Church than Jewish practice.[72]
- 1521 - The fall of Mexico to Cortés in the name of Spain. Converso soldiers were with Cortés.
- 1550 - Beginning of the Mercantile Age with Jewish involvement.

In the century from 1550 to 1650 the English and Dutch challenged the Spanish and Portuguese for control of international maritime trade and the American colonies, and Sephardic Jews were in leadership roles in that process. Their crypto-Jewish cousins occupied parallel roles in Spanish and Portuguese colonies, developing mining and the trade in mineral resources.

Part III

From Spain to the Americas

After the Expulsion, most Jews moved to the countries nearest to Spain, including Portugal, France, Italy, and Morocco, as the immediate first stage of migration. Eventually, many made secondary moves into other countries in the 1500s and early 1600s, migrating increasingly to Eastern Europe, the Muslim world, and the Americas.

Columbus and his crew sailed from the harbor in Palos which had been crowded with ships filled with Jews sailing into exile on the days leading up to the Expulsion deadline of August 2, 1492. As Columbus made final arrangements for his voyage, he would have been in the hustle and bustle of Jewish families boarding ships to leave. He probably competed with those ship captains to obtain supplies of food and other goods. What would Columbus and his men have felt or understand seeing these Spanish Jews being forced to leave their homeland with such uncertain futures ahead of them? Columbus set sail on August 3 the day after the last Jews had sailed.[73]

The first people of Jewish descent to land in the Americas were conversos who came on that first voyage with Columbus in 1492. Conversos and crypto-Jews were a part of the early conquistador expeditions, and when Hernan Cortes landed in Mexico in 1519, he was accompanied by four known conversos, according to Bernal Diaz del Castillo, the chronicler of the conquest of Mexico, who mentions the execution of soldiers accused of Jewish practice. Conversos continued their clandestine arrivals to the Spanish and Portuguese colonies in the Americas during the 1500s and early 1600s.[74]

Although the lives of openly practicing Jews and crypto-Jews had interwoven histories during the 1400s in Spain, those histories began to take significantly different trajectories during the 1500s and 1600s in the Americas. By 1700 most crypto-Jews had been separated from their religious roots for 200 years or so, and they no longer had contact with openly practicing Jews. Although their identity as Jews could be passed down from generation to generation, the practices of crypto-Jews from Brazil to Colombia, Peru, Mexico, and New Mexico began to develop along unique lines.

Chapter 5

Sephardic Diaspora

Figure 13
Rendering of Doña Gracia Nasi
by Gloria Abella Ballen

Sephardic Diaspora

THE NEAR ELIMINATION OF JEWS IN WESTERN Europe sent many Jews into Eastern Europe, as mentioned earlier, and they tended to be absorbed into the Ashkenazi communities.[75] Some 100,000 or more Jews, conversos, and crypto-Jews left Spain and Portugal for new centers of Jewish life.[76] Jewish populations formed in England, France, Italy, and the Americas. Poland replaced Spain as the anchor of Jewish life in Europe, and the mass exodus of Jews shifted the concentration of Jews from Western to Eastern Europe and Muslim lands. For example, Poland went from 25,000 Jews in the late 1400s[77] to as many as 150,000 by the late 1500s. The yeshivas and centers of Jewish scholarship, which had been destroyed in Spain, shifted to the East.

By the mid-1500s Doña Gracia Nasi was using the ships of her family's trading company to carry thousands of conversos to the Ottoman Empire,[78] which included communities from Greece to Istanbul and Israel.[79] Morocco and the Ottoman Empire were obvious choices for Jews fleeing Spain because the Muslim world was openly welcoming them. Although France and Italy were Catholic, they also welcome Jews, who have continued to live in those countries to the present day.

The Netherlands was a special case because it was ruled by the Hapsburg kings, who also ruled Spain. In 1579 the Netherlands broke from Hapsburg control and set up the Dutch Republic, which was Protestant and open to Jewish settlement. Many converso and crypto-Jewish families escaping the Inquisition moved there, and Amsterdam became an important center for Jewish conversos returning to Jewish life.[80] In 1601 Philip III temporarily lifted the ban on converso emigration augmenting the already existing clandestine emigration.

Crypto-Jews, who migrated to the Americas, were still confronted with the Inquisition.[81] By the mid-1600s English or Dutch colonies were accessible in Curaçao and Jamaica, where people could escape and live openly as Jews. In contrast, conversos who lived in remote interior regions of Mexico, Colombia, Peru, or Brazil had little or no opportunity to escape, and they were trapped geographically. They were still under Spanish or Portuguese authority, however tenuous, but there was no other country to which they could flee to re-establish themselves as practicing Jews.

These exiled Jews migrating to Muslim lands generally kept their identity as Jews from Spain. They tended to live in clustered communities or *mellahs*, and they developed Judeo-Spanish dialects. Instead of Yiddish, Sephardim have spoken versions of Judeo-Spanish (Ladino, Haketía, or Judezmo, Espanyolit), Judeo-Arabic, and Judeo-Berber. Sephardic cuisine is based on couscous, like the Muslim world, rather than potatoes like the Polish and Russian worlds.[82] Sephardic music is characterized by ballads, or romances in Judeo-Spanish that narrate stories of Jewish life and the interactions between Jews and Moors in contrast to the more dance-oriented klezmer music of the Ashkenazi world.[83]

The Sephardic Jews and their converso/crypto-Jewish cousins living in port cities around the Mediterranean had different social and cultural lives from Ashkenazi Jews, who lived in the eastern European agricultural plain from Poland to the Ukraine. Ashkenazi life tended to be based in agriculture with small town merchants and craftsmen.

In contrast, Sephardic life around the Mediterranean was more urban, and port city dwellers were involved in maritime world as merchants, navigators, or crewmen. They were multi-lingual and cosmopolitan and many developed sliding identities depending on whether they were in Catholic, Protestant, or Muslim lands. In comparison to the Ashkenazi experience, Sephardic/converso/crypto-Jewish identities were more fluid.

Sephardic Diaspora

Life in the Diaspora

Although honoring the history and culture of their Spanish past, the Jews of Spanish descent were normally against the Spanish government and its policies, repeatedly allying themselves with the enemies of Spain. In the Americas they supported the Dutch and the English, and in the Mediterranean they supported the Ottoman Empire. The English chartered Jewish sea captains as privateers to attack Spanish shipping. The Spanish called them pirates, but for descendants of Jews exiled from that country they were fighters in a war against the country that had destroyed their lives and lifestyles.[84]

Descendants of Jews from Spain and Portugal settled in Dutch and English colonies in South America, the Caribbean, and eventually in North America. When the Latin American countries gained their independence from Spain in 1820-1821, one of their first policies was to abolish the Inquisition, and eventually all allowed Jews to live openly in their lands. That led to a shifting of Sephardic populations from Dutch and English areas to the new Latin American republics in the mid to late 1800s. Today, the largest concentrations of Sephardic Jews are in Israel and Latin America.

Fluid Lines Between Jews and Crypto-Jews

Throughout the Spanish colonial period in the Americas the lines between Jewish and crypto-Jewish communities were porous, as they had been in Spain, and people could switch between living as Jews or crypto-Jews depending on their location. A person could be born into a crypto-Jewish family in Portugal, like Isaac Aboab da Fonseca, then move to a country open to Jews like the Netherlands and return to Jewish practice. Others like Paz Pinto or Lopez Mesa in Cartagena lived openly as Jews in Salonika, Amsterdam, and other places before migrating to the Americas for business opportunities and living as hidden Jews without converting to Catholicism.

The Jewish conversos, who left Spanish and Portuguese lands to live as Jews again in Amsterdam and elsewhere, were rejudaized, learned Hebrew, learned the prayers, and even became rabbis. Early Sephardic settlers in North America, such as the family of the businessman Aaron Lopez of Newport, were Jewish conversos arriving to return to life as Jews. Lopez had been born Duarte Lopez to a *converso* family in Portugal. His older brother had left Portugal for Newport and returned to Jewish practice, changing his name to Moses, and in 1752 Duarte and his family followed in the steps of his older brother, moving to Newport and returning to Jewish practice, adopting Jewish names. Today, changing ones identity has once again become part of the Catholic/converso/crypto-Jewish/Jewish experience as people are returning to Jewish life from their Catholic past.

The early Jewish communities in the United States from New York to Newport, Philadelphia, Charleston, and Savannah from the 1650s to the 1850 were Sephardic, and they included Jewish converso families migrating from Portugal. Among the latter was the family of the most famous Jewish American poet, Emma Lazarus.[85]

As the Spanish colonial period ended in 1820-1821, and the Latin American republics declared their independence, the Inquisition was abolished and could no longer threaten Jewish converso families. Rather than opening doors for them to return to open Jewish practice, the opposite seemed to occur. Most converso families continued as Catholics. By the 1820s, Jewish converso families had been in the Americas for 200 to 300 years, and they had been assimilated to the dominant Catholic culture and to their own crypto-culture of hiding. Many continued to preserve their hidden Jewish identity, and in the new Latin American republics from Mexico to Colombia and Peru, there was no Jewish community to which they could return. Slowly the new republics did offer religious freedom, but the return to open Jewish observance for converso families was not an option socially.

Cultural Hybridity

Jews in the Americas learned to blend with the cultural norms of the lands where they lived, either as crypto-Jews in Spanish Catholic territories or Sephardic Jews in English and Dutch Protestant lands. Cultural hybridity was a hallmark of survival as a Jew within the dominant religious cultural systems of Christianity, both Catholic and Protestant.

In the following chapters, we will look at Jewish converso life in the Americas, tracing the path of the conversos, who migrated to Mexico, thinking they could escape the Inquisition and then on to the lands of the Rio Grande and New Mexico in the north with the same intentions. The latter led to a unique experience of Jewish converso families living on the isolated frontier of the Spanish Empire and preserving elements of both their Jewish and Spanish heritage, and the surprising turn that has taken in recent decades.

Jews, Crypto-Jews and the Mercantile System

Conversos returning to Jewish life migrated to Dutch and English lands while those living as crypto-Jews migrated to the Spanish and Portuguese colonies in the Americas. The two groups were interlinked by family ties and culture, and they created trading networks in the early modern era. They had the cultural and linguistic skills to transcend the barriers of Catholic and Protestant realms and the geographic differences between Europe and the Americas.

For one hundred years between 1450 and 1550, the economic dynamic of the world changed fundamentally, bringing in a new world order. The Mercantile Age was beginning. By 1550, Spain, Europe and the world were transformed, as a result of contact with Asia and the Americas. The riches of the American colonies poured into Spain greatly increasing the wealth of Europe.

Mercantilism was a new political and economic philosophy of managing the economy to benefit the state. As it developed between 1550 and 1750, Sephardic Jews and crypto-Jews had important roles. The dramatic increase in international trade and growth in the European economy between 1550 and 1650 was fueled by the Spanish importation of thousands of tons of silver from the mines in the Americas. It tripled the supply of silver, transforming the economy and creating a new wealthy class of Europeans. Sephardic Jewish merchants and financiers had important roles in managing this influx of silver into Europe, and their crypto-Jewish counterparts in the Americas were on the supply end.

Jonathan Israel and Jonathan Ray [86] point out that the Sephardic Diaspora after the Expulsion from Spain created the scattered networks of Jewish merchant families that provided the infrastructure of the new trading networks of the Mercantile Age. These networks of family members and business partners lived in various parts of the world frequently in port cities because of their involvement in navigation and maritime trade. Sephardic Jewish merchants in Protestant and Muslim lands, and converso/crypto-Jews merchants in Spanish and Portuguese lands created commercial networks around the globe from Amsterdam to Lisbon, Seville, Istanbul, Mumbai, Goa, Manila, Acapulco, Veracruz, and back to Europe.

After England began re-admitting Jews openly in 1656, the Dutch-English axis became an important home for descendants of Jewish conversos returning to Judaism for the next 300 years. As the Dutch and English challenged the Spanish and Portuguese for colonial holdings in the Americas, these conversos had an important role in aiding them. Jews aligned with the Dutch, English, and later the United States because their policies of religious freedom allowed Jews to be part of their societies.[87]

Sephardic Jews were leaders in migrating to the Americas and developing sugar and tobacco plantations in English and Dutch territories. Crypto-Jews acted out these same roles in mining and other industries in Spanish and Portuguese colonies.

Important Conversos Who Returned to Jewish Practice

Some Jewish converso families accumulated extraordinary wealth in Spain and Portugal through international trade and/or banking, as did some in the Americas. If a family obtained a land grant from the king or a concession for a trade monopoly, they gave the king a percentage of the profits, and they both benefited. The spice trade was an early example in which Jews were particularly involved, and later diamonds and jewels would become important. In the sixteenth century the Mendes/Nasi family led the way for Jewish conversos in the eastern Mediterranean and the Ottoman Empire, and in the seventeenth century the Amsterdam Three made a major impact in the West.

The Mendes Family and the Ottoman Empire

The Mendes family, later known by their Jewish name Nasi, was a Portuguese Jewish converso family that was one of the wealthiest and most powerful families of the sixteenth century, and they are known through the well-documented lives of Doña Gracia Nasi and her nephew Joseph Nasi, the Duke of Naxos.[88]

Doña Gracia Nasi (1510-1569). Doña Gracia used her wealth and fleet of ships to save thousands of conversos from persecution by the Inquisition by transporting them to the Ottoman Empire that welcomed Jews. She built factories, housing, and synagogues to provide these displaced conversos, returning to Jewish practice, with communities where they could rebuild their Jewish lives. She pressured rabbis to challenge the Christian world when atrocities were committed against Jews. She was an extraordinary person and should be ranked as one of the important Jewish leaders of the last 500 years.[89]

The conversos who migrated to the Ottoman Empire became the Eastern Sephardim with a distinctive history and cultural development. They adapted to local societies of the Balkans, Greece, and Turkey. Since they were separated from hearing and speaking normative Spanish in Spain, they began to incorporate words and phrases from the new languages they were speaking, developing the Turkish Judeo-Spanish dialect Ladino. They not only returned to their Jewish way of life, but they also made important contributions to the Ottoman Empire in manufacturing, medicine, finance, scholarship, and international relations.

Joseph Nasi, Duke of Naxos (1524-1579). Joseph Nasi was an adviser to the Sultan of Turkey and was named the Duke of Naxos, a series of islands off the Turkish coast. He was also an important naval adviser and helped prepare the Turkish fleet that was challenging the Spanish for control of the Mediterranean. The Ottoman forces also fought Spanish shipping with privateers, a form of naval guerrilla warfare, and Jews were ship captains and crewmen in that war. As an adviser to the Sultan and supplier of military equipment to the Ottoman armed forces, Joseph Nasi, became an enemy to Christendom because he aided the Muslim empire that threatened the Christian power of Europe. He is said to have been the inspiration for Christopher Marlowe's historic play *The Jew of Malta* written in 1589, ten years after Joseph Nasi's death.⁹⁰

Joseph Nasi along with his aunt, Doña Gracia Nasi, who was a friend with the wife of the Sultan, received permission to settle Jewish converso families from Spain in northern Israel, which was a part of the Ottoman Empire. He was named the Lord of Tiberias with the purpose of bringing those families and creating industry in the area.⁹¹

The Amsterdam Three

As Portuguese converso families migrated to the Netherlands to return to Judaism, a new, vibrant Jewish community took shape, especially in Amsterdam. After the Netherlands broke from Spain in 1581, it became the most important safe haven in Western Europe for Jewish converso families. Amsterdam was a primary port for Europe, and the Dutch were known as a religiously tolerant society.

In keeping with its reputation for openness, it was a nation where Jewish doctors, butchers, and merchants could practice their professions. Thriving Jewish communities developed from Amsterdam to Antwerp. Three major figures emerged from these Jewish converso returnee families in the seventeenth century, and each of them had a significant influence of the future of Jewish life. Along with Doña Gracia and Joseph Nasi, these three Jewish conversos had major roles in shaping early modern Jewish history.

Menasseh Ben Israel (1604-1657)

He was born Manoel Dias Soeiro of crypto-Jewish parents on the Portuguese island of Madeira where they had moved from mainland Portugal to escape the Inquisition. When he was six years old, they moved to Amsterdam to return to open Jewish practice. Young Manoel took the Jewish name of Menasseh Ben Israel, learned Hebrew, and became a rabbi and an author, and eventually he set up the first publishing house in Hebrew in the Netherlands.

He wrote a dozen books, ranging from mysticism to the resurrection of souls to *The Hope of Israel*. He wrote about the arrival of the Messiah, which was a common theme in the despair of Spanish and Portuguese Jews in the Diaspora in the 1600s. One of his first books was *The Conciliator*, a Biblical commentary, which he wrote in Spanish for crypto-Jews and those returning to Jewish life. It was published in English in 1652 as his international reputation was growing.

In the mid-1620s he married Rachel of the well-known Spanish family Abarbanel, and they had two sons and a daughter. In the late-1630s he and the family moved to Brazil briefly, hoping to improve their financial status. When that did not work, they returned to Amsterdam where he was named as the head of a small yeshivah, giving him and his family some stability.

Menasseh ben Israel was a leader of the Jewish Emancipation Movement advocating Jewish rights in Europe, and he became known as the emancipator of the Jews. Perhaps, his most significant achievement was an appeal to Oliver Cromwell for the re-admission of Jews to England. Actually, there were Sephardic Jews living in England at the time, but they identified themselves only as Spanish merchants. They were living as crypto-Jews with no synagogue because it had been illegal to be Jewish in England since the Expulsion of 1290.

In response to Rabbi ben Israel's appeal, Cromwell's government granted Jews the right to begin returning to England in 1656. We do not know when religious services were first allowed, but Samuel Pepys makes reference to attending Simchat Torah in 1663 in a synagogue on Creechurch Lane, which is the street where current Bevis Marks synagogue is located today. It is the only synagogue in Europe that has held services continuously for 300 years. Bevis Marks is a Sephardic synagogue and seems to have been built by Jewish conversos who had returned to Jewish practice.

While Rabbi ben Israel was in England arguing for the return of Jews, his student, Baruch Spinoza, was called before the Portuguese synagogue in Amsterdam and asked to leave the congregation because of his ideas about God, which were thought to be too extreme for the religious atmosphere in Protestant Amsterdam at that time.[92]

Baruch Spinoza (1632-1677)

Spinoza was born in Amsterdam to a Portuguese family that migrated to that city and returned to Jewish practice. He grew up speaking Portuguese, Hebrew, Spanish, and Dutch among other languages. He was a leading rationalist in Enlightenment thought with a moral philosophy based on self and the universe. Spinoza was trained in Talmudic studies, but in his early twenties became more interested in philosophy and moved away from traditional Jewish thought.

The first problem for Spinoza was his radical conception of God as the summation of all that exists. He believed that God even went beyond material existence, and he believed that the greatest good was the knowledge of God. He did not believe in an anthropomorphic God, who intervened in human life. He saw the Torah as a human document and not the words of God, and as such, the laws of Moses were no longer applicable for contemporary society.[93] Spinoza also argued that the soul was not immortal, nor was there life after death.

As he espoused these ideas publicly, it seems that synagogue members were concerned that his rationalist thought would be offensive to the larger society of Christians, which had begun to challenge him. In fact, his writings were put on the *Index of Forbidden Books* by the Catholic Church. Spinoza was already moving away from the synagogue when the *cherem* or ban on him was approved, and it seems that the synagogue was as much making a statement about disassociating itself from Spinoza's writings, as it was banning him from their congregation. This was perhaps a preventive measure to protect themselves from potential reprisals from the Christian community and the fear of an expulsion from the city because his thought might have been interpreted as anti-religious and by implication anti-Christian.[94] With the ban, the congregation alienated its most famous member, Spinoza.

Isaac Aboab da Fonseca (1605-1693)

Aboab da Fonseca was born in Portugal of a crypto-Jewish family, and in 1612 the family moved to Amsterdam to return to Jewish practice. Young Isaac learned Hebrew and studied alongside another boy of his age, Menasseh ben Israel. In 1623 he was appointed rabbi for one of the three Sephardic synagogues in Amsterdam. In 1642 he was name rabbi of the Synagogue Kahal Zur in Recife, Brazil, the Dutch colony.

He was a rabbi, scholar, writer, and kabbalist of the Sephardic tradition. He epitomizes the experience of thousands of conversos, who fled Portugal for a return to Jewish life in Amsterdam. He became one of the most important rabbis of the seventeenth century. See his poem on the following page praising God, which he wrote when he was the rabbi in Dutch controlled Recife, Brazil.

When the Portuguese re-conquered Recife in 1654, he returned to Amsterdam where he was named the Chief Rabbi of the Sephardic community. In 1656 he was one of the scholars hearing the case of Baruch Spinoza and making the decision to ban him from the synagogue. The Jewish community in Amsterdam seems to have flourished under the direction of Rabbi da Fonseca, numbering in the thousands. In 1675 he led the congregation in building the largest synagogue in Europe at that time, the Portuguese Synagogue, which still exists. It became the model for Sephardic synagogues in the Western world from London (Bevis Marks) to New York (Shearith Israel).

Isaac Aboab da Fonseca
(1605-1693)
Crypto-Jewish family from Portugal returned to Jewish practice
in Amsterdam. First rabbi in the Americas, in Recife.
Composed in Hebrew, oldest known Jewish writing from the Americas.

Who is Like You?
Who is like You? There is none like You.
Who resembles You? None resembles You.
Great God, the Lord.
Exalted above all, dwelling in my abode.
I shall invoke His name in the assembly of the faithful.
We shall acclaim Him with songs of praise.
Due to my sins, I was cast off to a far-away land,
thus fulfilling the words of His prophets to me.
But even if I have fallen from the heights to the depths,
Happy is the man for whom God is his refuge.
Ocean waves passed over my head,
And even still my soul longed for Him.
I have not been false to my Holy One,
My covenant is faithful to Him.
My spirit has clung to Him,
My steps have not deviated from His steps.
My soul rejoices in His words,
Therefore I will hope in Him.
Declare that His name is exalted,
He has not given full vent to His fury.
He has raised up the horn of His people,
the people whom He has chosen for His possession.
-- Translation David Gilad and Orit Rabkin

Chapter 6

The Grand Conspiracy:

Fear of Jews and Protestants

Figure 17
Portuguese Synagogue in Amsterdam, 1675
Built under the leadership of Rabbi Isaac Aboab da Fonseca
Photo Courtesy of Vanessa Paloma Elbaz

JEWISH CONVERSOS AND CRYPTO-JEWS CONTINUED

to live for decades, and even centuries, in Spanish territories in the Americas. They controlled much of the trade between Spain and the Americas until the 1650s.

Jewish converso migration to the Americas came in two waves between 1550 and 1640 after which it was largely cut off. The predominantly Spanish wave came first, and it was mostly in the 1500s. That was followed by a predominantly Portuguese wave that came mostly between 1600 and 1640. By the late 1600s and 1700s, there were fewer converso/crypto-Jewish families remaining in either Spain or Portugal. There were isolated families and individuals still leaving, but they were going increasingly to English and Dutch lands in North America and the Caribbean.

The First Wave of Jewish Converso Migration

By the mid-1500s the first wave of Jewish converso migration to Mexico, Colombia, and Peru was underway, enticed by the vibrant mining economies in those areas. When the Spanish Crown took control of Portugal in 1580 that opened the possibility for Portuguese conversos to enter Spain and to migrate to the Americas, which had not been open to them.[95] The continuing arrests for Judaizing by the Inquisition pushed conversos out of Spain and Portugal, and the pull factor was economic opportunity, which enticed them to the Americas.

This initial period of migration to the three Spanish colonies was becoming more important in the late 1500s. In the first two *autos de fé* after the Inquisition was established in 1571 in Mexico, 105 people were arrested but not a single person for Judaizing.[96]

That would soon change because Jewish conversos were arriving in larger numbers.

The Inquisition reacted quickly to these new arrivals, and in 1590, 1596, and 1601 there were three rounds of arrests of people for Judaizing. They were imprisoned and either deported or executed. However, by 1604 there was only one person left in the Inquisition jails for Judaizing, indicating the ups and downs of these arrests. Examples of the acts of Judaizing for which people were arrested in Mexico included bathing and putting on clean clothes on a Friday, draining and disposing of blood after slaughtering an animal, fasting on a Jewish holiday, and observing Yom Kippur. Even eating tortillas, unleavened cornbread, during Passover is mentioned.

Who was a converso and who a crypto-Jew in the Americas? The line between being a converso with no Jewish practice and a crypto-Jew who was keeping Jewish practices might have been difficult to recognize or define for officials of the Inquisition. Both groups came from similar Jewish religious and cultural backgrounds and might have had family and friends in common, and they might have interacted socially.

The number of Spaniards in the population of Mexico was small, reaching ten percent or so by the mid-1600s, perhaps 200,000 or 250,000 Spaniards. Jewish converso families were a fraction of that ten percent, but still could number in the thousands. There was nothing in the Americas comparable to Belmonte in Portugal where the descendants of Jewish families lived for centuries in the same town and retained the identity of being Jews. In contrast to Portugal, complete and intact crypto-Jewish communities did not exist for centuries in the Americas. Jewish converso life was more dispersed and fragmented, especially after 1650.

Jewish conversos and crypto-Jews had to create new communities after arriving in Mexico, Colombia, or Peru if they wanted to maintain contact with others of their tradition. Inquisition records do suggest that people formed these communities, but they were immigrant communities, hidden within the Spanish elite.

The Spanish colonies in the Americas were not Spanish culturally, nor was Brazil culturally Portuguese. These colonial societies were conquered peoples, and 90 percent of the population was indigenous or African. They were not Catholic and could not speak Spanish or Portuguese. Soldiers and priests were everywhere to convert and control the subject peoples. The Spanish colonial elite was small and consisted of governing officials and those who became wealthy in mining, sugar cane, and other extractive industries.

In this colonial system the Crown gave land grants to selected Spaniards of the wealthy class to develop the land and control the Indians living on it. Indian resistance to Spanish rule continued for decades in some places and centuries in others, but these were lands rich in mineral wealth, and the Spanish were determined to stay. In addition to the indigenous people, Africans were brought as slave laborers in the sugar cane areas and some coastal mining areas.

Many Christian Spaniards were men by themselves who came as Crown officials, soldiers, or priests while freelancers came to make their fortunes in mining and other businesses. In contrast to English North America, Spaniards did not come primarily as families to settle the land and set up farming communities. Although the Spanish ideal in the Americas was to become wealthy return to Spain, marry, and live the life of gentlemen, many did not become wealthy, and they tended to stay and marry local indigenous women, living in the local economy. The Spanish and Portuguese territories in the Americas were colonies for the exploitation of natural resources for the mother countries, they were not primarily European settler driven communities. How did this affect Jewish conversos?

There were converso men who came by themselves to make their fortunes, just like the Christians, but records of the Carvajal settlement of Nuevo Leon mention Jewish conversos and crypto-Jews coming as settler families. Converso men who came alone frequently married local indigenous women, breaking the Jewish line. Conversos in Mexico were often merchants and craftsmen, and those who migrated to New Mexico were more likely to be landowners and farmers. Some came from Portugal, but others came from openly practicing Jewish communities in Ottoman realms. Some were Portuguese Jews who had fled to Amsterdam, then came to the Americas seeking a fortune. This was a new world with mixed populations and people coming from diverse Jewish backgrounds.

The knowledge of Jewish practices varied widely. Those who came from Muslim lands or Amsterdam and had been living as Jews knew prayers in Hebrew and were more familiar with the Jewish holidays and kosher practices. Those who came directly from Portugal or Spain knew less because of the decades of separation from active Jewish life. In fact, some people knew so little that they consulted the Inquisition list of Judaizing practices, "Edicts of Faith and Inquisition" [97] to identify what it meant to be Jewish.[98]

Given the gray and porous line between Jewish conversos and crypto-Jews, some of the people arrested by the Inquisition at this point might not have been crypto-Jews. Most of them did confess to Judaizing, but these confessions were often given under the threat of torture or even torture itself, which raises the question of how reliable they were. Some non-Judaizing conversos associating with crypto-Jews family members or friends might have been indistinguishable from the crypto-Jews to their accusers, who could have reported them erroneously to the Inquisition. As a Crown institution, the Inquisition needed to make a public, political point against Judaizing as a warning, so even if a few non-Judaizing conversos were caught in the process, it served the overall purpose of the Inquisition.

The Second Wave of Jewish Converso Migration

During the period that Spain ruled Portugal (1580-1640) tens of thousands of Portuguese *anusim* (forced converts) traveled to the Americas through Spain. This second wave of converso migration to the Americas, the predominantly Portuguese wave, started after 1580 and continued to 1640. It seems to have overwhelmed the budding Spanish converso wave of migrants, and it was described at the time as a virtual invasion because the numbers were so large. The term Portuguese became synonymous with being Jewish in the colonial Latin America in the seventeenth century. This was shortly after the establishment of the offices of the Inquisition in Mexico (1571) and Peru (1570).

Then, the unexpected happened and world politics intervened to favor Jewish conversos and crypto-Jews. Spain had the most powerful navy in the world and controlled the Atlantic Ocean. Since the defeat of the Ottoman navy in the Battle of Lepanto in 1571, Spain had also controlled the Mediterranean Sea. In May, 1588 it sent the Spanish Armada of 130 ships to ferry an army gathered in Flanders to invade England and overthrow the Protestant Queen Elizabeth I, take back England for Catholicism, and stop the English support of privateers attacking Spanish shipping in the Americas. The English navy outmaneuvered the Spanish ships and forced the Armada to change its course into more open water at which point it was hit by storms. One-third of the much-heralded Spanish Armada was destroyed in a stunning defeat that was seen as a crack in the wall of Spanish invincibility and a turning point in Catholic and Protestant power relations.

The Spanish defeat was interpreted as Protestantism triumphing over Catholicism. It strengthened the budding Protestant Republic of the Netherlands, which was welcoming Jews. For the Spanish it was a financial loss and a blow to their prestige. It showed that Spain was vulnerable. Spain could be beaten. That coincided with an uptick in converso migration out of both Spain and Portugal.

This second wave of Portuguese Jewish converso migration to the Americas continued Portugal broke away from Spain and re-established itself as an independent country until 1640. In response Spain closed the borders with Portugal, and the Inquisition in Mexico began the arrests of Portuguese people, using the accusation of Judaizing. The combined impact of the sweeping arrests in Mexico and the closing of the Spanish/Portuguese border, cut off the last remaining source of Jewish converso migration to the Americas.

With this new round of arrests by the Inquisition, the remaining converso families in Mexico had to leave, assimilate, or go into deeper hiding. Some joined the Oñate expedition to the north to settle New Mexico. Leaders of the converso/crypto-Jews communities in Mexico were arrested and either reconciled with the Church, executed, or sent into exile, and those who survived became more invisible. A new era was at hand.

Jews and the
Challenge to Spain in the Americas

The Spanish and Portuguese had been granted the lands of North and South America by a Papal Bull in 1493 by Pope Alexander VI. That was the authority for Spain and Portugal to claim the lands and peoples of the Americas as their subjects. The flow of silver from Mexico and the Andes and the wealth of sugar from the Caribbean and Brazil were enriching Spain and Portugal to the envy of the rest of Europe.

The English and Dutch had both initiated policies to obtain American territories and the potential riches from them but given that Spain and Portugal technically owned all of the Americas, the English and Dutch had to take territories by coercion or force. In late 1585 Sir Francis Drake attacked the city of Santo Domingo on the Caribbean island of Hispañola, then in early 1586 he attacked and occupied Cartagena, the richest Caribbean port of the Spanish, defeating the Spanish forces in both places.[99] These attacks heightened the existing Spanish fears of invasion by the Protestant powers.

The Spanish had paid little attention to North America, which they considered to be a backwater area with no immediately identifiable mineral wealth and not promising for sugar cane like Caribbean lands. Seizing that opportunity, the English and Dutch made agricultural and trading colonies in the undisputed lands of North America, even though their focus continued on the wealthier Caribbean islands. Eventually, England would gain control of Jamaica, Trinidad, and small islands in the Lesser Antilles. The Dutch gained possession of Curaçao and Aruba, and descendants of Jewish conversos had significant roles in all of these colonies.[100] In 1664 the English ceded Surinam in the Caribbean to the Dutch in exchange for New Amsterdam, renaming it New York.

Both the English and the Dutch allowed and even encouraged Jewish settlement, and the islands they controlled became escape havens for Jews from the Spanish and Portuguese lands. Sephardic ship captains engaged in contraband trade with Spanish cities without identifying themselves as Jews, so there was a flow of Jews in and out of Spanish held port cities around the Caribbean from Cartagena to Veracruz, Havana, and Santo Domingo.

Portuguese Jews coming from Amsterdam or Portuguese conversos coming from Lisbon could travel freely to Spanish colonies, such as Cartagena, a rich port attractive for young Jews who wanted to build capital. In the sixteenth and early seventeenth centuries there were few effective controls on the migration of Jews and crypto-Jews to the American colonies, and the distinction between them could be difficult to establish.

Spain's Fear of A Grand Conspiracy

From the 1500's to the 1800's all Jews in Spanish and Portuguese colonies were conversos or crypto-Jews, and many had experience in international trade. New Christians in Spain were dominating the trade with the Americas from Seville. They had links with Sephardic Jewish merchants in Amsterdam who became involved in financing trade with the Americas. Since the Americas were becoming an important center for trade, more and more Jewish conversos risked the consequences of migrating there aspiring to a better economic future.

Throughout most of the sixteenth century the Spanish and Portuguese were busy building Europeanized societies and economies in their colonies, and the Inquisition had not yet been established there, which meant that most Jews could live without fear of official persecution.[101] When Jews, conversos, and crypto-Jews arrived and established businesses, importing the goods needed to run these new societies, people did not ask much about their origins.

The Challenge of Recife

In 1630 the Dutch seized Recife, Brazil from the Portuguese and gained control of the rich hinterland of sugar plantations. Spanish officials feared that the Dutch or English might make attempts on their own colonies, and they feared that the Jewish conversos in their colonies could be a potential fifth column that would support such invasions. In 1626 the Inquisitors in Cartagena wrote to their Spanish superiors that their colony was being "infested with heretics", especially Portuguese (i.e. Jews).[102] In the meantime, trade between Sephardic merchants in the Netherlands and their compatriots in Spanish and Portuguese overseas territories continued in the Americas, Africa, and Asia even though it was illegal.

After the Dutch seized control of Recife in 1530 they were governing almost half of Brazil. The Dutch West India Company set up their headquarters in Recife and named the territory New Holland. They invited skilled craftsmen and merchants to increase immigration and build the economy. Jews could live openly, and large numbers migrated there, ultimately making it a majority Jewish city.[103] Crypto-Jews already living in the region were able to return to the active Jewish practice.

Jews built a religious community, [104] and in 1636 they established Kahal Zur Israel synagogue, the first in the Americas, and the synagogue still exists. Rabbi Isaac Aboab da Fonseca was rabbi of the synagogue from 1642 to 1654, and he was the earliest Jewish writer in the Americas.

New Holland lasted for a quarter of a century until the Portuguese invaded in 1654 defeating the Dutch. They expelled the Jews and provided ships for the approximately 1500 Jews to return to Amsterdam. One of the ships sailing from Recife to Amsterdam was damaged in a storm and attacked by pirates. Ultimately twenty-three Recife Jews were rescued by a French ship, Sta. Catarina, which was on its way to New Amsterdam in North America, and they were taken there, becoming the first Jews in what was to become New York City.

The Spanish saw the English and Dutch, backed by Jews and crypto-Jews, as direct threats to their American colonies. If the Dutch could take and hold Recife and much of the interior of Brazil, they might also be able to capture Cartagena or one of the other rich ports. Such an event would be a major blow to Spanish power, wealth, and prestige.

Up to this point, the Spanish control of Jewish converso migration to the Americas had been porous or even ignored in a "don't ask, don't tell" situation, but now they saw conversos as a dangerous element in their territories who would aid the English or the Dutch in the event of an invasion.[105]

The Spanish Response

Spanish authorities launched attacks on the Jewish converso populations of Colombia and Peru using the Inquisition. The Offices of the Inquisition in Mexico, Cartagena, and Lima launched massive arrests against conversos for Judaizing, leading to the highest number of *autos de fé* in the history of the Americas. These merchants had developed commercial networks in the early 1600's during a period when the Spanish Crown was more interested in the economic development of their colonies than religious purity. Now, world events were intruding, and those caught up in the dragnet of the Inquisition would pay the price.

During this critical period, the Spanish made two policy shifts. One was to use the Inquisition to suppress the Jewish converso populations, and the other was to militarize their valuable ports from possible Dutch or English attacks. They strengthened existing fortifications in Cartagena and other Caribbean ports and named governors with military backgrounds. The military governor of Cartagena charged with expanding the fortifications was Field Marshal Melchor de Aguilera (1638-1641). He had served in Italy and France before being named Governor in Cartagena.[106] His daughter, Doña Teresa Aguilera y Roche, was later to become the most important figure arrested for Judaizing by the Inquisition in New Mexico. Her story will come later.[107]

In the fused world of religion and politics in the sixteenth and seventeenth centuries, there are cases that indicate that the Inquisition was used for political purposes, including the events of the "Grand Conspiracy" and the arrests of Governors Luis Carvajal de la Cueva and Bernardo López Mendizábal in Mexico, both of which will be discussed later. Since Spain had two parallel legal systems, the secular one and the religious one (Inquisition), the accusation of Judaizing against a person was an effective mechanism for arresting a person even when the reason behind the arrest was political.

In reaction to the perceived "Grand Conspiracy", the Inquisition was used as a political and religious weapon to decimate the wealthy

Jewish converso networks within the Spanish colonies. The properties of those who were arrested were confiscated, and if they were convicted, the property went permanently to the Inquisition, and the people would either be reconciled with the Church, executed, or expelled from the Americas. As the Jewish converso merchant networks were eliminated in Cartagena, Lima, and Mexico, each of the colonies suffered an economic decline.

Cartagena

Throughout the late sixteenth and early seventeenth centuries there was a crypto-Jewish presence on the coast of Colombia, then known as Nueva Granada. They were a mixture of Portuguese conversos and Sephardic Jews from Amsterdam, Morocco, and the Ottoman Empire.[108] The leaders were involved in international commerce and maritime trade, but others came as doctors, managers, mine speculators, pharmacists, surgeons, tailors, shoemakers, silversmiths, sailors, and penniless adventurers. A few acquired landed estates and grew sugar cane, others established cattle ranches, and yet others were workers for these large landholders.

The Portuguese controlled the slave trade between Africa and the Americas, and crypto-Jewish merchants in Cartagena, were involved in that trade.[109] Mining was an important industry in Colombia, and crypto-Jewish merchants were among those who provided the tools and equipment for the miners and in turn bought the gold and silver they discovered.

Contraband trade was a bustling business in the Americas, and both conversos and openly practicing Jews were active in it. In Cartagena the Jewish converso merchants developed a system of offloading their goods in remote areas of the coast on land they owned, and later the goods could be brought into Cartagena in small shipments without attracting the attention of the customs officials.[110] A census of foreigners in Santa Marta, a smaller port to the east of Cartagena, was made in 1606, and they identified fifty-two foreigners of whom forty-one were Portuguese, usually indicating Jewish conversos.[111]

The Grand Conspiracy

The presence of conversos and crypto-Jews by the early 1600s, stimulated the Crown to establish an office of the Inquisition in Cartagena in 1610, which was responsible for Nueva Granada and the Spanish controlled Caribbean islands.[112]

Figure 18
Palace of the Inquisition in Cartagena

In Cartagena the Minyan (Jewish prayer group) met regularly in the house of Blas de Paz Pinto in the early 1630's. Some knew the prayers and blessings central to Jewish practice and observed Shabbat and other Jewish holidays. After Paz Pinto was arrested by the Inquisition, neighbors gave testimony that the group met regularly in his house, and that they heard songs or prayers that they thought were in another language.

The Inquisition records of those arrested indicate that many of them observed Shabbat without working or lighting fires, and they bathed and put on freshly laundered clothes for the day. They observed dietary restrictions against ham and other foods, and they observed the fasts on the appropriate religious holidays. They also observed the celebration of Esther, a crypto-Jewish counterpart to Purim.[113]

Among surviving correspondence with the crypto-Jews of Cartagena there are references to leaving the Spanish territories and migrating to safer English or Dutch lands. In one letter a father pleads with his son to return to the safety of Amsterdam. The son chose not to leave and continue his lucrative business selling mining supplies. Later he was arrested for Judaizing.[114]

The Inquisition targeted business leaders and leaders of the minyan in the arrests, which made a clear statement to the city that Judaizing would not be tolerated. One died from torture during the interrogations, and the others were expelled from the Americas with loss of property.[115] No one was burned at the stake, but there are no records about what happened to those who were expelled.[116] A common practice was to send people back to Spain, which was considered to be safe because it was free of Jews. In addition to being expelled, their wealth was confiscated, leaving them in poverty, and some had been wealthy before being arrested.[117]

Lima

In the 250 years that the Inquisition existed in Lima, it was mostly focused on issues of superstition among Old Christians and rarely questions of heresy with crypto-Jews other than the 1635-1640 Grand Conspiracy trials.[118]

Jewish conversos had a central role in the mining operations in the famous silver mines of Potosi, supplying miners and managing the transport and sale of the silver production. Lima was the port and primary staging area for supplies and later exportation of the silver. In 1635 the Inquisition initiated a series of arrests of conversos accusing them of Judaizing. More than 100 people were arrested under suspicion of involvement in the imagined Grand Conspiracy with the Dutch against the Spanish Crown. The arrests began with Antonio Cordero, a low-level employee in a local business.

Antonio Cordero

He was arrested on April 1, 1635, while he was working in a business owned by Antonio de Acuña and Diego López de Fonseca. A disgruntled customer reported Cordero to the Inquisition, leading to his arrest, and his subsequent confession led to the arrests of his employers, the first in the Lima crypto-Jewish business circle. At Cordero's first hearing he was asked to make a statement about his life, which was normal Inquisition procedure.[119]

At the end of his statement, he was asked if he knew why he had been arrested and whether he would like to make a confession. Cordero did. He went on to explain that he had learned crypto-Jewish practices in Seville before coming to the Americas, and once in Lima, he had gotten the job with Acuña and de Fonseca. At a subsequent hearing on May 11, 1635, he admitted that his employers were crypto-Jews and gave information about beliefs, prayers, and kosher customs that they practiced. His employers were arrested the same day along with other merchants, and the Inquisition seized all of their properties. The economic shock of these arrests led to the collapse of one of the most important banks a few days later. This led to a series of bankruptcies, which combined with the arrests of other crypto-Jewish merchants by the Inquisition, led to a business crisis in the economy of Peru.

Cordero was sentenced to reconciliation with the Church, which was a mild punishment.[120] The Inquisition tended to be lenient with people who confessed immediately, gave the names of other crypto-Jews, and agreed to return to the Church and stop practicing the Law of Moses, the teachings of the Torah.[121]

Manuel Bautista Pérez

He was perhaps the wealthiest crypto-Jew arrested. Bautista Pérez was a broker in the silver business in Lima, also involved in banking, and owned mule trains that brought the silver out of the distant mountain of silver in Potosí to the coast. He was reported to be the head of the Jewish community in Lima. He was arrested and under torture revealed the names of others practicing the Law of Moses, the Torah. In January 1639 Bautista Pérez and eleven others were burned at the stake.

His vast assets were confiscated by the Inquisition and sold at auction with the agent of the Chief Inquisitor, Andrés Juan Gaitan, bidding on the property. Afterwards, Gaitan was reported to have become quite wealthy riding around Lima in a silver coach. Although Gaitan was accused of arresting Bautista Pérez and other silver merchants out of greed, he defended himself invoking their supposed involvement in the Grand Conspiracy.[122]

What Happened to the Crypto-Jews after The Grand Conspiracy?

The Jewish conversos and crypto-Jews virtually disappear from Inquisition records after 1650, and there are multiple factors that explain it. One, the remaining crypto-Jews were more careful to hide their identity and practices. Two, many of the surviving crypto-Jews left the Spanish colonies, moving to Dutch and English territories. Third, many of those arrested by the Inquisition were expelled and not allowed to return to the Americas.

In Cartagena the governor expelled all Portuguese from the Province.[123] This required the Jews, who wanted to stay in Nueva Granada, to move to the inland provinces, such as the mining centers in Antioquia. Colombians have a common saying that the people from Antioquia are the Jews of Colombia, and some could be the descendants of those from long ago.

By 1650 the century long experiment of Jewish conversos and crypto-Jews being important actors in the new societies of Latin America was coming to an end. The Jewish presence in the Caribbean was shifting to the Dutch and English colonies, which began to replace the Spanish as centers of maritime commerce. The remaining crypto-Jews in Latin America fade from the public record.

The Grand Conspiracy

Crypto-Judaism and Anti-Clericalism

What was the mixture of "crypto-Judaism", "anti-clericalism", and Enlightenment thinking in the later generations of descendants of Jewish conversos that might have affected their estrangement from the Catholic Church? Historian Mercedes Garcia-Arenal points out the need to distinguish between religious dissent and the identity of being Jewish. The Crown and Church used the Inquisition to obligate people toward conformity to Catholic practice in Spain and its American colonies in the 1500s and 1600s. By the 1700s resistance to that uniformity was growing as Enlightenment thought grew. Baruch Spinoza, who was of a Portuguese crypto-Jewish background, was one of the leaders in the rational thought and overt skepticism of organized religion in the Enlightenment. [124]

This skepticism of religion emerges in the early 1800s in the independence movements in Latin America. Spanish colonial America was dominated by the Catholic Church and the State, both hierarchical institutions with power concentrated at the patriarchal pinnacle. As the new Latin American republics took shape after independence in the early 1800s, the movement to limit the power of the Church began. The confrontation between Church and State that had existed throughout the colonial period continued after independence. This has led to an anti-clerical tradition of opposition to the Church and its power among sectors of Latin American society. Crypto-Jews were largely external to the hierarchy of the Church, and one of the unknowns is to what extent they formed part of the anti-clerical resistance.

Statistics on the religious practice of people in Latin America usually are about 90 percent Catholic, but that is a misleading number. Latin American countries are culturally Catholic, but large portions of the population are secular and either non-religious or anti-religious and anti-clerical. Many are overtly against the Catholic Church and its power and wealth.

The anti-clerical Masons had leading roles in the independence movements in the Americas from Washington and Franklin in North America to Simon Bolivar and Jose de San Martin in Latin America.

The support of the Jewish community for the independence movement in the United States is well documented, but the records are not so clear for Latin America.

One indication of the role of anti-clericalism in the new Latin America republics was the formation of Masonic Lodges after the independence from Spain. It is impossible to know how many Jews were involved since Masonic Lodges are secret organizations, but in my interviews with Jewish families in Colombia and elsewhere, I have regularly been told of the men being Masons in families that tended to be anti-Church. That leaves this unresolved question, "To what extent were Jews and Jewish conversos in Latin America a part of that anti-clerical tradition?"

Part IV
United States and Mexico

In the American Southwest families who had a memory of having Jewish heritage commonly kept that information to themselves until recent decades. Having been separated from active Jewish community life for hundreds of years, most families did not know the details of Jewish observance. Since the Catholic Church controlled access to Bibles, descendants of converso families could not read the Bible or know the teachings of Moses. If people wanted to self-identify as Jews after learning about the family history, they had to rely on oral traditions to learn what it meant. Affirming Jewish identity secretly to one's self in an environment largely hostile to Jewish practice, required a special commitment. It is remarkable that families kept this hidden identity alive for hundreds of years under harsh and sometimes threatening conditions. During those centuries some people must have wondered if it was worth it, but clearly others continued to re-affirm the importance of preserving this unique identity.

Chapter 7

Crypto-Jews in New Spain 1520-1650

Figure 19
Palace of the Inquisition
Mexico City

In New Spain 1520-1650

THROUGHOUT THE 1500S AND EARLY 1600S, JEWISH conversos migrated to the Americas, even though it was illegal to do so. Some church officials are said to have been of converso background. Historian Alicia Gojman notes that well-known priests as Fray Bartolomé de las Casas, Fray Alonso de la Veracruz, and Fray Bernardino de Sahagún were rumored to have Jewish backgrounds.[125]

Crypto-Jews in Mexico

The Spanish colonies of New Spain (Mexico), New Granada (Colombia, Venezuela, Ecuador) and Peru were the most common destinations for crypto-Jews. A number of those who migrated to Mexico would eventually move on to the northern edges of the Spanish Empire in what is today New Mexico.

Gojman mentions that migration to the Americas was a dream for many conversos because of the possibility of escaping the Inquisition and still living in a society with the Spanish language and culture.[126] The horrors of the Inquisition in Spain in its first fifty years (1480-1530) drove conversos out of the country. By the mid to late 1500s they were leaving for Mexico where they could live with few restrictions and hopefully become successful.[127]

Historian Stanley Hordes says that crypto-Jewish communities existed from the late 1500s to the 1640s in Mexico City, Taxco, Veracruz, Oaxaca, Morelia, Guadalajara, Pachuca, Zacatecas, and in the northern territory of Nuevo León. In this early stage of Spanish migration, most crypto-Jews seem to have come for economic opportunities rather than religious reasons.[128] These communities were organized around extended-family and patron-client relationships, and each group was headed by a wealthy patrón.[129]

After the Inquisition was established in Mexico in 1571, crypto-Jews began to migrate to more remote areas where the Inquisition did not yet exist.[130] The three Offices of the Inquisition in the Americas (Mexico, Lima, and Cartagena) normally gave little attention to Judaizing, except for the period of the Grand Conspiracy in the 1630s and 1640s. The Inquisition in Mexico did have an earlier period of arrests for Judaizing in the 1590s. Each of the three Offices of the Inquisition arrested only a few hundred people for Judaizing in their 250 years of existence.[131] Most of those arrested were reconciled with the Church or expelled from Spanish territories, and rarely were people sentenced to be executed.

Betraying Family to the Inquisition

The Inquisition was a corrupting system that instilled fear in people to the point that they would betray their own family members to protect themselves. It even pressured people to inform on their parents and brothers and sisters. In one such family story in 1636 in Mexico, Maria de Zarate, the niece of an anti-Jewish cleric, married Francisco Botello, a crypto-Jew, and over time she adopted his practices as well. She then taught Jewish practices to her adopted son, Jose Sanchez. Eventually, Botello was arrested for Judaizing. The Inquisition had a requirement that anyone who knew a person who was Judaizing had to report them or be subject to arrest themselves for harboring a Judaizer, and they could be sentenced to jail and have their properties confiscated. In that climate of fear Jose Sanchez reported his mother.[132]

As we see in the case of Maria de Zarate, she adopted the practices of her crypto-Jewish husband and consequentially was arrested for Judaizing. So, a person did not necessarily have to be Jewish to be arrested for Judaizing.

Historian Roger Martínez-Dávila describes an incident of family betrayal in the Carvajal-Santa Maria extended family.[133] The Carvajal/Santa Maria family was mixed between Old Christians, conversos, and crypto-Jews. When the accusations of Judaizing were made against the

Luis Carvajal branch of the family in the 1590s, the Inquisition branch of the family closed ranks against them. Leonel Cervantes de Carvajal, Bishop Juan de Cervantes, uncle of Leonel, and the inquisitor Alonso de Peralta, a cousin of Leonel, were involved in their cases, and they acquiesced to the sentences of death to Carvajal mother, son, and daughters. The Bishop had told the son Luis that he would be tortured until he confessed, and Alonso de Peralta later signed the execution order for Luis, his distant cousin.

Martínez-Dávila suggests that these three family members collaborated to execute the Judaizers in the Carvajal branch of their own family to protect themselves from further attention or investigation by the Inquisition.[134] If one member of a family was convicted of Judaizing, the Inquisition kept records to watch other members of the family as potential Judaizers. People would betray their own family members to avoid becoming Inquisition suspects themselves.

The Carvajal Family

The story of the Luis Carvajal family has become legendary among the descendants of Jewish conversos in Mexico and the American Southwest. Many claim descent from the family, who represent a kind of nobility among people who identify with crypto-Jewish ancestry.

Luis Carvajal y de la Cueva

He was the rich uncle and the patron of this family, and he was authorized by the Spanish Crown to occupy and settle a large territory inland from the port of Tampico, called *Nuevo Reino de León*.[135] He had permission to bring settlers for the new territory, and he brought 259 people, who were exempt from the usual requirement to prove *limpieza de sangre*, or no Jewish blood. His sister, Francisca Nuñez de Carvajal, and her family were included in the group, and they, along with others, were New Christians and active crypto-Jews.[136]

According to anthropologist Schulamith Halevy, 177 (68 percent) of those original settlers with Carvajal had Portuguese Jewish converso backgrounds like Carvajal himself.[137] In 1581 they began the settlements in Nuevo Leon, but over time the Governor created political enemies, and in 1588 he was accused of being a Judaizer to the Inquisition.[138] He was arrested and at his trial in 1590, he was acquitted of Judaizing, but he was convicted of not reporting the Judaizers among the settlers he had brought to Nuevo Leon. He was sentenced to a six-year exile from Mexico, but he died in the Inquisition jail before he could be deported.[139]

The arrest of Governor Luis de Carvajal and members of his family was a high-profile case that alerted crypto-Jews to the dangers they faced in Mexico. The Governor's nephew, also named Luis, was an active crypto-Jew, and he was encouraging others to return to the practice of the Law of Moses, the Torah.

Luis de Carvajal, el Mozo

His name, *el mozo*, means "the younger". Under ideal circumstances el Mozo might have succeeded his uncle as a governor, but Judaism became the passion of his life. Later, in the Inquisition jail, he wrote extensively about his crypto-Jewish experience, and we see that he did not know what it was to be a Jew when he learned as a young man that his family was Jewish.[140]

He obtained clandestine sections of the five books of Moses and, not knowing about Jewish practice, began informing himself about the Mosaic laws through reading. In addition to that he would have learned from family oral traditions and the list of Judaizing practices made public by the Inquisition. From these elements he re-created his understanding of what it was to be a Jew. It was partly Bible, partly Inquisition, and partly family traditions.

Since his mother apparently retained some Jewish practice, why did he not know that the family was Jewish until he was a young man? Actually, that seems to have been common. The domestic Jewish rituals preserved by women could be carried out quietly without even the children being told the reasons for lighting candles, not eating pork, resting on

Saturday, death rituals, etc. Crypto-Jewish children were not told of the family legacy until they were old enough to keep the secret.

When Carvajal learned that circumcision was Jewish law, he circumcised himself. Then, he urged other men to do the same, as a marker of their return to Jewish practice, and he became known for encouraging people to observe the Law of Moses.

His mother, Francisca, and sisters Isabel, Catalina, Mariana, and Leonor were arrested by the Inquisition along with Luis in 1589. They asked for mercy as first time offenders and were given penance confined to a monastery for the next five years. After serving that sentence Luis was released with the promise to not continue Jewish practices, but he did return to his life as a crypto-Jew.

Figure 20
Luis de Carvajal, el Mozo
in Inquisition Jail
by Charlie Carrillo

Luis was articulate and multi-lingual. After leaving the Inquisition confinement, he began writing his story, a prayer guide for crypto-Jews, and other materials that are the only spiritual statement of its kind by a crypto-Jew in the Americas. Historian Ronnie Perelis has studied Carvajal's original manuscript and describes it as "an electrifying spiritual autobiography".[141] During these events Luis changed his name to Joseph Lumbroso. Joseph is from the biblical Joseph, the dreamer and prime minister to the Pharaoh. "Lumbroso" in Spanish means shining or light. So, he took the name of being an enlightened dreamer.[142]

In 1595 he was arrested again, now as a second offender. Knowing his fate, he apparently attempted suicide to avoid the torture that might force him to reveal the names of other crypto-Jews. In his second trial he was again convicted of Judaizing, and this time he was sentenced to death.

Priests walked along side Luis on the way to the pyre, trying to convert him at the last minute. He agreed to give a "confession" in which he renounced his sin of having identified eight others as being crypto-Jews when he was tortured. The priests accompanying him decided that his making confession was enough to consider him reconciled with the Church, and according to Inquisition protocol he was granted the privilege of being strangled before being burned because of his "reconciliation".[143]

The mother and sisters were also reconciled with the Church at the last minute, giving them the privilege of being strangled to avoid the excruciating pain of being burned alive. The the bodies of the Carvajals, mother, son and daughters were burned at the stake together on Sunday, December 8, 1596 in Mexico City.[144]

That created the Carvajal family legend as martyrs, and they are still known and respected in crypto-Jewish circles. Luis de Carvajal has become a folk hero to descendants of crypto-Jews because of his martyrdom and his reputation for passion in encouraging others to return to the practice of Judaism.

Crypto-Jews and the Inquisition in Mexico

Crypto-Jewish families set up networks of assistance and protection that could aid and direct newcomers. The arrival port was Veracruz, and the house of Fernando Rodriguez functioned as a "safe" house where crypto-Jews could arrive,[145] and he would direct them to families in the interior of the country from Mexico City to Taxco, Zacatecas, and other cities. In Mexico City, Antonio Váez was a community leader, and he would have Passover Seders in his house and visit crypto-Jewish families who were ill or in need.

After he was arrested by the Inquisition, his son, Simón Váez Sevilla, continued his father's work in community organization, helping disseminate information about the calendar of Jewish holidays and other activities. As one of the wealthier crypto-Jews, he successfully helped other families establish themselves economically in other parts of the country, forming a network of crypto-Jewish families. Eventually, he too was arrested, but others carried on responsibilities within the community, such as Margarita de Rivera, who prepared the dead for a Jewish burial, and Miguel Tinoco, who provided matzah for Passover.[146]

A last round of massive arrests for Judaizing by the Inquisition in Mexico started in 1642. These arrests targeted Portuguese conversos after Portugal broke from Spain in 1640. The Spanish Crown feared that the crypto-Jews, a majority of whom were Portuguese, might side with Portugal in a conflict.

The king banned Portuguese travel to the American territories and ordered that Portuguese already in the Americas could not live within fifty-two miles of strategic ports and mining centers. Crypto-Jews began preparing to protect themselves and their possessions. Over the next five years, 130 people were arrested for Judaizing, in an attempt to suppress Jewish converso sympathizers with the Portuguese independence movement.

Stanley Hordes tells about key cases, starting with **Blanca Méndez de Rivera**. In May, 1642 she and her five daughters were arrested by the Inquisition for Judaizing. She exclaimed, "Ay, how has so much misery come to me, they've just thrown us in here and already we're lost and without honor and no one will look us in the face..."[147] She was in the Inquisition jail for four years and eventually died there. Blanca Mendez and her daughters were known for their eagerness to talk, and their arrest sent fear through the crypto-Jewish community in Mexico City. In secret communications with her, the community offered a large amount of money to not implicate others, but subsequently the Inquisition began to make a series of arrests, suggesting that Blanca Méndez or one of her daughters did talk and identify people.

Simón Váez Sevilla. The night of July 12, 1642 Váez Sevilla and six others were arrested for Judaizing, and thirty more the next night. He had turned over most of his wealth to a friend and business partner for safe keeping, so that it would not be confiscated by the Inquisition. Váez Sevilla was in the Inquisition jail until the *auto de fé* of 1649, when he was reconciled with the Church and exiled to Spain.[148]

Luis Núñez Pérez. He was a Portuguese cacao merchant, who was a crypto-Jew. When he was arrested by the Inquisition, they found a copy of a treaty between the Dutch and the new king of Portugal, which made it appear as if he were an enemy agent, representing either the Dutch or the Portuguese, both of whom Spain feared might try to take Mexico. This seemed to confirm that crypto-Jews were supporting the Portuguese against the Spanish. Hordes points out that the inquisitors were more concerned about the threat posed by their allegiance to the leaders of the Portuguese revolt than about Judaizing.[149]

Eighty percent of the 130 arrested by the Inquisition from 1642 to 1647 confessed to Judaizing, and almost all (71 percent) were reconciled with the Church, promising to never do it again. Another twelve percent of those arrested were reconciled with the Church but had added punishments of confiscation of goods or exile because their offenses were deemed to be greater. Five percent, who were the most religious, were sentenced to serve as galley slaves at sea, which was usually the equivalent of a death sentence. In the largest *auto-de-fé* in Mexico in 1649, thirteen people were burned at the stake in April, 1649, putting a close to seven years of Inquisition arrests.[150]

Alicia Gojman points out that starting in the late 1640s the Inquisition deported the "reconciled" people to Spain, which was considered a safer, more Catholic environment. She says that active crypto-Jewish communities began to disappear at that time.[151]

Although the Inquisition in the Americas struck fear in crypto-Jewish families, it was not as devastating as it had been in Spain, which measured arrests in the tens of thousands and deaths in the thousands. In the 250 years from 1571 to its abolishment in 1821, the Inquisition in Mexico arrested a few hundred people for Judaizing but rarely sentenced anyone to be executed. The show trials of the 1590s and the 1640s had the purpose of putting prominent conversos on trial in public, which served as a warning to anyone who was following the Law of Moses, i.e. Judaizing. Then, burning them at the stake used the terror of death to emphasize the point that non-Christian behavior would not be tolerated.

The public displays of death at the stake for Jewish practice would have had the effect of driving crypto-Jews to leave Mexico, abandon their crypto-Jewish practices, or go into deep hiding. In the 1700s the Inquisition made only a couple of arrests for Judaizing, suggesting either that the Inquisition had eliminated active crypto-Jewish life in Mexico or that it was no longer interested in prosecuting crypto-Jews or that crypto-Jews had lowered their visibility to avoid the scrutiny of the Inquisition.

A Mikveh in Mexico?

Immersion in the *mikveh* is an important spiritual cleansing ritual in Jewish life, and the *mikveh* is required of Jews for spiritual purification and preparation for important events in life. Recently, three mikveh-like structures were discovered in Mexico in the town of Juliantla in Taxco, which is known to have had a Jewish converso population. Although these mikveh were authenticated by the *Instituto Nacional de antropología e historia* (National Institute of Anthropology and History of Mexico) as being from the colonial period,[152] their legitimacy has been questioned. Preparation for Shabbat included bathing and changing to fresh clothes, cleaning the house, and changing beds. The sacredness of Shabbat required cleanliness of the person and of the house. Regular bathing was not a common practice in Christian medieval Europe or the Americas. So, people doing such an unnatural and unchristian thing as bathing weekly, could be accused of being Jews.

The Settling of New Mexico

The first crypto-Jews in New Mexico would have come in 1598 with the expedition of Don Juan de Oñate y Salazar. Oñate was a Basque, whose father had become wealthy as a co-owner of mines in Zacatecas. As the son of a prominent family, he married Doña Isabel de Tolosa Cortés de Moctezuma, the granddaughter of Cortés and the great granddaughter of Moctezuma.

In 1595 Oñate was authorized by the king of Spain to colonize the northern frontier of the Viceroyalty of New Spain, what was to become New Mexico. Over the next three years he gathered a group of colonizers who were willing to move to the outer edge of the known world.

After initial explorations of the northern frontier by Francisco Vazquez Coronado (1540-1542) and others had failed to find sources of mineral wealth, such as silver and gold, the Spanish showed no interest in settling the area for the next fifty years.

With the defeat of the Spanish Armada in 1588, Spain lost some of its dominance in the Atlantic Ocean, and the English and Dutch had made clear their interest in establishing American colonies. The northern frontier of the rich Viceroyalty in Mexico had to be protected from potential encroachment by other European powers, and new settlements in that area would provide a buffer. It was in this context that Oñate's expedition was approved.[153]

The overlapping story of Oñate's expedition was the arrest and execution of the Carvajal family by the Inquisition for Judaizing in 1596. If such a prominent family could be burned at the stake, the implication was that any crypto-Jewish family in Mexico could be exposed and suffer the same fate. That incident could well have encouraged crypto-Jewish families to consider joining such an expedition that would take them far from the Offices of the Inquisition, and it also held the promise of wealth to be accumulated in the new land.

In the following decades, an untold number of New Christian conversos, and among them crypto-Jews, settled in northern New Mexico and southern Colorado. Oñate himself is said to have been a descendant of a converso family.[154] The Inquisition did not maintain an office in Santa Fe, but local priests could report suspicious activity to the Inquisition in Mexico City, which could then send an inquisitor to investigate. But the trip to Santa Fe from Mexico City was four months over sometimes grueling terrain, so that was a barrier that provided some protection from the Inquisition. Crypto-Jews still had to maintain a low profile, and keeping the secret of a Jewish background could be a matter of life or death, even in the distant Santa Fe territory.

Oñate's expedition included 130 families and 270 soldiers along with wagons and carts and thousands of animals, including horses, mules, donkeys, and oxen. In late April, 1598, they arrived to the Rio Grande where they rested. Oñate claimed the River and its drainage basin and all the adjacent lands for Spain. This newly claimed land was named *El Reino de la Nueva Mexico* (the Realm of New Mexico). The Rio Grande flows almost directly southward until El Paso where it turns southeastward to the Gulf of Mexico.

Oñate and his expedition basically followed the course of the Rio Grande on the trek northward from El Paso, and it became known as the *Camino Real de Tierra Adentro*, the "Royal Road Inland" between Mexico City and Santa Fe. They arrived in northern New Mexico in July, 1598 and established a Spanish settlement on the west bank of the Rio Grande across the river from the San Juan Pueblo. By 1610 it was decided to move the settlement further south to a better location, and Santa Fe was established.

Ten Franciscan priests were in the expedition, and their role was the evangelize the Native American people. The goals of conquering and subjugating the native peoples and at the same time "saving their souls" set up a struggle between Church and State that would continue throughout the Colonial period.

The crypto-Jewish community in New Mexico was spared the mass arrests of the 1640s, partly because they were cut off from the larger crypto-Jewish community in Mexico itself. Their remote mountain location 1400 miles away from Mexico City meant that they did not pose a threat to the Spanish Crown, nor to the main body of the Church. Caught in this splendid isolation, this community was left to develop relatively unscathed. Although we have a paucity of Inquisition records about Judaizing in northern New Mexico, we know they were there because their descendants have made themselves known over the last half century.[155]

The crypto-Jews on Oñate's expedition were starting a new life that would shape generations to come. Their ancestors had come to Mexico, and now their grandsons and granddaughters were decades removed from Jewish practice, still keeping the family memory of being Jewish, but they lived under the shadow of the Inquisition. Were they hiding because of the stigma of their past, or were they hiding because they wanted to protect something precious to them, their Jewish identity? Certainly, the reasoning was different for different families. Whatever their motivations, they had a common legacy, and as the records of the Inquisition in Mexico indicate, these families must have formed clusters of like-minded people. They would have shared recognizable cultural practices from lighting candles on Friday night to not eating pork.

How would these crypto-Jews have understood their spirituality and their religious condition? How did they balance their Spanish identity and their religious identity? If they continued living in Spanish lands, they could not live openly as Jews. It seems like a conundrum, but maybe it was more than that.

Chapter 8

Secret Santa Fe:
Jewish Conversos in New Mexico

Figure 21
Colonial Adobe Church (1760)
Las Trampas, New Mexico

Crypto-Jews would have attended churches like this one in small towns in northern New Mexico.

AFTER SANTA FE WAS ESTABLISHED IN 1610 LIFE for the next fifty years was mostly uneventful. When Bernardo López de Mendizábal was appointed governor of the territory in 1659, it became a time of conflict. During Don Bernardo's tenure as Governor, he was repeatedly in conflict with the Church, and "succeeded in agitating and alienating virtually every friar in the province with his irreverent words and hostile polices..."[157] He came into conflict with the local Franciscan priests when he prohibited them from forcing the local Pueblo people to work on Church projects without paying them. He also defended the right of the Pueblo people to do traditional religious dances in spite of the fact that the Church had prohibited native religious practices for decades. His conflict with the local clergy also included irregular attendance at mass and confession.

As he left office, he was confronted with accusations of abuse of power for financial gain, and to expedite his removal from Santa Fe, they added the charge of Judaizing. So, similar to the case of Don Luis de Carvajal, Governor of Nuevo León, discussed earlier, the charge of Judaizing could be used for political purposes.[158]

In 1662 the Inquisition arrested Governor López and his wife, Doña Teresa Aguilera y Roche. The dramatic nighttime arrest of Doña Teresa in the Palace of the Governors in Santa Fe was filled with political intrigue, as described by anthropologist Frances Levine in her book *Doña Teresa Confronts the Spanish Inquisition*.[159]

Doña Teresa and the Inquisition

The incoming governor demanded forfeiture of properties that López had accumulated as governor. When López refused, he was arrested, and Doña Teresa received word that she would be next. She invited her two best women friends to stay with her in the Palace of the

Governors, as she awaited her fate. The Sheriff and his men arrived in the early hours of pre-dawn to take her into custody in the name of the Inquisition. She and her husband were held in a detention facility in Santo Domingo Pueblo south of Santa Fe until they could be transported to Mexico City.

Figure 22
Palace of the Governors, Santa Fe, New Mexico

Don Bernardo and Doña Teresa were taken on the months long trek along the Camino Real to Mexico City to stand trial. The trip across the deserts of Mexico along rough roads and trails took their toll. The conditions of travel were so precarious that four of Doña Teresa's maids died en route.[160] The Governor and his wife were displayed in towns and villages along the way as examples of what can happen if one were to be accused of Judaizing.

Don Bernardo died in the Inquisition jail before completing the trial, but he was later absolved *en absentia*. Doña Teresa did have a trial that lasted two years, and the accusations against her ranged from drinking chocolate on Holy Friday, to bathing and changing to clean clothes for the weekend, and reading novels in a foreign language.[161] Drinking chocolate on Holy Friday was seen as an indulgence that disregarded the sanctity of Good Friday, indicating that she was not a good Catholic. Bathing and changing clothes on Friday were considered to be Jewish practices, preparing for Shabbat on Saturday. Spanish was considered to be the Christian language, so reading a book in a foreign language was a suggestion that she was reading material that was not Catholic.[162]

Doña Teresa was cosmopolitan and multilingual, and the servants in Santa Fe, who made these accusations against her, seemed not to understand her foreign ways. Her father was a diplomat, and she had lived in Italy and France before her father was named Governor of Cartagena, as discussed earlier. She seems to have read French, Italian, and Latin in addition to Spanish.

On trial before the Inquisition, she made a strong defense of her innocence, and eventually the charges against her were put into abeyance, and she was released from the Inquisition jail. Her Catholic background, fluency in Latin, and knowledge of Catholic prayers by memory were in her favor. Her Catholic practices could be traced to her maternal grandfather John Roach, an Irish Catholic, who had migrated from Ireland to Spain because it was more Catholic.[163] She seems to have convinced the Inquisitors that she was a literate, educated Catholic although she was lax in her practice. The suspicions about her behavior meant that she would not be absolved, but neither could they convict her.

When a person was arrested by the Inquisition, their goods were confiscated and used to pay for their cost of living while in the Inquisition jail. In the case of Doña Teresa, she was charged 4,000 pesos for her cost of living for the two years she was in jail. One of the curiosities about her bills for food were the ten to eleven pounds of chocolate she would order monthly. While it seems impossible to eat or drink that much chocolate each month, Levine thanks that she might have been using it to bribe the guards for other needs. If a person was acquitted of the charges against them, their remaining goods would be returned to them, but if a person was convicted, their goods became property of the Inquisition.

Levine notes that Doña Teresa was the only woman from New Mexico tried before the Inquisition for secretly practicing Judaism, and she faced thirty charges of alleged Jewish practice. Governor Don

Bernardo, Doña Teresa, and four men arrested with them constitute half the cases before the Inquisition from New Mexico and all the cases alleging Jewish practice.[164]

Since the case against Doña Teresa was suspended and she was not acquitted, her money and property were not returned. She fought the rest of her life to have her name cleared, on the one hand, and for the return of her wealth on the other. The refusal to exonerate her left her family under a cloud of suspicion. The Inquisition kept records of those who were convicted or who had open cases against them, and that information was attached to the files of their relatives. That made family members people of record in case they were ever to fall under suspicion for unCatholic behaviors.

None of the four men, arrested with Don Bernardo and Doña Teresa, were convicted of Judaizing. The cases of Francisco Gómez Robledo and Cristóbal de Anaya Almazán were dismissed, and they were released. Diego Romero and Nicolas de Aguilar were convicted on minor counts of heresy, but not Judaizing, and they were sentenced to a ten-year exile from New Mexico, but it was not clear if they were ever actually exiled.[165]

The Decline of the Inquisition

Crypto-Jews became less relevant to the Inquisition after the 1650s, and there were a couple of factors to explain that. Crypto-Jews became less of a threat, but the Church and the Inquisition also lost influence during that time.

The Pueblo Revolt of 1680

When the New Mexico colony was established in 1598 under Oñate, both the secular forces and the Franciscan friars exploited the indigenous Pueblo people and engaged in open cruelty. After a battle with the Acoma Pueblo people, Oñate had the right foot cut off of men over twenty-five-years-old, and they were enslaved for twenty years. Young women were also enslaved and assigned as servants in houses of the Spanish or for the Church.

The Franciscans were known for drafting Indian laborers to work for them for free building large adobe churches and the personal living quarters for the priests. The priests prohibited the traditional dances and religious practices that were an integral part of the native agricultural cycle. Given the disruption in their lives, the insistence that they convert, and the forced labor, the indigenous people were hostile toward the Spanish, including soldiers, settlers, and priests.

We do not know what the role of converso families was during this process. Spanish families, including conversos, were given plots of land to farm, which would have impinged on the land used by the indigenous people for farming or hunting. When the native people struck back in the Pueblo Revolt of 1680, they seem to have treated all the Spaniards as the same. In the revolt some 400 Spanish settlers and priests were killed and the remaining 2,000 fled to El Paso.

When the Spanish were able to return in 1692, it was on the terms that the power of both the Church and State would be curtailed. That benefited not only the indigenous people but also the converso families. The Church had lost power.

The Bourbon Reforms

In 1700 another event in Spain would ultimately weaken the Inquisition and make life easier for any converso families in the Americas. The last Hapsburg king died without an heir and named Philip, Duke of Anjou of the Bourbon family to succeed him. The Bourbons brought a more liberal French attitude toward religion and governing. The power of the Holy Office of the Inquisition was reduced, and the Bourbon kings initiated broad reforms in the administration of the American colonies, giving more rights to local populations. Although the Bourbon kings did not abolish the Inquisition, they reduced its importance in contrast to the power it had under the Hapsburg kings.

After Inquisition lost power in the late 1600s and early 1700s there were virtually no arrests for Judaizing and no records about crypto-Jewish life. Priests lost influence to impose religious orthodoxy, and crypto-Jewish families had less to fear from the Inquisition than from the social pressure of their own neighbors, many of whom still found it shameful to have a Jewish past.

A century later in 1812 the Inquisition was abolished in Mexico at the start of the Mexican War of Independence, briefly reappearing before being finally abolished in 1821.[166] The Inquisition was initially abolished in Spain when Napoleon invaded in 1808, but it was re-established when the French were driven out before being finally abolished by the Regent Maria Cristina in 1834.[167]

Although the Inquisition lost power and became less of a threat in the 1700s, the culture of secrecy was well established in crypto-Jewish families. The larger society was Catholic, and having Jewish ancestry was not acceptable. Jews were still denounced from the pulpits, and they were said to be the people who had killed Jesus. Even without the Inquisition, the shame and fear of being identified as Jewish was too great to be publicly admitted.

Crypto-Jewish families did attend mass and observed Catholic holidays like their neighbors. The result was that through the generations and centuries, their descendants gradually became more Catholic. Adobe churches from the Spanish colonial period like the ones they would have attended still exist in the small towns in the northern mountains of New Mexico, such as Chimayó and Las Trampas.

The Hybridity of Ritual

The research of Stanley Hordes, David Gitlitz, and others has documented elements of crypto-Jewish life in Mexico, some of which seem to have survived in New Mexico, according to interviews with descendants. Any given family or community of families would not have necessarily observed all of these practices, but these are some practices that have been recorded.

- **Observing Shabbat.** Observing Shabbat was the one custom that was most persistent in families that retained the memory of being Jewish.[168] Common practices in preparation for Shabbat were bathing, changing to fresh clothes, changing the bed, cleaning the house, and preparing the food for the day. Shabbat itself was a day of rest, and not working.[169]

- **Centrality of Moses, Esther and Job.** The central figures in crypto-Jewish veneration were Moses the lawgiver, Esther of stalwart faithfulness, and Job the one faithful in spite of suffering and adversity. The Fast of Esther was an important day in Mexico and New Mexico.
- **Dietary laws.** A common practice was to not eat pork and to avoid the mixing of meat and milk in the same meal. In spite of not eating pork at home, some people would make displays of eating pork publicly, which was like a vaccination to prevent the Inquisition. Animals were slaughtered in a kosher-like process in which the blood was drained from the animal.
- **Lighting candles.** Many families report lighting candles on Friday night with prayer. Early on, it seems that women did remember the Hebrew prayer, but by the twentieth century, women were saying Catholic prayers with the candle lighting.
- **Death rituals.** In keeping with Jewish custom, the person who passed away was buried quickly after the body was bathed, wrapped in a shroud, and buried in virgin soil.[170] Mirrors were covered in the house of the deceased during the initial period of mourning. It is common among descendants of crypto-Jews to place small stones on graves.[171]
- **Marriage.** Young men and women seem to have continued the practice of choosing marriage partners from within the crypto-Jewish community. Hordes confirms this in Mexico.[172] Families in New Mexico have reported similar marriage patterns. This was not only a normal practice among crypto-Jewish families, but also among active Sephardic families in America.[173]
- **Circumcision.** This practice was common among crypto-Jews in Mexico.[174] Inquisition records show that men arrested for Judaizing were checked to see if they were circumcised and 80 percent were. Another 11 percent showed cuts or scarring that Inquisitions thought worth noting.[175]
- **Holidays**. Yom Kippur was commonly observed with a fast in classic Spanish crypto-Jewish life. Yom Kippur was known as *el*

día grande or the Big Day, and reference to it appears regularly in Inquisition records.

- **Fear of the Power of the Church.** The phrase "wearing the *sanbenito*", an overshirt for those arrested by the Inquisition became a euphemism for being discovered as a practicing Jew and punished. The use of the phrase "wearing the *sanbenito*" has continued into recent times.

Figure 23
Reconstruction of a New Mexico Farm House Patio of the 1700s
Las Golondrinas

In addition to the practices described above Loggie Carrasco describes a funerary practice in New Mexico. Sand was rubbed on the feet of a dying person to symbolize that they were walking on the native soil of Israel as they were leaving this earth. Then, at the burial, earth would be thrown into the grave, representing soil from Israel. Since Israel was a desert land like New Mexico, people used local sand to represent the holy land.[176]

What Survived

As crypto-Jews in Mexico became less visible in the 1700s, only two cases were tried before the Inquisition: Diego Rodriguez of Tlaxcala in 1723 and Maria Felipa Alcazar from Oaxaca in 1739. Veracruz was known for the floating population of illegal foreign Jews because of the maritime trade. They would arrive on ships from English or Dutch lands, but it was not a continuous resident population, and they were not persecuted by the Inquisition. The other port, Acapulco, also had a Jewish converso population, as did Mexico City, Puebla, and Guadalajara.

The crypto-Jews who left Mexico for New Mexico had less to fear from the Inquisition, but they had no opportunity to return to Jewish practice if they wanted to do so. It was a golden cage. Unlike crypto-Jews in Spain, they could not flee to Morocco or Amsterdam, and unlike crypto-Jews in Veracruz, they could not flee to an English or Dutch island in the Caribbean. The crypto-Jews of New Mexico were surrounded by Native American nations, and their only lifeline back to life as Jews was through Mexico, which was fraught with the potential danger of the Inquisition. With their cultural and religious lifelines cut off, the Catholic descendants of hidden Jewish adjusted to being invisible with a thread of memory that became thinner and thinner.

Figure 24
Retablo
Charlie Carrillo

Chapter 9

Oral Tradition, Folklore, and the Arts

Figure 25
Adam and Eve Retablo
Charlie Carrillo

AS CRYPTO-JEWISH LIFE EVOLVED FROM ITS CLASSIC stage in Spain to the Twilight period in Mexico and New Mexico, it had fewer elements of normative Judaism and more from the Catholic context in which it existed. Oral traditions became more important as stories filled in for the study of Torah. Since rabbinic teachings were not available, crypto-Jewish stories and interpretations of Biblical stories filled the vacuum, providing the understanding of religion and legacy. Like Midrash in Judaism, oral traditions filled the gaps in knowledge about the Bible and Jewish traditions.

How Crypto-Jews Might Have Lived

Contemporary novelists, such as Isabelle Medina Sandoval, Marcia Fine, and Corinne Brown have created narratives in their novels of what crypto-Jewish life might have been like historically.

Medina Sandoval is a spokesperson for her own journey of discovery and reclaiming Jewish identity in addition to being a leading poet and novelist. She is well-known in New Mexico and the American Southwest for writings and talks about her personal story. She is a researcher on crypto-Jewish life, and in her historical novel *Guardians of Hidden Traditions*, she weaves a story around her own line of women ancestors. Based on her research, this is Medina Sandoval's reconstruction of how her ninth-generation grandmother, María Paula Mascareñas de Trujillo, might have lived.[177]

1787 Chimayó

The afternoon of July 3, the priest baptized the new Trujillo daughter. The priest in the Santa Cruz Church baptized the baby in the presence of the parents and the godparents, Damasio Trujillo and María Dionisa Borrego. The new mother claimed she was not feeling well and asked to host a fiesta later in the month. As was the custom, the padrinos handed over the newborn criatura [child] to the mother saying:

Reciba esta prenda amada	Receive this dear being
Que de la iglesia santa salió	That came from the Holy Church
Con los santos sacramentos	With the holy sacraments
Y el agua que recibió.	And the [baptismal] water it received.

Feigning keen tiredness after the ceremony, María told everyone she was feeling ill and needed to go home to bed. The madrina, María Dionisa Borrego, expressed her satisfaction that the baptism had taken place because she had feared that the baby might be a heretic and was in danger of dying without being baptized. Dionisa's best friend, Beatriz Vigil, voiced her satisfaction that the baptism had taken place because she did not want María Jésus to be a judía for lack of the blessed baptism.

After José left the house to feed the cows and goats, María took her newborn daughter into her private bedroom. Baltazar was a good Catholic man and she did not want him to know how she was going to perpetuate the female custom of washing off the Catholic baptism and asking for a guardian angel for her daughter. She waited to get out of bed until she heard Baltazar leave the house.

María Paula's mother, Paula Romero died several years ago. Had Paula been alive, the grandmother would have assisted her to wash off the Catholic baptismal fluids. In her conversa family, this was the custom of the women.

She would perform this holy ceremony by herself and G-d would witness the faith of her heart and soul. G-d had answered Hannah's prayer and she knew that this blessing of generation to generation must be honored by her actions.

María poured water into a basin to remove all traces of the baptismal liquids from her baby's head. Gently placing her daughter in the lukewarm water, she scrubbed the baby so much that her pale brown skin turned blotchy red. She washed the baby all over and placed some seed pearls, turquoise and coral nuggets in the basin filled with the clean mountain water. She followed this same procedure with all her children. Drying the baby with a thick towel, she took the baby out to the mountain behind the house and lifted her up to heavens. In the pure air of the high altitude surrounded by royal purple wild irises, her melodic voice halted the celestial melodies of the songbirds as she chanted:

Eterno Altísimo	Eternal Holy One
Mis sueños son Tuyos	My dreams are Yours
Mi hija es Tuya	My daughter is Yours
Tus hadas protegen mi hija	Your angels protect my daughter
Alabado es El Eterno	Praised is the Eternal One
Siempre, siempre, amén.	Always, always. Amen.

María Jésus was a lovely child. Her hazel eyes sparkled against her medium brown skin. Rarely having to be reminded or scolded for misbehaving, she was an intelligent and loving child. She spent time asking her mother and father philosophical and religious questions while demonstrating a bottomless thirst for knowledge. In her soul, María recognized how much her daughter mirrored herself. It warmed her to know that the Jewish faith burned like the blue flame of the Shabbat candle in the next generation of her blood.

From the wilderness of New Mexico, the chime of time stopped to marvel that three centuries of the Spanish Inquisition had tolled the bell in remembrance of the conversa *women from the Iberian Peninsula still providing Jewish support and spirituality for their children.*

Medina Sandoval portrays a life in which the Jewish heritage was quietly interwoven with every aspect of life without making it so obvious to trigger reactions from the ecclesiastical authorities. It was the life of farmers at the end of the Camino Real in the mountains of New Mexico, the far northern frontier of the Spanish Empire.

Crypto-Jews and Biblical Figures

Although the descendants of Jewish conversos do not have written histories of their families, they do have oral traditions. Although these traditions might not have followed the interpretations of normative Judaism, they did fit the reality that crypto-Jews were living. They interpreted Biblical stories in terms of converso and crypto-Jewish experience. The distance from Jewish practice and the ever presence of Christianity led to a fusion of religious imagery between the two. This hybridization can be seen in the crypto-Jewish trinity of Moses, Esther, and Job.

The Catholic Church used visual iconography to convey the stories of Bible and Church history in the high art of churches and cathedrals, and crypto-Jews were able to use the folk art imagery of the common people known as *retablos* for their homes. These were small format paintings (twelve to eighteen inches or so) on commonly available materials, such as wood, leather, or tin made them easily accessible and affordable to the public. Since retablos were commonly made about Christian figures, crypto-Jews could adapt their own Biblical figures to that format without suspicion.

These retablos were sold in the street markets in Mexico City, and Gojman points out that,

> *The Inquisition suspected these shopkeepers of being Judaizers who had no respect for religious images and found a profitable business in the sale of these small panels painted with saints. Therefore, the Inquisition made a decision to stop the worship of these images and prosecute the sellers as Judaizers.*[178]

"Saint Moses" was a popular crypto-Jewish icon, and crypto-Jews could pray to him in a Catholic-like practice asking to be helped or for deliverance from their difficult situation. Expectant mothers are known to have prayed to Moses that their child might be the Messiah, who would bring a new age for Jews and deliver crypto-Jews from their problems.

Moses became much like a Jewish Jesus to some, a figure who could be an intercessor with God. He was a Christian-like saint that could be shared without suspicion between reverent Catholics and crypto-Jews. Moses was even a God-like figure for some. Ana Núñez confessed to the Inquisition that she had been taught that Moses was the only God and that the Messiah was to be born of a Mexican Jewish woman. People were known to light candles before images of Moses much like Christians would do for Catholic saints.[179]

Esther, the Biblical queen of Persia was also an important figure in retablos. The Bible account says that Esther fasted before she went uninvited to plea with the King to reverse the decision about allowing a pogrom against Jews in the empire. The Fast of Esther became a regular practice in the crypto-Jewish worlds of Mexico and New Mexico.

In Jewish life the Esther story was part of Purim, but such a celebration would have been difficult to hide from the Inquisition. So, it was transformed into a fast, and the Fast of Esther became the substitute for Purim. Esther gained importance with the crypto-Jews of Mexico and New Mexico perhaps because they identified their own plight with the Jews of Ancient Persia.

In New Mexico some families celebrated a Saint Esther's Day, which was primarily for women teaching domestic skills to their daughters. The fast would typically be during the daylight hours, and they would break the fast at night with fish and vegetables. The celebration was with a special local meat turnover (*empanada*) and wine during which they would light candles to Saint Esther.

Job was the third popular figure in retablos because he represents suffering, which was a theme for many crypto-Jewish families, who looked for an end to the persecution. Since the suffering Jesus is a popular theme in Catholicism, Job became the counterpart for crypto-Jews.

Although not common today, people still mention their mothers or grandmothers venerating "crypto-Jewish" saints in retablos, including the three mentioned above. Such veneration would be acceptable in a Christian context, and it can now be identified as a crypto-Jewish practice.

Charlie Carrillo
Twenty-First Century Retablos

The tradition of retablo painting is still alive in New Mexico, and Charlie Carrillo is a widely known and respected retablo artist. He is a *santero*, a carver of wooden images of saints and a painter of retablos, depicting images of Biblical figures. His pieces are in the collections of Smithsonian Museum, including both the Museum of American Art and the Museum of American History. His pieces are also in the collections of the Denver Museum of Art and the Museum of International Folk Art in Santa Fe among others. He acknowledges having Jewish ancestry, but he identifies as Catholic. He fuses of the two religious traditions in his artistic work, giving recognition to both.

He borrows the format of the colonial retablos but rendered with contemporary materials. He combines Jewish elements in what is considered traditional Catholic imagery, a characteristic of this style of art. That has led to criticism from some about commercializing a religious legacy, but these images are important to others, who are embrace this hybrid tradition of Jewish memory combined with loyalty to the Catholic Church.

> *New Mexicans are aware of their multi-cultural background, both artistically, linguistically, and religiously, all those things that make us who we are. I had ancestors that were Jewish way, way back. Usually, the first reaction is, "Are you a converso?" And, I tell them, "No, I am very much a practicing Catholic, but I understand that [Judaism] is part of my ancestral heritage. As a Catholic santero [creator of religious images] I can take the pen in my hand, or the brush, and go further back. I can paint images that are copied or inspired by fifteenth, sixteenth, and seventeenth imagery from the Sephardi community in Spain and incorporate those ideas and motifs into my own work. What it says is that I, Charlie Carrillo, as a Catholic, am tremendously proud of my Sephardic ancestry, and I cannot deny it. The three cultures, the Jewish, Catholic, and Muslims were all mixed up in Spain, and we are still mixed up in New Mexico. We don't separate them. Then, I think how much of my Catholic practices are couched in Jewish traditions like lighting candles on Friday*

night, putting stones on graves, or putting earth on the burial. People say, "Well, that's Sephardi tradition." What I realize is that both traditions are mixed, but they stayed separate to a certain degree. I can't tell which is the Catholic tradition and which is the Sephardi, all I know is that they mix, and it builds my culture.

Charlie Carrillo[180]

Figure 26
Joseph's Dream
Charlie Carrillo

These retablos by Carrillo are carved in relief and painted in bold colors with red, yellow, blue, and green dominating his palette. Carrillo's painted retablos are an important genre of folk art that has become widely popular in recent years.

In twenty-first century New Mexico, Moses, Esther, Job no longer dominate the retablo tradition, and retablos are no longer venerated. In keeping with contemporary society, retablos have mostly become collector's items, rather than religious ones. They are folk art to adorn a house, giving memory to this tradition. The veneration of these figures that was common in the Spanish Colonial period has largely drifted into the past, remembered vaguely like horse drawn carriages and remote ancestors.

Family Oral Traditions

Many people, who identify as having a Jewish ancestry have oral traditions about their origins, usually emphasizing the Jewishness or Spanishness of their family. Oral traditions are valid, but they are not always historically accurate. The very nature of passing information orally lends itself to changes from generation to generation. With no written sources from the past as reference, each generation can add new words and ideas with old ones dropping out. Oral traditions are a reflection of family histories, and their validity is not based on historical accuracy but on the meaning they reflect to the people who tell the stories. Since oral traditions do not necessarily follow historical facts, some skeptics have questioned whether the crypto-Jewish experience reflects history or is a mixture of unsubstantiated folk beliefs. These are some of the oral traditions today.

Baptism and Jewish Heritage

Families have stories of the baptismal water being washed off newborn babies, or strategies to avoid the baptism altogether. Loggie Carrasco in a 1978 interview with anthropologist Paula Sabloff commented on the lack of baptismal records in her family. [181]

> *I started doing the research on my family to see if I could make a claim, a legacy claim. [Atrisco land grant claim] I ran into a Carrasco, but I couldn't find the certification I needed because you had to have baptismal records. My mother said that I would not find baptismal records - they were Marranos. If Marranos got baptized they did under force, but evidently they tried to avoid baptism. My paternal grandmother, the story was told that as to why I could not find her baptismal certificate. Her name was Maria Lucero,*

they always chose a Christian name to cover up for the Inquisition. But she was never baptized to my knowledge...I never could find a legacy claim for Carrasco directly in the grant court case 833715 because if you were known to be a Marrano you could hold no legacy...

Later, she mentioned that when her mother learned that she was inquiring about the land grant, her mother warned her to avoid it. "She said, 'Don't, you will discover fire. They were Marranos.' And, she kept telling me this."

Jewish Last Names

A common belief is that Spanish or Portuguese family names that end in "ez" or "es" are Jewish last names, such as Sanchez, Gomez, Rodriguez, Gonzales, and Fernandez. The "ez" or "es" endings actually refer to being the "son of". Names ending in "ez" were common Spanish names, and Jewish conversos could have adopted them after converting to Catholicism. These are names shared by Christians and Jews but not necessarily Jewish. There is the question whether the common New Mexico family name of Rael is a derivative of Israel, but it is actually a German family name. There were uniquely Jewish names in Spain, such as Abulafia, Abarbanel, Benveniste, Cohen, Halevi, Senior, but those names are not usually found among the descendants of Jewish conversos in the Americas.[182]

Crypto-Jews and Ladino

In New Mexico some people have thought that the sixteenth or seventeenth century colonial Spanish spoken among the older families in northern New Mexico was actually the Judeo-Spanish dialect called Ladino.

The Jews in Christian Spain (Castile, Aragon, and Navarre) spoke varieties of Castilian Spanish and other Ibero-Romance languages, and the Jews of Muslim Spain (al-Andaluz) spoke Arabic, and as they moved into Morocco after the Expulsion they developed the Arabic influenced Judeo-Spanish dialect called Haketia which was parallel to the Turkish version called Ladino. These Judeo-Spanish dialects did not arrive to New Mexico.[183]

A version of colonial Spanish is spoken by people in northern New Mexico, and it does have features in common with the Judeo-Spanish dialects, but it is not Ladino. The fact of speaking a colonial era Spanish is unique, and it is a carryover from the sixteenth and seventeenth century Spanish brought by the early settlers. It is a survival from that time and could be a parallel to the survival of Jewish practices.

Origins of Jewish Converso Families

A professionally educated member of a synagogue in northern New Mexico, who identifies as having Jewish converso background, told me that his converso family had arrived to New Mexico in the 1400s and that they had kept their Jewish identity to the present. In discussing the date of his family's arrival, I mentioned that the earliest settlers had come with the Oñate expedition in 1598. He knew that history, but he insisted that his family had arrived in the 1400s. That was his families' identification, as being the earliest Spanish settlers in this region.

In a similar oral tradition about the origin of a converso family, a woman told me that her family had arrived with Columbus to New Mexico. To clarify if I had understood her comment, I questioned whether Columbus had arrived to New Mexico, and she re-affirmed that he did and that her family came with him. Of course, arriving with Columbus would have authenticated the Spanish origins of her family, which was, perhaps, the real point of her family story.

I am a Sephardic Jew

A professional friend recently discovered a Jewish person with her family name in a historical document and came to me saying, "I am a Sephardic Jew". She is Catholic and identifies with the Catholic Church and has no known link to a Jewish past in her family, but she made the leap from finding one Jewish individual with her last name to assuming that her family might be of converso or crypto-Jewish background. Then, going further she conflated the possibility of having had a converso ancestor with being a Sephardic Jew herself. That kind of assumption

Oral Tradition, Folklore and the Arts

has entered the public narrative, and for some people having a Sephardic ancestor has become an adornment in their family tree, a matter of curiosity, even though it does not alter their Catholic identity.

Crypto-Jewish Villages in the Mountains of New Mexico

At one point I received inquiries from a rabbi in the eastern United States, asking how to visit a crypto-Jewish village in New Mexico. He had the impression that such villages had survived, and that they could be visited. This misconception perhaps fuses the Belmonte experience in Portugal with New Mexico. Misconceptions like this are the result of the lack of historical information about crypto-Jews with people filling in their understanding of what it could be. That has resulted in oral traditions and beliefs that do not correlate with known historical information.

Oral traditions, folklore, legends, or myth have an element of truth in that they represent the understanding that people have about the subject being discussed. Even family narratives about ancestors arriving to New Mexico with Christopher Columbus or arriving in the 1400s have the affirmation that the families arrived very early, and that they were direct Spanish descendants. Although this might be historically incorrect, yet these statements reveal how the person perceives their family history and status. The crypto-Jewish oral traditions give us an insight into how these families defined their experiences and their histories to themselves, and that is their validity.

The contemporary narrative about the survival of crypto-Jews in northern New Mexico has grown to legendary proportions. Perhaps, the inherent secrecy of crypto-Jews has contributed to this, leaving a void filled with oral traditions.

All Spanish and Portuguese Have "sangre judia" (Jewish Blood)

I have heard frequently the saying that all Spanish and Portuguese people have "Jewish blood". But at the time of the Expulsion in 1492, the Jewish population was between one and two percent of the total Spanish population, 100,000 to 200,000 people out of 8,000,000. That suggests that 98 to 99 percent of Spaniards were not of Jewish descent. Jews were a minuscule part of Spanish society.

Another claim says that there are tens of millions of descendants of Jewish conversos in Latin America today. Again, the population numbers do not suggest that. The Spanish and Portuguese inhabitants of the colonies in the Americas were approximately 10 percent of the local populations, which were predominantly indigenous from Mexico to Peru and indigenous and African in Brazil. The Latin American colonies were not settled by Spaniards and Portuguese. They were conquered and ruled by a small elite that came from the home countries and commonly returned "home" after their tour of duty. The European population in the Americas was a fraction of the larger population, and the Jewish converso population was a fraction of that. Although there would have been thousands of Jewish conversos and crypto-Jews in the various Spanish and Portuguese colonies in the Americas, they were a fraction of the colonial elite.

Part V
The Jewish Identity Movement

Spanish and Portuguese-speaking people of Latin America are claiming and re-claiming the identity of being Jewish. Some return to Jewish religious practice, but others only adopt an identity as a descendant of Jewish conversos. For yet others it is a novelty aspect of their overall identification. In recent decades, this Jewish movement has grown to thousands of people, and it is emerging as a new element in Latin American life from Brazil to the American Southwest. For the descendants of Jewish conversos or crypto-Jews, this is a reclaimed identity. After twenty-five generations of being Christian, some are finding a well-spring of religious and ethnic heritage in Jewish identity.

For the last 500 years, the descendants of Jewish conversos and crypto-Jews have lived as Catholics, and for 300 of those years they lived under the shadow of the Inquisition, which led to a culture of secrecy and hiding Jewish memory or identity. The unique cultural and religious legacy of the descendants of conversos and crypto-Jews is only beginning to be understood. Given a centuries old culture of hiding their heritage, many descendants of crypto-Jews are hesitant to be public, but the international distribution of people repeating similar accounts lends a credibility to these family traditions.

There have been two historic moments of a wave of converso families returning to Jewish life: first in the 1600s and 1700s and the contemporary one, starting in the late 1900s. Spanish-speaking Americans, who assume Jewish identity, in the twenty-first century are not like the conversos of the sixteenth and seventeenth centuries, but they share something in common, the desire to return to Jewish practice in spite of odds to the contrary.

Chapter 10

Reframing Jewish Identity

Reframing Jewish Identity

JEWS LIVE THE CONUNDRUM OF A GOD-GIVEN IDENTITY with porous social and ethnic boundaries. Abraham and Sarah's son, Isaac, was a Jew, but Abraham's other son, Ishmael was not. Isaac had two sons, and one followed the Jewish tradition, but the other did not. So, is a person Jewish by genes, religious and cultural practices, upbringing, or choice? While some Jews choose to leave their identity, other people choose to adopt it, as we see in the Jewish identity movement.

During the three centuries of Spanish colonial rule thousands of Jewish *conversos* migrated to the Americas, some of whom were crypto-Jews, estimated to be several hundred or more in Colombia and in the thousands in Mexico and Peru. Not all remained in the Americas, some of them left later or were arrested by the Inquisition and exiled or sentenced to death. Even with those limited numbers, the descendants of Jewish conversos in Latin America today could number in the tens of thousands or multiples of that.

Hybridity and Crypto-Jews

The line between being a Jew or crypto-Jew was often a shifting one. Blas de Paz Pinto came from a crypto-Jewish family in Spain before moving to Salonika and returning to Jewish practice and studying to be a rabbi. Then, he moved to Cartagena, which made him once again a crypto-Jew. Since he knew about Jewish liturgy, he was active in the *minyan* (a men's prayer group). Like so many others, he shifted between being an openly practicing Jew and a crypto-Jew at different stages in his life.

The divide between the descendants of converso/crypto-Jewish families that chose to remain in Spain in 1492 and religious families that chose to leave seems to have created a different attitude toward the "Spanish homeland". Sephardic Jews are distinguished by an aversion toward Catholic Spain and its anti-Semitism and have been hesitant to return to that country. On the other hand, some descendants of conversos or crypto-Jews have a nostalgia for Spain, a continuing identification with their Spanish legacy.

The Twilight Period 1650-1950

The inherent qualities of surviving crypto-Jewish families were hybridity, selective assimilation, and secrecy. We have a paucity of information about the networks that might have been created in the interior of Brazil, the mountains of New Mexico or Colombia or the borderlands region between Mexico and the United States in this time period. Surviving Inquisition documents from the 1600s suggest the struggle to live as crypto-Jews then, but from the 1650s to the 1950s even that goes dark.

What happened in that period eclipsed from history? We know that family memories of having been Jewish survived, and we know that fragments of Jewish practice survived, even though the Jewish meanings might have been lost. After the 1950s the interest of people in reclaiming Jewish identity began emerging from that long interlude of silence.

The descendants of crypto-Jews seem to have assimilated to the larger Catholic and later Protestant society during those three centuries between 1650 and 1950. When historian Stanley Hordes began doing research in the 1980s, he did not find active crypto-Jewish life, but people came to him with accounts of their grandparents lighting candles on Friday night and doing other rituals that reflected Jewish practice. He says that "specific knowledge of their Jewish heritage ceased being transmitted in the mid-twentieth century. While certain customs continued to be passed down..."[184]

At that time, when the teaching of crypto-Jewish practices to the younger generations was being lost, the movement of reclaiming Jewish identity by the following generation was beginning, and across the

Americas, Spanish-speaking people began to explore the possibility of Jewish roots in their families. People coming out of Christian backgrounds and identifying as Jews mention a variety of factors that have influenced them to make that decision, ranging from family memory to feelings of wanting to be Jewish.

Some people focus on genealogy to establish Jewishness, and others look to DNA as scientific evidence of their link to Spain and Jewish identity. DNA and genealogy can show links to Jewish ancestors, but what does it mean to be a Jew? For that people are looking to conversion or return to Judaism rituals and becoming involved in Jewish communities.

Being a Jew is not a belief system, it is being a member of a Jewish family and community and learning the traditions that come with it. It is more than synagogue attendance; it is a multi-faceted role in social and cultural life. The culture of being Jewish is different from the culture of being Catholic and becoming Jewish is an acculturation to a way of life and thinking. There is no Jesus to give salvation; Jews have to create their own repentance (*teshsuvah*). Jews have no saints to intervene with God; you have to do it yourself. Jewish life is more about practice than belief.

Being Jewish is partly religious, partly ethnic and cultural, and partly social. Jews have a unique world view in which Biblical accounts of Abraham, Moses, David, and others are not just sacred literature, they are familial stories.

Narratives of Jewish survival exist on most continents of the world from Europe (Belmonte, Portugal) to Africa (Beta Israel, Ethiopian Jews), South Asia (the Bnei Menashe in India), East Asia (Kaifeng Jews, descendants of Jewish traders at the eastern end of the Silk Route), and North and South America (crypto-Jews).

Vanessa Paloma Elbaz.[185] has reported the same phenomenon in North Africa where descendants of Jews, who have converted to Islam, are also exploring the Jewish ancestry of their families.

Returning Jews and the Jewish Identity Movement

People are identifying as Jews out of a mosaic of factors from what people were and what people want to be. Identity might be based on knowledge of fragments of Jewish practice, on family memories, on the identification of Jewish connections based on genealogies and DNA tests, or on the feeling of affinity with being Jewish.

Upon independence from Spain in the early 1800s the new Latin American republics gradually adopted policies of religious pluralism, making it legal to be Jewish. After the Treaty of Guadalupe Hidalgo in 1848, freedom of religion was introduced to New Mexico. The arrival of Protestants and German Jewish merchants and settlers brought new attitudes and information about Jewish practice.[186] Having a Jewish background began to be more acceptable.

The Latin American Jewish movement gained momentum in the latter half of the twentieth century. Why did it emerge at this particular time? Four backgrounds factors can be considered:

1. The Second Vatican Council. In 1963 the Second Vatican Council altered official Church policy toward Jews, and it specifically repudiated the centuries old charge of the collective guilt of Jews for the death of Jesus. The document *Nostra aetate* says,

> *Furthermore, in her rejection of every persecution against any man, the Church, mindful of the patrimony she shares with the Jews and moved not by political reasons but by the Gospel's spiritual love, decries hatred, persecutions, displays of anti-Semitism, directed against Jews at any time and by anyone.*

The late twentieth century upsurge in reclaiming Jewish roots among Spanish speakers came after the Second Vatican Council conferred new respectability on being Jewish.

2. Ethnic Roots Movement. In the 1970s, searching for family and cultural origins became a movement across the Americas, as seen in Alex Haley's 1976 novel *Roots* and the television mini-series of the same title. At the same time people became interested in their Jewish roots from family and cultural origins to religious roots. For many this identification with being Jewish goes beyond family memory or history to an identity for the soul.

3. The 500 Year Anniversary of the Expulsion. The 1992 anniversary of the Expulsion of Jews from Spain sparked interest in the history of Spanish Jews, Jewish conversos, and crypto-Jews. With this increased awareness and information about Jews and crypto-Jews, many people began to consider the possibility of their own roots as descendants of conversos.

4. Access to Information. Publications from David Gitlitz in 1996 to Janet Liebman Jacobs in 2002, Stanley M. Hordes in 2005 and Seth Kunin in 2009 have heightened interest and given awareness to converso and crypto-Jewish history. The availability of the Internet and social media in recent years has had a major role in facilitating information to people about crypto-Jewish history. Until the Internet, information was not available on Jewish practice and crypto-Jews in Catholic Latin American countries, but now it is readily accessible.

Publications have had an important role in disseminating information about both converso and crypto-Jewish ancestry, including *HaLapid* and *La Herencia*. The Society for Crypto-Judaic Studies re-activated the name *HaLapid* of the original journal on crypto-Jewish life, published by Barros Basto in Portugal. The contemporary *HaLapid* features research and personal narratives about crypto-Jewish practices and family memories in the Americas and beyond and has become a major source of information about the converso and crypto-Jewish experiences and the movement of return.

The quarterly magazine *La Herencia*, about New Mexico Hispanic history was published from 1994 to 2009, and it included a column entitled, "Sephardim" that focused on references or memories of New Mexico traditions that had Jewish themes.[187] This magazine reached a popular reading audience and heightened attention to practices identified as crypto-Jewish in New Mexico culture.

After hiding identity for centuries, the discovery and redefinition of public identity from being Catholic to being Jewish is complex and emotionally fraught. Janet Liebman Jacobs[188] suggests that people returning to Jewish practice overtly emphasize their Jewish origins as a counter measure to the generations of Christianization that they inherited. She notes that the "persistence of a culture of secrecy poses certain dilemmas for descendants…faced with the challenge of constructing Jewish origins out of collective memory and remnant ritual behavior."[189]

The Jewish Identity Movement

Who has the drive to identify with being Jewish? Who are the individuals who piece together fragments of memory and practice and re-establish Jewish identity from it? Why would someone want to reclaim the Jewish practice that their ancestors distanced themselves from in the past? Many Portuguese and Spanish-speaking people in the Americas are reclaiming Jewish ancestry by the thousands. What are the roots of this Jewish identity movement after 500 years of Catholic identity? Why do some people have the longing or desire to return to Jewish practice while others do not? For different people there are different reasons, but some of them could be:

Homeland as Identity
The identification with homeland is important in the roots movements of recent decades. For descendants of conversos and crypto-Jews homeland can exert a strong pull on identity and legacy. An identification with an ethnic or religious identity in the distant Iberian past, combined with a dissatisfaction with the current identity, can contribute to this movement. Although Spanish-speaking Americans from the United States to Chile are Catholic, there is an anti-clerical countercurrent in the population. Jewish identity with Spain can be an alternate non-Catholic identity that holds the promise of a new religious path and meaning in life.

Authenticity of Judaism
Many, who are anti-clerical and anti-Catholic, are really looking for a religious path that is authentic and meaningful. Protestant churches, African derived religions, and Asian religions have made major inroads in this part of the world, as people look for an alternative to the uniformity of Catholicism. Judaism is one those paths, and for some people, Judaism is the primal religion of the Western world. It can be seen as an authentic religious identity.

The "Proto-Jewish Consciousness"
David Graizbord[190] describes the identity of conversos in the Sephardic Diaspora as people who felt Spanish or Portuguese but also felt

rejected by the Old Christian society and disillusioned with aggressive "Ibero-Catholicism". He goes on to say that the "echoes of the tribal solidarity" and the common experience of crypto-Jewish life led to a "proto-Jewish" group identity for some, but that did not always lead to "full-fledged, normative Judaism". So, the identity of crypto-Jews as Jews could be ambiguous and not well defined.

Seth Kunin[191] uses the French term bricolage, or cobbling together, to describe how people construct their combination of Jewish, Catholic, and Spanish or Mexican cultural elements within their lives. He gives an example reported by one family of the grandmother making wheat tortillas in the Spring and toasting them until they were burned. Although the grandmother did not identify the practice as Jewish and there was no specific association with Passover, the man reporting the practice thought that it might have had left over from Passover with tortilla substituted for matzah.[192]

The Cobbling Together of Jewish Identity

Out of the mosaic of interests, motivations, and backgrounds, that have led Spanish speakers to identify as Jews, some want to learn how to be Jewish. From avoiding pork, some are taking a step further to learn kosher dietary laws. They are not Sephardic Jews in the traditional sense, but they have an identity shaped out of the crucible of crypto-Jewish life in colonial Latin America, the Inquisition, and years of isolation and secrecy.

In the nuanced world of crypto-Jewish religious practice, what originally might have been a Jewish practice can be performed with Catholic meanings and purpose today. When the boundary between the two religious traditions becomes porous, the Catholicness or Jewishness of an individual depends on what their intentions as they combine the elements of their experience.

The Role of Women

In one of the earliest studies on the subject, Cecil Roth notes the important role of women in crypto-Jewish families in Mexico, and he goes on to say that women could act as spiritual leaders in the crypto-Jewish community.¹⁹³ Jacobs points out that women were at the center of maintaining the memory of the family having been Jewish. The vestiges of Jewish practice that survived in the Americas were from the world of the household, and the path back to Judaism is frequently through those same domestic Jewish practices.¹⁹⁴

Artur Carlos de Barros Basto:
And the Jewish Identity Movement

Barros Basto (1887-1961) was the early twentieth century leader of the movement of Jewish identity. He lived in Portugal, and when his grandfather was dying, he told his grandson that the family had Jewish ancestors. His family had not kept the identity of being Jewish, nor observed any Jewish practices, and that information launched Barros Basto on a campaign to understand what that legacy was. As a young man, He began studying Hebrew and went to Morocco to study Jewish law and practice. He was circumcised and converted before a rabbinical court, a *Beit Din*, taking the Hebrew name Abraham Israel Ben-Rosh. He returned to Lisbon as part of the Jewish community and married Lea Israel Montero Azancot. Her maternal last name, Azancot, is an important Sephardic name in Tangier, Morocco.

They returned to his hometown of Porto and started organizing a synagogue. Later the Baron de Rothschild in Paris and the Hong Kong branch of the Kadoorie family learned of his efforts and provided financial support. People began attending the synagogue, identifying themselves as descendants of crypto-Jews who had maintained Jewish rituals in the privacy of their homes. With time, he was able to build the Kadoorie Synagogue, which continues as the focal point of Jewish life in Porto.

Barros also established a yeshiva for theological training in Jewish scholarship, called The Israelite Theological Institute of Porto, and he set up a Jewish newspaper, called *HaLapid*, the Torch, which he continued to publish until 1958. As the movement of return to Jewish life has grown in recent decades, he has been honored as a founding figure.

In 1917 Barros' work received a boost from the contact made by Samuel Schwarz with Belmonte, a Portuguese village in the northeastern mountains, in which descendants of Jewish converso families from the 1500s continued to be recognized as Jews. Realizing that people who preserved memory of their Jewish descent still lived in villages and towns in nearby regions, Barros Basto began traveling looking for those who wanted to return to Jewish practice. "The Community of Portuguese Jews" in London heard of his work and established a committee to assist this Jewish identity movement.

Schwarz wrote about his experience in *Os Cristã os-Novos em Portugal no Século XX* in 1925 and since then Belmonte has become known beyond Portugal. Outside groups raised funds for Belmonte to build a synagogue, which was inaugurated in 1997. Five hundred years of hidden tradition is not easily unraveled and rewoven as a fully functioning Jewish community, as commented by David Augusto Canelo,[195] a local historian, wrote about the ritual life of the Belmonte community.

Learning that You are a Jew

Information about being Jewish is a family matter. From Luis de Carvajal, el mozo to Artur Barros Basto we can see how parents or grandparents informed their adolescent children of the Jewish background of the family when they are old enough to keep the secret. For Juan Mejia and Barros Basto the information came from their grandfathers, and often it was a deathbed confession. Angelina Muñoz Huberman tells of her mother taking her out to the privacy of a balcony of their house when she was an early adolescent to tell her about the family's Jewish history.

A male colleague told me of his experience of learning about the Jewish heritage of his family from his sister when he was a mature adult. The mother had told the sister when she was an adolescent because in that family the information was passed from mother to daughter. Later, the sister developed a terminal illness, and she told her brother so the family memory would not be lost. As we can see, there were many paths for passing along the information about Jewish history in the family.

Rejudaization

What is rejudaization, and how do conversos rejudaize? For descendants of Jewish conversos who were returning to Judaism in sixteenth century Salonika or seventeenth century Amsterdam, they no longer knew the details of Jewish practice, and many had little more than the idea of being Jewish. But they had Sephardic synagogues to which they could turn to start the process of re-establishing their Jewish lives. They came with little or no knowledge of the songs or prayers in Hebrew, and the information they did have was occasionally mixed with Christian or folk beliefs and practices. They might continue to speak with Catholic-like terminology about salvation but now in reference to the Law of Moses rather than Jesus. They would say Catholic prayers when lighting candles because they did not know Jewish ones.

Miriam Bodian[196] describes how crypto-Jews returning to Jewish life in Amsterdam had to come to their own understanding of their lives under Catholicism, and what it meant in light of their return to Jewish practice. For many, their focus in reclaiming Jewish identity was focused on specific religious-ethnic cultural practices, such as lighting candles, bathing and changing clothes on Friday, not working on Saturday.[197] The practices that survived the longest after conversion were the first markers of Jewishness to be re-claimed when returning to Jewish life. This was a reification of their identity through recognizably Jewish acts. The process of rejudaization in our contemporary era seems to be similar to what it has been for centuries.

As the movement of Jewish identity has been taking shape in the Americas, rejudaization has a plethora of meanings from genealogy to synagogue membership, learning Hebrew, Jewish prayer, and *aliyah* or return to Israel. For some it is returning to Spain, and for others it is little more than identifying as being Jewish.

Reframing Jewish Identity

In Amsterdam, crypto-Jewish men returning to Jewish practice affiliated with the synagogue and began functioning in the community. Although they had been separated from Jewish practice for 100 to 150 years, they sought out a Sephardic synagogue and community that in turn supported them in their return to Jewish life. In contrast, in the Americas today the separation from Jewish practice has been 500 years, and the synagogues do not always provide a support system for those who want to return, especially for men in synagogue practice.

People in the Americas have been separated, not only from Jewish practice but from Spain and Portugal, for five centuries, which includes generations of cultural experiences that are Latin American, not Spanish or Portuguese. Rejudaization in the Americas has been a quilt work of different experiences that vary widely from entire communities establishing themselves as Jewish, such as the example in Bello, Antioquia in Colombia to the rogue synagogues in Brazil. More common in the American Southwest is the individual return to Jewish practice,[198] and women have led the way sometimes starting that path of discovery with little or no support from Jewish institutions.

Identity and Culture

Identifying as a Jew and living in a Jewish social and cultural context is usually a basic definition of Jewishness, but within that there is a broad diversity. Are you religious or non-religious? Do you speak Yiddish, Hebrew, Judeo-Spanish, Judeo-Arabic, or Amharic? Is your tradition patriarchal or egalitarian? What foods do you eat, and what songs do you sing?

Culture is multi-dimensional and functions on different levels, beginning with the shared communal level, which tends to be public, and the personal culturing level which tends to be private. The paragraph above is referring to communal aspects of shared culture. However, in addition to that people have individual cultural operating systems that are less visible to the outside observer. It is in this personal culturing system where crypto-Judaism could survive. Individualized patterns of behavior follow an internal algorithm that involves biology and genetics, learned forms of behavior (communal culture), social and economic contexts, and personality and psychological issues among other elements. The personal culturing system requires a link to a communal cultural reference point, which would be the family memory and practice of being Jewish, and beyond that in some cases a link to a cluster of families who were keeping the tradition.

Within that context the individual must decide what he or she is going to activate in their own behavior. What is meaningful to them as a person? These are the building blocks of person-hood. We construct who we are through our choices from the smorgasbord of behaviors available to us. Being a crypto-Jew is the acting out of the personal combination of identity, attitudes, and behaviors, the building blocks of who we are as a person.

We might not know where an individual's personal behaving lies along the converso/crypto-Jewish spectrum, which is private and not always apparent to an observer. Did the person convert to save their lives but remain in limbo, neither actively becoming Catholic nor retaining Jewish practice? Or, after converting did the individual make a choice of personally identifying with Catholic practice? Did they make the choice of retaining Jewish practice in their private lives? Since Jewish practice was illegal in Spain and Portugal and their colonies, those who made the choice of retaining Jewish practice could only do so in secret, leaving few if any records of how they were leading their lives.

Chapter 11

Jewish Identity Movement

When we would ask him things about our families' history, my grandfather would say to us, "If I were you, I would be very careful who you told these things to because it is not popular, and in some cases it is not very safe to reveal a Jewish heritage. The name Carvajal resonated with a lot of people of both Sephardic and Ashkenazic backgrounds here in El Paso. We have a very tight Jewish community. We had a lot of friends in the community, and a lot of them would tell us that we had a Jewish last name, a famous Jewish name related to Luis Carvajal.

Luis Carvajal's experiences and the tragedies that he endured because of his faith and his religious beliefs and his conviction to Judaism as his religious identity really resonate with me, and I think it makes my Judaism much stronger because it tells me that if someone was willing in our family to give up their life and be burned at the stake, but they were willing to preserve that at all costs then it is important to our family. It is important today, and it was important back then, and I believe it will be important to the future of the Carvajals. Those that are Jewish, and those that are not, but they need to know how strong our Jewish faith is in the history of our family.

Bill Carvajal[199]
President, Anusim Center
El Paso, Texas

THE JEWISH IDENTITY MOVEMENT EXTENDS FROM Mexico and the American Southwest into South America. This international movement has had considerable response throughout this region of the world, and it has uniquely different manifestations from country to country and from one cultural region to another.

South America

Although the Jewish identity movement in South America can be found in many countries, I would like to highlight two: Brazil and Colombia.

Brazil
This is the leader in religious pluralism in South America with the largest Protestant population in the region and large African-based religious groups. A significant movement toward Jewish practice is occurring in parts of Brazil, especially the Northeast. This country has a history of converso and crypto-Jewish families, probably arriving in Brazil in the 1500s when sugar cane production was brought from Africa.

Then, the New Holland era from 1630 to 1654 brought more Jews, making Recife a uniquely majority Jewish city. Portuguese Jewish families from Amsterdam came to settle, and conversos from Brazil returned to open Jewish practice.[200] When the Portuguese re-conquered Recife twenty-four years later, most Jews left, but some must have stayed managing or supplying the rich sugar cane industry, rather than leaving for Amsterdam.[201] That would have made them crypto-Jews.

In the 1970s a movement started in Brazil of people identifying family practices as indications of Jewish heritage. Lighting candles, eating tapioca during Lent instead of bread, finding items with Hebrew letters, and Jewish-like burial practices have led people to ask about the possibility of a Jewish background. Sonia Bloomfield Ramagen[202] has written about these families and their understanding of their history. She found that the oral traditions they inherited were not always consistent with the known historical information, which reflects the disjuncture that can exist between what people think about their heritage and what it might have been.

Rabbi Gilberto Ventura of Sao Paulo has established the *Sinagoga sem Fronteiras* or the Synagogue without Borders with an outreach program to descendants of Jewish conversos. He teaches converso families about Jewish traditions and leads them through conversion and return to Jewish practice if that is their desire.

Arthur Benveniste[203] interviewed people in Brazil, who identified with having a Jewish background. Gilvanci ben Shmuel Portillo told Benveniste about practices of lighting candles on Friday nights, circumcision in the family on the eighth day after birth, and a version of kosher slaughtering of animals. He personally adopted Jewish practice and lifestyle, but other members of his family have not accepted it.

Brazilian conversos or crypto-Jews have not been accepted by the established Jewish community, and a version of rogue Jewish life has developed in response. João Madeiros gathered followers and set up a synagogue in Natal, and he has helped people convert to Jewish practice. He acted as rabbi to the congregation, but he was never converted by Jewish law himself and was not trained to be a rabbi. Neither he nor the congregation have been accepted by the Jewish leadership in Brazil, and the Natal community has functioned independently.[204]

Another group that is reclaiming recognition as Jews are the descendants of Sephardic men, largely from northern Morocco, who came to the Amazon River Basin during the rubber boom in the late 1800s and married local women. Their descendants, called *Judeus Amazônicos* (Amazon Jews) continue to live in the Amazon, and a movement has been growing among them to reclaim Jewish identity.[205]

Colombia

The origin of the converso and crypto-Jewish settlement in Colombia dates back to the port Jews of Cartagena of the early seventeenth century described earlier.[206] After the Inquisition trials in Cartagena in the 1630s, a number of crypto-Jewish men who were supplying the mining industry in Antioquia hid their Jewishness, rather than leave Colombia. Today some families in Antioquia preserve Jewish identity, raising the question whether they could be descendants of those men.

Among the first acts of the newly independent government of Gran Colombia (Colombia, Ecuador, Panama, and Venezuela) in 1819 was to grant the rights of residence, religious freedom, and political participation to the "members of the Hebrew nation". Curaçao had the largest Jewish population in the Caribbean, and many of those families migrated to the emerging port of Barranquilla and eventually to the capital in Bogotá.[207]

As the Jewish identity movement has grown in Colombia over the last couple of decades, Rabbis Juan Mejia and Daniel Mehlman have led the teaching of Jewish practice to people who wanted to convert, and in ceremonies in Santa Marta and Barranquilla, they have supervised the conversions of dozens of people.

The new Jewish converts in Colombia do not always meld into the existing Jewish communities, and in at least one instance they have set up their own, the *Comunidad Sefardita de Antioquia* (Sephardic Community of Antioquia), led by Rabbis Elad Villegas and Ezra Rodriguez. It is located in the city of Bello, a suburb of Medellin.

Organized in 2004, the *Comunidad Sefardita* is an active multi-generational community of 300 people, featuring a synagogue, a Jewish school, kosher bakery, and the infrastructure of a Jewish community. It also has an adult Jewish education program, including Hebrew language classes. This is a group of Colombians who have converted to Judaism. They do not have the same cultural traditions as the predominately Ashkenazi synagogues in Medellin, so they established their own community.

Schulamith Halevy
on Mexico and the Rio Grande Borderland

When Mexico gained independence from Spain and abolished the Inquisition in 1821, it immediately defined itself as a Roman Catholic nation. The Constitution of 1824 stated that, "The religion of the Mexican nation is and will permanently be the Roman Catholic, Apostolic religion."[208] That began to change in 1865 during the aberrant reign of the French-born Emperor Maximilian when he issued the Edict of Religious Tolerance, giving rights to Jews. By 1867 there were twenty openly Jewish families living in Mexico City. During the twentieth century, the Jewish population of Mexico grew to an estimated 40,000 to 50,000 people and more than twenty-five synagogues, mostly in Mexico City.

Although Mexico was a focal point for crypto-Jews during the colonial period, the Inquisition was effective in decimating the community in the seventeenth century. But there were survivors, and their descendants are a part of the Jewish identity movement in Mexico.

The anthropologist, Schulamith C. Halevy,[209] has done research interviewing dozens of descendants of the Carvajal and other converso and crypto-Jewish families in northern Mexico. Drawing from her background in rabbinic studies and comparative religions, she interviewed people who had Jewish-like customs combined with a sense of a "separate cultural identity". When she could trace practices to rabbinic law or Spanish Jewish practices, which were not Catholic customs, she gave credibility to their being descendants of conversos or crypto-Jews. Based on this research, Halevy concluded that there had been a crypto-Jewish presence in northern Mexico into the 1900s, and that their practices did conform with verifiable Jewish ones.[210]

In extensive interviews with local people in the state of Nuevo Leon, capital Monterrey, she documented a complex set of Jewish related practices in a number of families,[211] including: observing Shabbat, intermarriage within the group, birth practices from circumcision to a 40-day period of sexual abstinence after birth, mikveh practices, death, burial, and mourning practices, candle lighting on Friday evening, Yom Kippur observance, Passover-like Spring celebration, fast of Queen Esther, kosher-like dietary practices from the slaughter to separation of meat and milk, not cleaning the house through the front door, and fasting on Monday and Thursday.

For Halevy this suggests an integrated complex of behaviors with Biblical and rabbinic foundations that can be considered as constituting a Jewish heritage. She summarizes her work saying, "Alongside the winding path of mythology lies the truth. Complex, explicable, and logical, the truth about the culture of the anusim was passed down the generations, guarded via endogamy, along with the preservation of Jewish practices and identity." [212]

This area was originally settled by the group recruited by Governor Luis Carvajal, two-thirds of which seem to have been crypto-Jews. There is a growing acceptance and interest in the possibility of Jewish ancestry among many families in the region. As people have migrated from Monterrey to San Antonio, Texas, they have carried that awareness with them. So, the lower Rio Grande Valley and the corridor from Monterrey in Mexico to San Antonio in Texas has a concentration of people who identify as having Jewish heritage.

Other studies in the region by the Israeli anthropologist Rafael Patai[213] and by local historians[214] give additional information on the converso families of Northern Mexico.

El Paso/Juarez and Rabbi Stephen Leon

In the Borderland region of El Paso and Juarez, Mexico, a Jewish movement has been growing for the last thirty years. Rabbi Stephen Leon of Congregation B'nai Zion in El Paso, Texas tells of a Spanish-speaking family who came to his office a number of years ago and gave him an empty *tefillin* box, saying that they knew that it was a Jewish sacred object, and they felt that it should be in Jewish hands. As Rabbi Leon heard more stories of Spanish-speaking families with memories of Jewish connections, he welcomed those who were interested to attend services and join classes on Jewish practice.[215]

Over time, a significant number of people have converted, and the congregation now has a number of Spanish-speaking families as members and some in leadership roles. He has also organized an Anusim Center which has an active program of talks and Jewish learning events. They have annual Anusim Conferences that focus on the experiences of people who have become Jewish, and those who are interested in that possibility.

In his book, *The Third Commandment*, Rabbi Leon describes the incident with the family and *tefillin* box. He describes it as follows:

> *One of the most moving B'nei Anusim stories occurred just a few years ago. While sitting in my office at the synagogue, the secretary told me that three people had just come in and were anxious to speak with me. Then, in walked an elderly, short dark-haired woman wearing a plain dress, accompanied by a younger woman, about forty-five-years-old who was wearing jeans and a brown jacket, and a man in his mid-forties also in jeans and a blue denim jacket.*
>
> *Without asking permission the elderly woman took the seat directly in front of me, and the couple asked permission to sit down. The younger woman, whom I shall refer to as Beverly, told me that she, her husband Jimmy, and her mother Maria had spent the last few days in San Antonio attending her son's graduation from college. The family lives in Los Angeles, but Maria, who had a terminal illness, did not like to fly, and so they drove from Los Angeles to San Antonio. They were on their way home traveling along Interstate 10 when Maria told her son-in-law, to get off the highway and find a synagogue.*
>
> *Beverly could not understand her mother's request, because she was a religious Catholic, and it was the first time she can recall her mother even using the term, "synagogue". Nevertheless, Maria was insistent, and so they turned off the next exit, which was Exit 13 Sunland Park, and pulled into the first gas station and asked where the nearest synagogue was located. The attendant directed them to Congregation B'nai Zion, which he knew was on Cherry Hill Lane about two miles from there.*

Jewish Identity Movement

'And now,' Beverly said, 'we are here, Rabbi, and I don't know why. Mom, tell the Rabbi why we are here.' Maria's eyes were old and black and filled with emotion, and she spoke with a deep Spanish accent, 'My dear Rabbi,' she began and went on to say,

'I am so grateful that you were willing to speak with me on short notice. I am sure that you are a very busy man. Rabbi, I am eighty-six-years-old, and I will die soon, but before I die it is very important that I tell you something. I have practiced the Catholic religion my entire life, as has my family. When I was a little girl living in Mexico, my grandfather invited me into a private room in our house, every single morning but Sabado, Saturday. And he would place on his arm and his head two black boxes and black straps. He would pray for a few minutes wearing these items, and then he put them away in a blue velvet bag. I was the only family member to witness this event and the only one to know about it.

'When my grandfather was about to die, he called me into his bedroom and revealed to me that he was Jewish, these items were Jewish, and that they had belonged to his grandfather's grandfather from Toledo, Spain and that they were the only remnant of the family's Jewish ancestry. He made me promise to him that somehow, when no one was looking, that I would bury one of these boxes with him, and the other box I would keep and when I was ready to die, I would tell my children, so that they would bury that Jewish box with me. And so, my grandfather passed away many years ago, and I saw to it, that next to him in the coffin, I managed to place that Jewish prayer box.

'I haven't slept so well in recent days, dear Rabbi, because I know that I will be in heaven, soon, next to my Saba, as he told me to call him, next to my grandpa. But I shouldn't be buried with my grandfather's other Jewish box. It isn't right, and it isn't fair to him and to his Jewish grandparents. I am not Jewish. I have loved Jesus Christ my entire life. I go to Church every Sunday. I do not want to disrespect my grandfather or the Jewish people. That is why I haven't slept so well, Rabbi.

'But then last night after my grandson's graduation I fell asleep for the first time in weeks, and I had a dream. In that dream my grandfather came to me and told me, Maria, I see that you are very *troubled by the promise you made to me on my death bed. I will release you from that promise on one condition. You must make me a new promise, that you will find a religious Jew, and you will tell him of your promise to me. If he agrees to promise you that he will bury that religious object with him when he dies, then you can be released from your vow. For then, I will know, you will know, and my Jewish ancestors will know, that this Jewish box will be buried in a Jewish cemetery with a religious Jew and in that way it will surely be returned to our family, who kept it part of us from generation to generation.'*

She looked directly into my eyes, and we both began to cry. She opened her purse and took out the black box that contains part of the Torah scroll in which the commandment to bind these words upon our arms and between our eyes is found. The beautiful, old, tear-drenched tefillin, was the most beautiful religious item that I had ever held in my hand. She handed it to me and took my hands in hers and asked me to swear to her in her grandfather's name that I would agree to have this tefillin buried with me when I die. I promised her, and I will keep that promise.

That tefillin is always kept nearby me, and I will take it to my grave. With a big sigh of relief, Maria smiled and thanked me, we hugged for a few minutes and said, "Shalom". She left my office, and her daughter and son-in-law remained. Beverly revealed to me that she had no clue about her mother's Jewish background or that she had this Jewish prayer box for over twenty-five years.

Although Beverly was almost speechless, she thanked me for understanding and doing this for her mother. I told her that I was really the one to thank her for bringing Maria to me, and that maybe it was really God that had arranged the meeting. I further told her that I wasn't doing this just for her mother, but for the generations and generations of Jews who had given blood, pain, and their very lives to keep Judaism alive.

I thanked God for her mother and told her that this meeting was not just a coincidence, but as it is said in Yiddish, "Beshert". It was "destiny" that made this meeting happen. As I reflect on this incident, I really believe that this was not just a coincidence. Maria lives *in Los Angeles where there are hundreds of rabbis, and yet she had never said a word about her Jewish ancestry until this moment. How did she just happen to stop in El Paso, at the exit on the highway where my synagogue is located, and come to me, a rabbi, who has devoted a good part of his life welcoming the B'nei Anusim home?*

The sacred tefillin of Maria's grandfather is connected to the past history of the crypto-Jews from the time of the Inquisition and is also connected to the future generations of the crypto-Jews who continue to return every day. The tefillin are worn on the arm, so that we will make a physical commitment to follow the commandments, and they are worn between the eyes, so that we will think with devotion and dedication as the reasons why this commitment must be from the depths of our hearts. For the crypto-Jew it is the same. The sincere return inspires a physical action, to become involved in performing the rituals and customs which were forcibly taken from them generations ago, and it also requires learning the meaning of the Torah, the rituals, and the Mitzvot which identifies them with their Jewish ancestors and the Jewish progeny to come. Like the tefillin of Maria's grandfather, the commitment of the B'nei Anusim is bound by each arm and mind.

Rabbi Stephen Leon[216]
El Paso, Texas

Chapter 12

Hidden Traditions

Crypto-Jews

My name is Timothy Herrera, and my family has been here for many generations. Where did the journey start as far as finding out who are we, where did we come from? These are family secrets that never meant to be told to anybody, and it is still something that is hidden. When we made a decision to really start pushing as far as doing Shabbat and not eating pork, there was a huge push back. That felt lonely in the midst of the people that I grew up with. But now, this is who we are. I took on my forefathers' trials. We talk about the things that happened as if we were there, and with that understanding I can read these stories and see these things, and I get the feeling that I was there. These were my people. That was almost me that had to go through that [torture of the Inquisition].

I have done a lot of family history back to Abraham Halevy in Spain. The first ancestors that I found on this journey were Solomon Halevi and Abraham Halevi in the 1300s. I was able to find Solomon Halevi because he was a very well-known rabbi and also finding who he was when he converted, he actually became a bishop...and the tutor to the heir [of the throne]. With that type of influence he was able to protect the family. Now, that I have become me, this is not only an attachment to the Jewish people of today, it is an attachment to an entire heritage. And, that is tremendous to me. This became mine. It was lost. It had not been in my family for many, many years. And, now here it is, and I am holding this identity, not only from this point, but it attached me to every Jew in the world and to everyone that came before me.

Timothy Herrera[217]
Cuba, New Mexico

Hidden Traditions

NORTHERN NEW MEXICO WAS AN AREA OF REFUGE FOR much of the seventeenth, eighteenth and nineteenth centuries where people could live rarely disturbed by the larger Catholic world around them. The fact that crypto-Jews tended to migrate to the region as families was a critical factor in the preservation of Jewish identity. Crypto-Jewish mothers could teach the hidden identity to their children in a way that a crypto-Jewish father with an indigenous mother would not have been able to do.

Commenting on the unique character of crypto-Jewish identity in the region, Seth Kunin says, "Crypto-Judaism in the American Southwest is both an individualized and complex phenomenon that draws from historical evidence as well as contemporary practices. Its preservation and expression are dependent on both the passage of cultural traditions through labyrinthine genealogical paths and through the idiosyncratic nature of individual discovery and recovery."[218]

Kunin,[219] David Gitlitz,[220] and others have noted the importance of secrecy is an inherent part of crypto-Jewish life and identity, and yet they suggest that Jewish life can continue within that veil of secrecy. Why did New Mexico become a focal point of research and information about converso and crypto-Jewish life?

The New Mexico Converso/Crypto-Jewish Heritage

New Mexico does have a legacy of Jewish converso and crypto-Jewish memories and family identity, and hundreds identify themselves as having Jewish ancestry. There is no census of this population and getting exact numbers of how many people have knowledge of a Jewish connection in their background would be difficult. When Spain and Portugal offered citizenship to the descendants of Jews and Jewish conversos, hundreds of people from New Mexico applied to the programs although few if any actually plan to move to either country. Jewish memories, identity, and practices have been reported and documented repeatedly in the work of Stanley Hordes, Seth Kunin, Cary Herz, Gerald Gonzalez, and Isabelle Medina Sandoval among others, giving a basis to the historicity of Jewish conversos and crypto-Jews living in the mountainous villages of this region.

The research of Stanley Hordes has highlighted this converso/crypto-Jewish legacy. Early in his research in the 1980s, people began telling him about their families lighting candles on Friday night, covering mirrors at the passing of someone, and other traditions that were Jewish-like practices. His background of archival research in the Inquisition records on crypto-Jews in colonial Mexico gave him a basis as he interviewed people about New Mexico, and he began to see patterns of Jewish-like practices emerging. Although there were no written records about converso and crypto-Jewish life in New Mexico, many people had oral traditions about Jewish-like practices and family memories.

In recounting instances of people self-identifying as descendants of Jews from Spain, Hordes comments,

> *Given the long and rich history of crypto-Judaism in Spain, Portugal, Mexico, and the far northern frontier of the Viceroyalty of New Spain [i.e. New Mexico], it seemed logical to consider the question of whether there existed a connection between the beliefs expressed and practices followed by twenty-first-century native New Mexicans and those of the conversos of fifteenth and sixteenth-century Iberia.* [221]

He goes on to say that the purpose of his book, *To the End of the Earth*, is the historical examination of the secret practice of Judaism in New Mexico. Although many scholars agree that crypto-Jewish practice in Spain and Mexico can be documented into the 1600s, some question whether crypto-Jewish life could have survived into the twentieth century.[222] These questions focus on whether it is valid to assume that Jewish-like practices, such as lighting candles on Friday night (now done with Catholic prayers) can still be considered Jewish. Was it more folklore than survival of Jewish practice?

Although there are practices with Jewish roots, are they practices that have been absorbed into Christian ritual and have lost their Jewish meaning? Folklorist Judith Neulander argues that interference of fundamentalist Christian Churches, such as the Iglesia de Dios (Church of God) and the Seventh Day Adventists since the 1850s, has shaped the behavior that we see today, altering the perceptions that descendants of conversos have of themselves.[223]

In response to the questioning of the authenticity of crypto-Jewish life in New Mexico, David Gradwohl [224] points out that the Jewish-like practices that have been reported in New Mexico are consistent with those reported in numerous other locations, which tends to confirm that there is a consistency to these experiences across the Americas.

Commenting on the question of the authenticity of crypto-Jewish practices, Seth Kunin says, "One of the primary concerns of the crypto-Jews and those that critique them is whether or not they are authentic and historically linked to Judaism...A practice...gains its Jewish authenticity by being practiced by individuals who consider themselves to be Jews or crypto-Jews."[225]

Questions arise whether Jewish-like practices, such as not eating pork, observing Shabbat, and covering mirrors at death, whose provenance has been forgotten, are still legitimate Jewish practices. The argument is that if these practices do not occur as part of a larger complex of Jewish life, they are no longer Jewish. Some question whether identifying as a descendant of crypto-Jews is a valid claim to being Jewish. The argument is that being Jewish is determined by having a Jewish mother, and some would add by growing up Jewishly.

Some argue that a continuous line of Jewish biological descent over the last 500 years cannot be proven, so descendants of crypto-Jews would have to convert, as would be required of a non-Jew. The second argument questions whether growing up without overt Jewish learning and practice can qualify as truly being Jewish. These arguments have made it difficult for the descendants of crypto-Jews to have full acceptance in normative Jewish synagogues, and this is true in most of the Americas.

These questions get at the heart of the difficulty that some crypto-Jews have in associating with Jews in synagogue life. The experience of the descendants of crypto-Jews is unique and different from that of the descendants of Ashkenazi, Sephardi, and Mizrahi Jews creating a challenge with many different and conflicting responses within Jewish communities.[226]

The Impact of the Laws of Return

The laws of return to citizenship in Spain and Portugal for the descendants of Sephardic Jews had a major impact on awareness of Jewish ancestry among Spanish-speaking people throughout Latin America. In 2015 both countries passed laws giving citizenship to descendants of Jews and Jewish conversos who could identify that their ancestors were discriminated against and either expelled from the country or forced to convert. In less than four years 130,000 people applied for Spanish citizenship and 50,000 applied under the Portuguese law.

As part of the application for citizenship, people needed to provide a genealogy or other documentation that traced their ancestry to Jewish family members in Spain or Portugal. For people of converso backgrounds, this offer can be complicated because when distant ancestors converted, they frequently changed their names to Christian ones and created false genealogies, eliminating references to Jewish family history. For many people documenting their connections to a Spanish or Portuguese Jewish past represents a validation of their Jewish roots.

The laws of return stimulated the reclamation of Spanish or Portuguese Jewish identity that was already growing. These laws allowed descendants of conversos and crypto-Jews to validate Spanish or Portuguese ancestry because of the Jewish connection through a secular path that did not require them to become religiously Jewish.

The Unique Converso Path to Jewish Identity

The descendants of conversos and crypto-Jews in the Americas have a unique hybrid Catholic/converso path to their return to Jewishness, and as they reclaim that identity it is important to understand their experience. Although some Jewish conversos call themselves "Sephardic Jews" that blurs and confuses the understanding of their uniqueness. They are descendants of Sephardic Jews, but the Spanish Judaism of 1492 from which they are descended disappeared long ago. From 1492 to 1947 most Sephardic Jews lived in the Muslim worlds of the Middle East and North Africa which has tended to Arabize Sephardic traditions.

The shared legacy of Sephardic Jews and the descendants of conversos and crypto-Jews goes back to The Alhambra Decree, the Edict of Expulsion of Jews in 1492. When Spanish Jews had to convert or leave, the decisions they made in the weeks leading up to the deadline of July 31, 1492 shaped how their descendants would live for decades and even centuries. Many who chose to leave Spain and live as Sephardic Jews went into the Muslim world, especially the Maghreb. At the same time those who decided to convert and stay in Spain became Jewish conversos, and their descendants would eventually arrive to Colombia, Peru, Mexico and the mountains of northern New Mexico as hidden Jews. This historical moment of decision-making in 1492 had momentous impact shaping the lives of so many people for centuries.

Of the Jews who chose to stay and convert, how many truly became Catholics and assimilated and how many feigned conversion and became crypto-Jews? Religious rituals and holidays were synthesized with Catholic practices. Purim morphed into the Fast of Esther, and Moses was Catholicized as St. Moses. Although some converso/crypto-Jewish families kept a semblance of kashrut by not eating pork, others slaughtered pigs using kosher techniques. Lighting candles on Friday night would be done with either Catholic prayers or family prayers said in Spanish.

Crypto-Jews

The Layers of Jewish Converso Experience

The descendants of conversos and crypto-Jews have had their particular path of hidden identities, communities, and practices for over 500 years, and the Spanish Jewish life to which they trace their ancestry vanished long ago. The conversos and crypto-Jews in the American Southwest and Latin America have lived in Catholic lands, a life quite different from their Sephardic cousins in Arab lands. Even within the converso/crypto-Jewish groups of Latin America, the experience of people in the northern mountains of New Mexico has been unique.

Time Period Identity Layer Formed	Layers of Crypto-Jewish Identity by Historical Period
2000-2020	Openness to reclaiming Jewish identity
1900-2000	Twentieth Century Awareness of Sephardic Heritage
1800-1900	Post-Independence Crypto-Jewish Identity
1600-1800	Colonial Crypto-Judaism in the Americas
1500-1600	Classical Crypto-Judaism in Spain & Portugal
1400-1500	Spanish/Portuguese Jewish Identity

Chart 12.1
Layers of Experience in Crypto-Jewish Identity

Cultural, ethnic, and religious identities are usually multilayered, and Jewish identity is no exception. Over the last 500 years, Jewish and crypto-Jewish identity has not been one seamless experience. Crypto-Jews have passed through various layers of cultural and religious identity, either imposed or chosen. Understanding that experience of the descendants of crypto-Jews has to include this layering of identity across the centuries. A contemporary Latin American with a Jewish converso background inherits customs from ancestors who were Spanish in the 1500s, Spanish colonial ancestors in the 1600s and 1700s, and citizens of Latin American republics in the 1800s and 1900s.[227] Today they live in the internationalized world of study, travel, and the Internet.

For many the path to Jewish identity from Catholicism goes first through conversion to one of the Protestant Churches in which they are exposed to the Hebrew Bible (Old Testament), and for some that awakens an interest or reconnects them to family memories, leading to the exploration of Jewish ancestry.

One version of contemporary Protestantism is "Messianic Judaism" or "Jews for Jesus". Messianic Judaism is a movement connecting Jewish traditions with Christianity, appropriating the name of Judaism because it adds Jewish-like practices to normative Christian beliefs. People in this group might learn Hebrew and say Christian prayers in Hebrew, and they might adopt dress patterns, such as the men wearing a *kipa* and *tzitzit*, but it is Christian.[228] In some cases, people with converso or crypto-Jews backgrounds have followed the path of Messianic Judaism in their process of exploring Jewish identity.

Jewish Sepharad exists today only in tourism, literature, and the imagined past. Most Jews who live in Spain today come from elsewhere, especially Morocco or Latin America, and there are few native Spanish Jews. Most Sephardic Jews do not live in Spain, and there is a chasm of cultural and linguistic differences between them and the descendants of conversos and crypto-Jews after 500 years of different lifestyles.

In the plethora of Jewish paths, the descendants of conversos and crypto-Jews today have inherited 500 years of experience that they might not have chosen. Their ancestors took a different road, and they inherited a trajectory that does not match that of other Jews.

Some descendants of conversos and crypto-Jews think of an idealized Sepharad, as Spanish-speaking Spain to which their DNA and genealogies can be traced, but the idealization of Catholic Spain as a homeland for Jews does not conform with historical reality. The myth of Sepharad is a vision of utopia in the distant past, but the historical Spain was one in which the Church and the Crown could collude to permit 100,000 Jews to be killed in a single year and another 100,000 could be forced to convert or go into exile.[229]

Spain has historically identified itself as a Roman Catholic country. To be Spanish is to be Catholic. Identifying as Spanish and Jewish at the same time seems to be a contradiction. The culture of anti-Semitism still comes to the surface quickly in Spain. An Anti-Defamation League global survey of anti-Semitism documented a 29 percent rate of anti-Semitic attitudes in Spain, among the highest in Western Europe. [230]

In spite of the seeming contradiction of identifying as Spanish and Jewish, it is a wave movement in the Americas.[231] Questions, such as the following, continue to be asked.

> *Contemporary research...has demonstrated that Jewish-like practices have been preserved by families that in some cases also preserve a memory of the family having been Jewish. Around this information an aura of the incredible has developed, and many have interpreted that these people have kept their Judaism in secret for centuries. This is a phenomenon of cultural memory, but what religious or ethnic significance does it have?*[232]

How do the descendants of conversos or crypto-Jews reconnect to Jewish identity today? What decisions will they make, and how will those decisions affect their descendants, as the decisions of their ancestors so long ago affected them? They are a piece of the emerging puzzle of Jewish life in Latin America. In the open religious plurality of the Americas, people have the freedom to define themselves with the knowledge of genealogy, DNA, family history, memory, and personal values to decide if they embrace the open identity of being a Jew.

The laws of return in Spain and Portugal have encouraged and facilitated the interest of the descendants of Jewish conversos in these countries.[233] For those identifying as Jews, they could migrate to Israel, but the laws of return to Israel (making *aliyah*) can be more difficult and forbidding, which have pushed people toward the Iberian alternatives. Spain and Portugal represent memories that have a historical basis and can be traced through genealogy, but Israel is distant, if not mythological and more abstract. For the descendants of crypto-Jews returning to Jewish practice, the pull of Spain and Portugal is more about history and family legends in contrast to the pull of Israel that is more about primal myths and distant religious history. Genealogy and DNA links them to Spain and Portugal, not Israel.

Descendants of conversos and crypto-Jews have had an experience of hidden identities, communities, and practices for over 500 years. The memories of a long distant Jewish practice in Spain have eroded, and in the meantime Jewish life itself has evolved, becoming more Eastern European, Middle Eastern, and Israeli, which is foreign to the Spanish-speaking descendants of crypto-Jews.

Like Ethiopian Jews, the Cochin Jews, or Jews of Goa the descendants of Jewish conversos and crypto-Jews come with the unique path of Jewishness that they have inherited. Now, for the first time in 500 years they can openly decide what that background means to them and how they want to relate it to their lives.

Crypto-Jews are not the only group to preserve religious identity and practices for centuries in hiding. The *Kakure Kirishitan* were Christians in Japan who preserved their religious tradition after it was outlawed by the Tokugawa shogunate in the first decade of the 1600s, and some have retained their practice even after Christianity was legalized in the late 1800s. The hidden version of Christianity was synthesized with Buddhism, and its practice has been renounced as unorthodox and rejected by the Catholic Church.[234]

Conclusion

The descendants of conversos and crypto-Jews are creating new identities and cultural patterns as they adapt to the contemporary internationalized world. The question is how to be Jewish with a cultural heritage from the Spanish-speaking world of Jewish conversos. They are not like either Ashkenazi or Sephardic Jews today.

The descendants of crypto-Jews have their own unique path to life and heritage in the twenty-first century. As individuals they are making decisions about their lives accordingly, sometimes following individual spiritual paths, sometimes converting and joining established Jewish communities, and sometimes forming their own Jewish communities where they build their Judaism within their own cultural sphere.

Notes

1   Graizbord, David. 2019. "Men and Women of the Nation: How the Inquisition's conversos defined Jewish religious and ethnic identity in ways that are still prevalent today," *Tablet Magazine*. https://www.tabletmag.com/jewish-arts-and-culture/289739/men-and-women-of-the-nation.

2   Hordes 2005:235 and 279

3   Kunin 2009:196-197

4   Kunin 2009:116-121; Hordes 2005:243f

5   Atencio 1996:59ff; The term "manito" comes for the word "hermano" (i.e. brother) or "hermanito" (i.e. term of friendship or brotherhood).

6   Atencio 1996:65

7   Netanyahu 1999:4

8   Graizbord, David. 2019

9   Ferry and Nathan 2000:85-96

10   Schwarz 1925; Duncan Hart 2016a:100

11   Gerber 1992:178-181

12   Hordes 2005: 201f

13   Martínez-Dávila. 2018a:12; Moore 1987:5

14   Number 70 of the Fourth Lateran Council says, "Jewish converts may not retain their old rite. Certain people who have come voluntarily to the waters of sacred baptism, as we learnt, do not wholly cast off the old person in order to put on the new more perfectly. For, in keeping remnants of their former rite, they upset the decorum of the christian religion by such a mixing…For it is a lesser evil not to know the Lord's way than to go back on it after having known it."

15   Marcus 2012: 137

16   McKay, John P., Bennett D. Hill, John Buckler. 1996: 421

17   Chazan. 1991:48

18   Gerber 1992:101-109

19   Matt 2017. These twelve volumes document this.

20   Rabbi Martin Levy. 2015. Personal communication.

21   Sharot 1980:394ff; Bodian 1997:122

22   Israel 1998a: 4-28

23   Israel 1998a:4

24   Duncan Hart 2002. "St. Vicente Ferrer and the Anti-Semitism of Fifteenth Century Spain." *HaLapid*. Vol.IX. No. 2. Spring.

25   Gerber 1992:120

26   Duncan Hart 2002

27   Gerber 1992:113

28   Gerber 1992:113-114

29   When Ferrer launched his campaign against Jews, his purpose was to eliminate all Jews from Spain, and over the next three decades he came close to achieving that goal. After he died, Ferrer was canonized, not only because he was an eloquent preacher who stirred Christians to their faith, but also because he was credited as the most successful evangelist of the age against the Jews.

"Agora, buena gente, catad que esto faze mucho contro los jodíos, en quento dyze: 'Maldicho es el home que confía en el home'. ¡Aquí los tomaré! Catad que vosotros, jodíos, confiades en el rey Mexías e dezides que rey Mexías non ha de ser omne dios, mas omne solamente. Pues parsçe por este propheta que sodes maldichos, porque confiades en omne e dezides que vos ha de levar a salvaçión…"

"Pues tanbién seredes vosotros maldichos, porque confiades en Ihesú Christo, que es omne"…Dize: 'Dixieron: el rrey Mexías non es Dios, e por esso son corruptos e aborreçidos de todas las gentes'. (Cátedra García 1994:341)

30   These restrictions were similar to the ones that the Nazis would impose on Jews in the twentieth century.

31   These laws had provisions such as: Jews were to be restricted to living only in the *juderia*, or Jewish ghetto. Jews could no longer provide services to Christian clients. Jews were no longer allowed to work in governmental or judicial offices. Jews had to wear distinctive clothing. Jews could not hire Christians nor be in supervisory positions over Christians. No improvements could be made to synagogue buildings.

32   Gerber 1992:125-126

33   Gerber 1992:120

34   He used his knowledge of the Talmud and Jewish scholarship to try to convert other Jews. He wrote a treatise called, Dialogues of Paul and Saul Against the Jews, which became the basis for the anti-Jewish writings of other Christian scholars.

35   Martínez-Dávila, Roger L. 2018. *Creating Conversos: the Carvajal-Santa Maria Family in Early Modern Spain*. South Bend: University of Notre Dame Press.

36   Martínez-Dávila 2018:11ff

37   Dimont, Max. 1962. *Jews, God and History*. New York: Simon and Schuster. Page 226.

38   Gerber 1992:123

39   The numbers of crypto-Jews were never large in comparison to the overall Spanish society, but the Church saw any foreign religious elements among its citizens as corruption that had to be eliminated.

40   Kunin 2016:88

Notes

41 Halkin 2009:15-34
42 Graizbord 2013:16-18
43 Graizbord 2013:21
44 Elbaz 2018:86
45 On January 1, 1492 Boabdil, the last Muslim ruler, surrendered to the Christian forces of King Ferdinand and Queen Isabella, and al-Andalus was incorporated into the Kingdoms of Castile and Aragon that they ruled.
46 He set the standard for early inquisitorial practice, arresting thousands and burning many at the stake.
47 Roth 1964:96ff
48 Kamen 1997:192ff
49 Kamen 1997:60
50 Beinart 2002:33-54. The Muslim elite left, but all Muslims were not expelled until the early 1600s. The conundrum is why did they expel the Jews and not the Muslims in 1492?
51 Beinart 2002: 207ff, Sloan 2009:26
52 Gitlitz 1996:38f
53 Beinart 2002:413ff
54 Beinart 2002:33ff, Perez 2005:35-36
55 Kamen 1997:23
56 The House Key. Some families, leaving into exile, took their house keys with them perhaps thinking that they would be able to return at some time in the future. As the years wore on, the house key began to symbolize their former lives in Spain. Although house keys were lost over the decades and centuries, the legend of the keys has continued. The key has become a symbol of the nostalgia of what life once was.
57 Martínez-Dávila 2018:2
58 Pike 2000:12
59 Pike 2000:xi
60 Monter 2003:323. The anti-*converso* movements of the sixteenth century, such as the Comunero Revolt of 1520-21, became progressively racial in nature. This became another incentive for *conversos* and crypto-Jews to leave Spain.
61 In the Spanish colonies of South America, the terms Portuguese and Jewish were synonymous. If a person was from Portugal, it was assumed that he or she must be Jewish.
62 Gitlitz 1996:43
63 Bel Bravo 1988:78
64 Melammed 2004:166-168; Bodian 1997:26
65 Anti-Semitism dominated the day, and Jewish life in Spain was slowly terminated.

66 Israel 1998:46-47.
67 Israel 1998a:146
68 Israel 1998a:27
69 Gitlitz 1996:54; Gerber 1992:xvi-xx
70 The original date of Expulsion had been July 31. Isaac Abarbanel had negotiated to suspend the Expulsion, but all he got was a respite for a couple of days, which made the Expulsion on the 9 of Av in the Hebrew calendar, Tisha B'Av, or August 2, the same day Columbus sailed on his historic voyage to the Americas.
71 Garcia 2012. As the High Renaissance was unfolding in Italy between 1500 and 1520 with humanistic literature, painting and sculpture with the encouragement of the Catholic Church, in Spain the Crown and the Church were focused on religious genocide against the Jews. While the Church was commissioning the best art of the Western world in Rome, it was condemning thousands of people to burn at the stake in Spain and by the end of the 1500s the Crown and the Church had achieved their purpose of eliminating the last vestiges of Jewish life in the country. That history cut Spain off from the Renaissance occurring in European and later would limit its participation in the Enlightenment.
72 When Martin Luther wrote his 95 theses in 1517 challenging the Church, Europe would soon split into Protestant and Catholic spheres. As Kings and Popes focused on this split in Christendom, the expulsions and persecutions of Jews became a secondary concern. That gave the Jews an opportunity to rebuilt Jewish life, and they did just that in the Rhineland and Eastern Europe. The Ashkenazi communities that developed there largely flourished for the next 250 years until Christian anti-Semitism would drive over two million Jews to the Americas in the late 1800s and early 1900s.
73 Sloan 2009:26
74 Diaz del Castillo 2009; Gojman 2016:56
75 Israel 1998a:27
76 Ibid.
77 Israel 1998a:4
78 Sloan 2009:101-126
79 Sephardic life prospered there until the Greek communities were destroyed by the Nazis. The Sephardim in Greece and the Balkans had the highest rate of loss in the Holocaust of all Jewish communities in Europe.
80 Bodian 197:27
81 Hordes 2005:33-34
82 Duncan Hart 2016c: 23; Duncan Hart 2015:13
83 That experience gave them a unique dimension not shared with Jews from Germany, Poland and Russia.
84 Kritzler 2008

Notes

85 Birmingham 1971:102-115

86 Israel 1998a:145; Ray 2013:11

87 Sephardic merchants played a central role in the development of international trade for the Dutch and other newly developing commercial powers of Europe, and in doing so Sephardic Jews and crypto-Jews spread out around the world. (Israel 1998:145) They could be found in the port cities from Europe (Amsterdam) to the Americas (Recife, Cartagena and Lima) and throughout Asia (Goa, Macao, Manila). They became known as the Port Jews and became major figures in managing international commerce as the global economy developed. This group included families, such as the Sassoon and Senior. The Portuguese historian Juan Alberto Rodriguez also describes the porous boundaries between Christians and Jews. Sometimes Jewish conversos who returned to Jewish practice reconverted to Christianity and life in Spain or Portugal as they reclaimed their Iberian identity. (Rodriguez Da Silva Tavim, 2011:175ff).

88 Brooks 2004; Sloan 2009:124-126; Toro 2010, 2011.

89 Gerber 1992:166-169

90 Ten years after he died in 1579 in Istanbul, Christopher Marlowe wrote the play, The Jew of Malta, which is about religious conflict and revenge set in the struggle for supremacy of the Mediterranean between the Ottomans and Spain. The story is strikingly similar to the life of Joseph Nasi, and Marlowe seems to have known the myth that surrounded his life as the Jew, who lived his life fighting Spain and Catholicism. The image of the Jew in Marlowe's play also has parallels with Shylock, the Jew in Shakespeare's play, "The Merchant of Venice".

91 Stillman 1979:90

92 Nadler 2018

93 Garver 2018: 25ff; Schama 2013:34

94 Spinoza was a central figure, and he links the other two famous figures from that time period in Amsterdam, one Rabbi Menasseh ben Israel, his mentor, and Rabbi Isaac Aboab da Fonseca, who was the rabbi of the Portuguese synagogue, and was involved in the trial against him.

95 Kamen 2003:343. Many of the first wave crypto-Jews who arrived in the early to mid-1500s would have still had memories of the Jewish practices of their families, but the second wave crypto-Jews, who arrive later in the 1600s, would have been separated so long from Jewish life that they would have begun to lose the original Jewish meaning of their practices.

96 Gitlitz 1996:55f

97 Halevy 1996:69

98 The Inquisition itself could become the source for identifying Jew-

ish practices for those wanting to return to Jewish practice.

99   After occupying Cartagena, considered a permanent occupation that would have made it an English city, but ultimately decided that they did not have the resources to hold it.

100   A large prosperous Jewish community was located along the Surinam River and was called Joden Savanneh (i.e. Savannah of the Jews). In 1694, there were 500 Jews in Surinam owning forty sugar plantations and 9,000 slaves, and by 1730 that had grown to 115 plantations. Jonathan Israel. 1998. *The Dutch Republic: Its Rise, Greatness, and Fall 1477-1806.* Oxford: Oxford University Press.

101   Duncan Hart 2016c:164

102   Vila Vilar, 1979:147-149. It continued to be illegal for Jews to enter Spanish territories, but it was a law that was not enforceable. While there were a few hundred crypto-Jews in the provinces of Cartagena, the Jewish population was in the thousands in Mexico and Peru.

103   Klooster 2009:34-36

104   Feitler 2009:123ff

105   Jews came to be seen as a fifth column that would support the Dutch or English in case they invaded a Spanish or Portuguese colony. English and Dutch privateers were successfully attacking Spanish shipping, and the crypto-Jewish merchants were successfully smuggling trade goods and African slaves into their colonies. The Crown saw the crypto-Jews as a multi-dimensional threat to their wealth, prestige, and sovereignty in the Americas.

106   Hordes 2005:149

107   Melchor de Aguilera's daughter Doña Teresa Aguilera y Roche, who was born in Italy and lived part of her childhood in France, became an interesting historical figure in her own right. While they were in Cartagena, she married an ambitious young officer, Don Bernardo López de Mendizábal, who was later named to be the Governor of New Mexico in 1658. The two made history by being arrested in Santa Fe (today New Mexico) by the Inquisition in 1662, accused of Judaizing.

108   Sugar became the largest export from the Americas, and Amsterdam was the primary port for sugar coming into Europe. Jewish merchants played a major role in both ends of that trade network.

109   McKay, et.al. 1996:529

110   By law the colonies in the Americas could only trade with Spain, not with each other and not with merchants of any other European nation. The problem was that supply ships from Spain were infrequent and did not satisfy demand in the colonies. Spanish-speaking Jewish entrepreneurs stepped in to fill that demand.

111   Vila Vilar, 1979:147-149

Notes

112 Duncan Hart 2006. Crypto-Jewish merchants helped these early colonies grow economically.

113 Duncan Hart 2006. Slaves were frequently converted to being Jews and circumcised so that they were complicit with the owner and thus obligated not to report his Jewish practices.

114 Navarrete 2002:8788

115 Splendini, et.al. 1997:429438

116 The leaders arrested were Juan Rodríguez Mesa, Francisco Piñero, Blas de Paz Pinto, and Luis Gómez Barreto.

117 Splendini, et.al. 1997:458-459

118 Schaposchnik 2015:12-13

119 Schaposchnik 2015:115ff

120 Schaposchnik 2015:115ff

121 Cordero did all the right things and was reconciled with the Church. Like anyone in his position, he did have a record with the Inquisition, but provided that he would not have any further arrests, he could expect to live a more or less normal life.

122 Kritzler 2008:151-152. Schaposchnik 2015:108f. Other people accused of Judaizing and arrested by the Inquisition as a part of the Grand Conspiracy included Antonio de Acuña, Diego López de Fonseca, Sebastián Duarte, Franciso Nuñez Duarte, Roque Nuñez, Rodrigo Váez Pereira, Rodrigo de Avila, Jorge de Silva, Antonio Gómez de Acosta, Manuel de Espinosa, Enrique Nuñez, Antonio de Sosa, Jorge Rodríguez de Acosta, Duarte Nuñez, Bartolomé de León, and Sebastián de Acuña.

123 Vila Vilar 1979:187

124 Garcia-Arenal 2013:14

125 Gojman 2016:55

126 Gojman 2016:53

127 When the Inquisition was established in Mexico in 1571, crypto-Jews had to hide their identities.

128 Hordes 2005:34

129 Hordes 2005:35

130 Gitlitz 1996:76

131 Gojman 2016: 58-59

132 Harboring a crypto-Jew was tantamount to treason against the Church. Family members, like Jose Sanchez, would betray relatives, even their mother, to protect their own lives.

133 Martínez-Dávila 2018:10

134 Hordes 2005:72f; Martínez-Dávila 2018:253

135 Hordes 2005:75

136 Gitlitz 1996:56; Hordes 2005:78f

137 Halevy 2011:7
138 Hordes 2005:78
139 Greenleaf 1969; Toro 1993:207f
140 Cohen 2001
141 Cohen 2001; https://www.khanacademy.org/humanities/art-americas/new-spain/viceroyalty-new-spain/a/the-manuscripts-of-luis-de-carvajal
142 Halevy 2011:16
143 Cohen 2001:255-257; Liebman 1970:182
144 Diaz, Duncan Hart, and Martínez-Dávila 2016:188
145 Liebman 1970:255-256
146 Gitlitz 1996:57f
147 Hordes 2005:1, 55-56
148 Hordes 2005:56-57
149 Hordes 2005:54
150 Of the sixty-three heads of households arrested during the 1640s, they represented a broad range of socio-economic status. Since the Inquisition confiscated the properties of those arrested, they kept records of their wealth. Fourteen percent of those arrested during this period were very wealthy with large estates; 43 percent were moderately wealthy with modest estates; 21 percent had small holdings and were "poor"; and 22 percent were among the very poor. Approximately one-half owned their house. Hordes 2005:45 and 58
151 Gojman 2016:59
152 https://www.lajornadaguerrero.com.mx/index.php/entretenimiento/cultura/item/8395-confirma-el-inah-autenticidad-de-banos-judios-descubiertos-en-juliantla-taxco.
153 Hordes 2005:110-123
154 Hordes 2005:109f
155 See the statements in the Introduction, *Somos Judios*
156 Kunin 2016:87
157 Hordes 2005:150
158 Hordes 2016:77
159 Hordes 2005:148-165; Levine 2016:63ff
160 Levine 2013:54
161 Levine 2013:54
162 As mentioned earlier, Spanish was considered to be the Christian language, and the expression is still used in parts of the Americas, "Hablo cristiano," which translates as "I speak Christian", but it means I speak Spanish.
163 Hordes 2005:149
164 Levine 2016:69
165 Hordes 2005:161-162

Notes

166 Hordes 2005:224

167 Jews were not permitted to practice openly as Jews in Mexico until after 1865, and in fact they did not arrive in significant numbers until the early twentieth century. As the Ottoman Empire disintegrated, Sephardic Jews began to migrate to the Americas and tens of thousands would locate in Mexico City.

168 Gitlitz 2002:317

169 Halevy 1996:82

170 Hordes 2005:49

171 This could be a practice acquired after the arrival of openly practicing Jews in the mid-1800s.

172 Hordes 2005:46

173 In Newport, Aaron Lopez (Portuguese *converso* returned to Jewish practice) and his wife Sarah Rivera Lopez had fifteen children, including seven daughters. As mentioned earlier, the Jewish communities were small and finding marriage partners could be a problem. Cousin marriage was a common solution, and it also responds to the belief that family members will be more suitable marriage partners. In economic terms, cousin marriage also keeps property or wealth within the extended family. The marriages of the Lopez daughters give an example of this pattern. Two of the daughters married Gomez brothers who were their cousins, and another daughter married a Lopez cousin. One daughter married a Hendricks, who was a cousin of the Gomez, and another daughter married a non-cousin, Jacob Levy, but when she died, one of her younger sisters married him. Another daughter married an uncle. Duncan Hart (2016c:208-209)

174 Gitlitz 1996:204

175 Hordes 2005:49

176 Sabloff 1978b:1

177 Medina Sandoval 2009:183-190

178 Gojman 2016:59

179 Gitlitz 1996:227

180 "A Long Journey: The Hidden Jews of the Southwest" Documentary Co-Produced by Cinewest-NMPBS.

181 Sabloff 1978a:1-2

182 Beider 2019

183 Bunis 2008:177ff; Bunis 2018:64

184 Hordes 2005:235

185 Elbaz 2015a:41ff

186 Atencio 2003:10f

187 Pacheco 2016

188 Jacobs 2002:149

189 Jacobs 2002:42
190 Graizbord 2008:53f
191 Kunin 2009:150
192 Kunin 2009:161-163. Although he admitted it had been distorted through time and lost its meaning, for him it was a signifier of the family's heritage.
193 Roth 1932:175
194 Jacobs 2002:42ff; Kunin 2016:89
195 Canelo 2001
196 Bodian 1997:76ff
197 Bodian 1997:98
198 In B'nei Zion synagogue in El Paso, Rabbi Stephen Leon has given classes to those wanting to return to Jewish practice and has created a path for them to do so.
199 "A Long Journey: The Hidden Jews of the Southwest" Documentary Co-Produced by Cinewest-NMPBS.
200 Klooster 2009:34-36
201 Feitler 2009:123ff
202 Bloomfield Ramagen 1994, 1997
203 Benveniste 1997
204 Primack 1997:107ff
205 Heller 2010
206 Duncan Hart 2006
207 Bibliowicz 2001
208 Pacheco 2016
209 Halevy 1999, 2011
210 Halevy 1999:82
211 Halevy2011:87-125
212 Halevy 2011:231
213 An early exploration of Jewish traditions of this area was by Raphael Patai, the Israeli anthropologist/folklorist, who did research in the region in the late 1940s and again in the early 1960s. Rather than the urban and town populations with which Halevy did research, he was looking into reports of "Indian Jews" that lived in more rural areas. In his research on these groups, Patai concluded that they were not Jewish. Although they did self-identify as having Jewish ancestry, he was not convinced that their practices linked them to a Jewish past. Patai 1983
214 In 1987 Ricardo Elizondo wrote *Los sefarditas en Nuevo León, reminicencias en el folklore* (The Sephardim of New Leon, Reminiscences in Folklore). He recorded the customs associated with Jewish practice, such

as separating milk and meat. Richard Santos followed up that work with *Silent Heritage: The Sephardim and the Colonization of the Spanish North American Frontier* in 2000 in which he raises the question of crypto-Jews in Texas. There was local opposition in Monterrey to being publicly identified as descendants of Jews although some of the same people would privately agree that their family was of Jewish descent.

215 Leon 2017: 29-33

216 Ibid.

217 "A Long Journey: The Hidden Jews of the Southwest" Documentary Co-Produced by Cinewest-NMPBS.

218 Kunin 2016:87

219 Kunin 2009:170

220 Gitlitz 2002; Gitlitz 1996:76

221 Hordes 2005:xv

222 Neulander 1996:19ff and 2014: 69ff

223 Neulander 1994:64-67

224 Gradwohl 1996

225 Kunin 2016:90

226 Are more in the category of other groups that have Jewish roots but have lost connection with the main body of Jews, such as the Russian Jews or others, such as the Ethiopian Jews and B'nei Menashe people, all of which have been accepted into Israel.

227 Aliberti, 2018:27-30.

228 Dell Sanchez is a popular west Texas television Messianic evangelist, who has a considerable following, and some people waver between thinking of themselves as crypto-Jews or Messianic Jews. Rev. Sanchez is a compelling speaker, some people with the memory of having had a Jewish background leave the practice of Catholicism for his teachings.

229 Gerber 1992:120.

230 Anti-Defamation League Global 100

231 The modern Jewish population in Spain includes many Ashkenazim of Latin American origin and Sephardim from Morocco with concentrations in Barcelona and Madrid with a growing presence in the Malaga/Marbella region in the south.

232 Duncan Hart 2016a:100

233 Although the Edict of Expulsion of Jews from Spain remained in force legally until December, 1968, different Spanish governments have been accepting Jewish residents for more than one hundred years. When the First Spanish Republic was declared in 1868, the new constitution of 1869 provided religious freedom to "all foreigners resident in Spain." Jews were

considered "foreigners". A Royal Decree promulgated on December 20, 1924 during the dictatorship of General Primo de Rivera gave full citizenship to individuals of Spanish origin who applied. Three thousand Sephardim, many from former Ottoman Empire countries, took advantage of that opportunity, and it was credited with saving large numbers of Jews from the Holocaust in the Second World War.

234 Turnbull 1998: 18f; Whelan 1996: 20f

Acknowledgments

Over the last twenty-five years scholars have made important additions to the literature on Jewish conversos and crypto-Jews in the Americas. Starting with David Gitlitz' *Secrecy and Deceit: The Religion of the Crypto-Jews* (1996), Janet Liebman Jacobs' *Hidden Heritage: The Legacy of the Crypto-Jews* (2002), and David Graizbord's *Souls in Dispute: Converso Identities in Iberia and the Jewish Diaspora, 1580-1700.* (2004) The work of Stanley Hordes, *To the End of the Earth* (2005) and Seth Kunin, *Juggling Identities* (2009), on crypto-Jewish practice in New Mexico has been invaluable.

Schulamith Halevy's "Descendants of the Anusim (Crypto-Jews) in Contemporary Mexico" (2011) and Roger Martínez-Dávila's *Creating Conversos: the Carvajal-Santa Maria Family in Early Modern Spain* (2018) have continued to add to the depth of historical research that have given us a more complete understanding of crypto-Jewish life and history. The body of literature on Sephardic Jews and converso/crypto-Jews continues to grow. The research of Vanessa Paloma Elbaz in Morocco has been an important source of my understanding of the surviving Sephardic life in that country.

I want to thank Corrine Joy Brown, Frances Levine, Roger Martínez-Dávila, Isabelle Medina Sandoval, and Paula Sabloff for reviewing early drafts of the manuscript. I especially thank historian Stanley Hordes for his meticulous and insightful reviews of this work on two different occasions. Each pointed out concepts to be clarified, data to be specified, and copy-editing issues that made this a better book.

Professors Robert Chazan, Jeremy Cohen, and Irven Resnick among others at the Oxford Centre for Hebrew and Jewish Studies facilitated my understanding of Jews in Spain and the later crypto-Jewish experience. I am especially indebted to Prof. David Bidney of Indiana University, who gave me insight into the interaction between religion and culture. Based on his own study with Ernst Cassirer, he introduced me to the analysis and understanding of culture and symbolic forms. From the classroom to Shabbat dinner in his house and long hours of conversation in the labyrinth of his book-lined office, I came to understand more about the cultural basis of religious traditions.

Thank you to my wife, Gloria Abella Ballen, who is an accomplished scholar and artist. I appreciate her sharing of information and debating concepts and the interpretations given here.

I thank those, who are on their unique spiritual journeys, for sharing their research and stories, from Rabbi Juan Mejia to Rabbi Jordi Gendra-Molina, Gerald Gonzalez, Isabelle Medina Sandoval, Sonya Loya, John Garcia, Blanca Garza Enriquez Carrasco, Maria Apodaca, Charlie Carrillo, Tim Herrera, the Jewish community of Juarez, and others who cannot be named here.

It has been a pleasure to work with Isaac and Jude Artenstein of Cinewest and their film crews in the making of the PBS documentary, "A Long Journey: The Hidden Jews of the Southwest," a Cinewest-NMPBS Co-Production, Directed by Isaac Artenstein, Produced by Paula Amar Schwartz, Mel Schwartz Executive Producer.

I thank Ilan Stavans for permission to use his translation of the poem by João Pinto Delgado and David Gilad and Orit Rabkin for their translation of the poem by Isaac Aboab da Fonseca. I thank Isabelle Medina Sandoval for permission to quote her poem "Marginal Threads" and also from her book *Guardians of Hidden Traditions*. I thank Rabbi Stephen Leon for permission to quote from his book *The Third Commandment*.

Photographs are by the author, except for those indicated from Wikimedia Commons (Public domain images or files licensed under the Creative Commons Attribution-Share Alike 3.0 Unported license.), images from "A Long Journey: The Hidden Jews of the Southwest" by Cinewest, and the Portuguese Synagogue in Amsterdam (courtesy of Vanessa Paloma Elbaz).

I appreciate the support of family, friends, and the Jewish community that have supported me in every stage of this exploration from Ines Abella to Nina Friedemann, Tirzah Sowa, Ira Schlezinger, Helene Harpman, Ariel Lazarus, Art Benveniste, Dolores Sloan, and so many more. Un abrazo.

About the Author

Ron Duncan Hart is a cultural anthropologist (Ph.D. Indiana University) with postdoctoral work in Jewish Studies at the University of Oxford, Centre for Hebrew and Jewish Studies. He is former President of the Jewish Federation of New Mexico and has awards from the National Endowment for the Humanities, National Endowment for the Arts, National Science Foundation, Ford Foundation, UNICEF, and New Mexico Jewish Historical Society among others.

Duncan Hart has done research on Sephardic traditions in Spain, North Africa, and South America with special attention to the Andalusian exchange among Jews, Christians, and Muslims. He is former Dean of Academic Affairs at InterAmerican University of Puerto Rico. He was Project Director in Latin America with the Ford Foundation, the International Development Research Centre of Canada, and UNICEF. He is a former Research Associate of the Latin American and Iberian Institute at the University of New Mexico.

He served a number of years as editor of *HaLapid*, the journal of the Society for Crypto-Judaic Studies. He is author of several books on religion, cultural history and social change, including *Fractured Faiths: Spanish Judaism, the Inquisition and New World Identities* (author/editor), and historical consultant for the exhibition of the same name at the New Mexico History Museum in Santa Fe (2016). *Fractured Faiths* won the Gold Medal for the best book on a religious topic in 2018. Other books include *Judaism, Sephardic Jews: History, Religion and People*, and *Jews and the Arab World*.

He has been an invited lecturer on Jewish life and culture for the New Mexico History Museum (Santa Fe), Neustadt Lecture (Oklahoma City University), the National Labor Relations Board (Washington, D.C.), and the Schlezinger Annual Lecture (Ohr Kodesh in Chevy Chase, Maryland) among other venues.

Glossary

Alhambra Decree - The Edict of Expulsion of Jews from Spain.

Anusim - The forced ones in Spanish, referring to Jews who were forced to convert.

Bima - The raised platform with a Torah reading table that is located in the center of the Sephardic synagogue.

Converso - A Jewish person who converted to Catholicism.

Convivencia - Spanish word referring to the living together of the three cultures in Spain, Christian, Jewish, and Muslim.

Crypto-Jew - Under Spanish and Portuguese rule this referred to a *converso* who continued Jewish practices in hiding. In the twentieth century it has been used to refer to someone who identifies as a descendant of people who were crypto-Jews.

Disputation - A system of argument used in Christian Spain to convince Jews that Christian theology was correct, and that they should convert.

Kabbalah - A system of mystical thought about spirituality and the Divine essence.

Limpieza de sangre - Meaning "purity of blood" in Spanish, referring to not having any Jewish or Muslim ancestry.

Marrano - A derogatory term used by Christians toward *conversos*, who wished to return to Jewish practice.

New Christian - A Jew who converted to Catholicism.

Reconquest/Reconquista - The recapturing of Spain from the Muslims by the Christians.

Sefarad, Sepharad - The Hebrew word for Spain.

Sephardic, Sephardi - Related to Spanish Jewish life.

Sephardim - The Hebrew plural term for a group of people of Sephardic heritage.

Spanish Inquisition - The political and religious arm of the Spanish Crown to police crypto-Jewish behavior.

Yeshiva - School for the study of Torah and Talmud.

Recommended Additional Readings and Films

For more detailed histories of conversos and crypto-Jews in Spain, Mexico, and New Mexico, consider these titles:

General:
Diaz, Joseph, Ron Duncan Hart, Roger Martínez-Dávila, editors. 2016. *Fractured Faiths: Spanish Judaism, the Inquisition and New World Identities*. Albuquerque: Fresco Books.

Spain:
Gerber, Jane S. 1992. *The Jews of Spain: A History of the Sephardic Experience*. New York: The Free Press.

Martínez-Dávila, Roger L. 2018. *Creating Conversos: the Carvajal-Santa Maria Family in Early Modern Spain*. South Bend: University of Notre Dame Press.

Menocal, Maria Rosa. 2003. *The Ornament of the World: How Muslims, Jews and Christians Created a Culture of Tolerance in Medieval Spain*. Boston: Back Bay Books.

Mexico:
Cohen, Martin. 1973. *The Martyr: Luis de Carvajal, A Secret Jew in Sixteenth-Century Mexico*. Albuquerque: University of New Mexico Press.

Hordes, Stanley M. 2005. *To the End of the Earth: A History of the Crypto-Jews of New Mexico*. New York: Columbia University Press.

American Southwest:
Hordes, Stanley M. 2005. *To the End of the Earth: A History of the Crypto-Jews of New Mexico*. New York: Columbia University Press.

Kunin, Seth D. 2009. *Juggling Identities: Identity and Authenticity among the Crypto-Jews*. New York: Columbia University Press.

Fiction, American Southwest:
Brown, Corinne Joy. 2016. *Hidden Star*. Victoria: Friesen Press.
Fine, Marcia. 2017. *Hidden Ones: A veil of Memories*. L'Image Press, LLC.
Medina Sandoval, Isabelle. 2009. *Guardians of Hidden Traditions*. Santa Fe: Gaon Books.

Online Documentary Films:
www.jewishlearningchannel.com

List of Figures

Frontispiece - Santa Fe
1. Rabbi Juan Mejia   15
2. Sonya Loya   18
3. Rabbi Jordi Gendra**   20
4. Maria Apodaca   22
5. John Garcia   24
6. Blanca Garza Enriquez Carrasco   25
7. Medieval Jewish Quarter, Besalu   38
8. Queen Isabella's Castle Segovia   46
9. Jew in Disputation*   47
10. *Auto da Fé*, Portugal*   52
11. Dominican Preacher*   54
12. Palace of the Inquisition, Lisbon   70
13. Doña Gracia Nasi   90
14. Menasseh Ben Israel*   98
15. Baruch Spinoza*   100
16. Aboab de Fonseca*   101
17. Portuguese Synagogue, Amsterdam***   104
18. Palace of the Inquisition, Cartagena   115
19. Palace of Inquisition, Mexico City   124
20. Luis Carvajal in Inquisition Jail**   129
21. Colonial Adobe Church, Las Trampas   138
22. Palace of the Governors, Santa Fe   140
23. Reconstruction of New Mexico Farm House Patio 1700s**   145
24. Retablo, Charlie Carrillo   148
25. Adam and Eve Retablo**   150
26. Joseph's Dream Retablo**   157

List of Charts

3.1. Jewish Population Trend in Spain, 1300-1492   63
3.2 Conversion Rates of Jews in Spain, 1300-1492   64
12.1. Layers of Cultural Identity   198

Photos are by the author unless another source is indicated.
* Wikimedia Commons (Public domain images or files licensed under the Creative Commons Attribution-Share Alike 3.0 Unported license.)
** Courtesy Cinewest
*** Vanessa Paloma Elbaz

Bibliography

Abrevaya Stein, Sarah.
- 2016. *Extraterritorial Dreams: European Citizenship, Sephardi Jews, and the Ottoman Twentieth Century.* Chicago: University of Chicago Press.
- 2014. *Saharan Jews and the Fate of French Algeria.* Chicago: University of Chicago Press.
- 2006. *Making Jews Modern: The Yiddish and Ladino Press in the Russian and Ottoman Empires.* Bloomington: Indiana University Press.
- 2008. *Plumes: Ostrich Feathers, Jews, and a Lost World of Global Commerce.* New Haven: Yale University Press.

Abrevaya Stein, Sarah and Julia Cohen. 2014. *Sephardi Lives: A Documentary History, 1700-1950.* Stanford: Stanford University Press.

Abrevaya Stein, Sarah and Aron Rodrigue. 2012. *A Jewish Voice from Ottoman Salonica: The Ladino Memoir of Sa'adi Besalel a-Levi.* Stanford: Stanford University Press.

Alberro, Solange.
- 1981. *La Actividad del Santo Oficio de la Inquisicion en Nueva Espana, 1571-1700.* Mexico City: Instituto Nacional de Antropologia e Historia. Coleccion Cientifica No. 96.
- 1988. *Inquisición y sociedad en México, 1571-1700.* Mexico City: Fondo de Cultura Económico.

Aliberti, Davide. 2018. *Sefarad: Una comunidad imaginada (1924-2015).* Madrid: Marcial Pons, Ediciones de Historia.

Alcalá, Angel, Editor.
- 1995. *Judíos, Sefarditas, Conversos: La Expulsión de 1492 y sus consecuencias.* Valladolid: ámbito Ediciones.
- 1987. *The Spanish Inquisition and the Inquisitorial Mind.* Boulder: Social Science Monographs.

Alexy, Trudi. 1993. *The Mezuzah in the Madonna's Foot: Marranos and other Secret Jews.* New York: Simon and Schuster.

Alpert, Michael. 2001. *Crypto-Judaism and the Spanish Inquisition.* New York: Palgrave.

Alvarez Alonso, Fermina. 1999. *La Inquisición en Cartagena de Indias durante el Siglo XVII.* Madrid: Fundación Universitaria Española.

Amador de los Ríos, Jose. 1960. *Historia Social, Politica y Religiosa de los Judíos de España y Portugal.* Madrid, Aguilar.

Angel, Marc D.
- 2009. *Maimonides, Spinoza and Us: Toward an Intellectually Vibrant Judaism*. Woodstock, Vermont: Jewish Lights Publishing.
- 2006. *Foundations of Sephardic Spirituality: The Inner Life of Jews of the Ottoman Empire*. Woodstock, Vermont: Jewish Lights Publishing.
- 1982. *La America: The Sephardic Experience in the United States*. Philadelphia: Jewish Publication Society.

Anti-Defamation League Global 100. (http://global100.adl.org/)

Arbell, Mordechai. 2000. *Portuguese Jews of Jamaica*. Kingston: University of the West Indies Press.

Archivo General de la Nación.

1949. Libro Primero de Votos de la Inquisición de Mexico. Mexico.

1642. Ramo de Inquisición. "Proceso y causa criminal contra Antonio Caravallo. Folios 327v-328. Tomo 409, exp. 2.

Archivo Histórico Nacional, Fondo Inquisición. Madrid, Spain.

Atencio, Tomás.
- 2003. "The Converso Legacy in New Mexico Hispano Protestantism." *El Caminante*, No. 2, pages 10-15.
- 1996. "Crypto-Jewish Remnants in Manito Society and Culture." *Jewish Folklore and Ethnology Review*. Vol. 18. Nos.1-2, pages 59-68.

Ayllon, Fernando. 1997. *El Tribunal de la Inquisicion: de la Leyanda a la Historia*. Lima: Ediciones del Congreso del Peru.

Baer, Yitzhak.
- 1981. *Historia de los Judíos en la España Cristiana*. Barcelona: Riopiedras Ediciones.
- 1961. *A History of the Jews in Christian Spain*. Philadelphia: The Jewish Publication Society of America.

Bango, Isidro G. 2003. *Remembering Sepharad: Jewish Culture in Medieval Spain*. Madrid: State Corporation for Spanish Cultural Action Board.

Beinart, Haim.
- 2002. *The Expulsion of the Jews from Spain*. Oxford: Littman (The Littman Library of Jewish Civilization).
- 1992. *Los Judíos de España*. Madrid: Editorial Mapfre.
- 1992. "La conversión en masa y el problema de los conversos en el siglo 15," in *Morešet Sefarad: El Legado de Sefarad*. Edited by Haim Beinart. Jerusalem: Hebrew University. Pages 355 to 392.
- 1981. *Conversos on Trial: The Inquisition in Ciudad Real*. Jerusalem: Magnes.

Beider, Alexander. 2019. "Why Do So Many Sephardic Jews Have Christian Lastnames?" in *Forward*. January 22.

Bibliography

Bejarano Butierrez, Juan Marcos. 2016. *Secret Jews: The Complex Identity of Crypto-Jews and Crypto-Judaism.* Tel Aviv: Yaron Publishing.

Bel Bravo, María Antonia.
- 1988. *El auto fe de 1593: los conversos granadinos de origen judío.* Granada: Universidad de Granada.
- 1997. *Sefarad: Los Judíos de España.* Madrid: SÍLEX.

Bell, Dean Phillip. 2007. *Jews in the Early Modern World.* Lanham: Rowman & Littlefield Publishers.

Bentley, Jerry H. and Herbert F. Ziegler. 2006. *Traditions Encounters: A Global Perspective on the Past.* Third edition. New York: McGraw Hill.

Bentolila, Yaakov. 2008. "La lengua común (coiné) judeo-española entre el Este y el Oeste," in *El Presente: Estudio sobre la cultural sefardí*, editores Tamar Alexander and Yaakov Ventolila. Vol. 2. December. pp. 159-176.

Ben-Ur, Aviva.
- 2009. "A Matriarchal Matter: Slavery, Conversion, and Upward Mobility in Suriname's Jewish Community," in *Atlantic Diasporas: Jews, Conversos, and Crypto-Jews in the Age of Mercantilism, 1500-1800.* Richard L. Kagan and Philip D. Morgan, editors. Pages 152-169.
- 2012. *Sephardic Jews in America: A Diasporic History.* New York: New York University Press.

Benveniste, Arthur. 1997. "Finding our Lost Brothers and Sisters: the Crypto-Jews of Brazil," in *Western States Jewish History.* Vol. XXIX, No. 3.

Bibliowicz, Azriel. 2001. "Intermitencia, ambivalencia y descrepancia: historia de la presencia judía en Colombia," in *América Latine Historie et Mémoire*, No. 3.

Bidney, David. 1953. *Theoretical Anthropology.* New York: Columbia University Press. Second, augmented edition, 1967. New York: Schocken Books.

Bidney, David, editor. 1963. *The Concept of Freedom in Anthropology.* The Hague: Mouton & Co.

Birnbaum, Pierre. 2004. "French Jews and the 'Regeneration' of Algerian Jewry," in Ezra Mendelsohn, editor, *Jews and the State: Dangerous Alliances and the Perils of Privilege. Studies in Contemporary Jewry, Vol. XIX.* Oxford: Oxford University Press. Pages 88-103.

Birmingham, Stephen. 1997. *The Grandees: The Story of America's Sephardic Elite.* Syracuse: Syracuse University Press.

Blazquez Miguel, Juan.
- 1994. *La Inquisicion en America (1569-1820).* Santo Domingo, D.R.: Editora Corripio.
- No date. *Inquisición y Criptojudaísmo.* Madrid: Ediciones Kaydeda.

Bodian, Miriam.
- 2014. "The Formation of the Portuguese Jewish Diaspora," in *The Jews in the Caribbean*. Jane S. Gerber, editor. Oxford: The Littman Library of Jewish Civilization. pp.17-27.
- 2007. *Dying in the Law of Moses*. Bloomington: Indiana University Press.
- 1997. *Hebrews of the Portuguese Nation: Conversos and Community in Early Modern Amsterdam*. Bloomington: Indiana University Press.

Brooks, Andre Aelion. 2004. *The Woman Who Defied Kings: The Life and Times of Doña Gracia Nasi, a Jewish Leader during the Renaissance*. New York: Paragon House.

Brown, Corinne Joy. 2016. *Hidden Star*. Victoria: Friesen Press.

Bunis, David M.
- 2018. "Echoes of Judezmo in Syria," in *Caminos de leche y miel*, edited by David M. Bunis, Ivana Vucina Simovic, Corinna Deppner. Barcelona: Tirocinio. pp. 64-115.
- 2008. "Differential Impact of Arabic on Haketia and Turkish on Judezmo," in *El Presente: Estudio sobre la cultural sefardí*, editores Tamar Alexander and Yaakov Ventolila. Vol. 2. December. pp. 177-208.

Canelo, David Augusto.
- 2001. *Belmonte, judaísmo e criptojudaísmo*. Belmonte: Câmara Municipal de Belmonte.
- 2001. *Os Ultimos Criptojudeus em Portugal*. Grigny: Ammareal.

Caro Baroja, Julio. 1996. *Inquisición, Brujeria y criptojudaismo*. Barcelona: Galaxia Gutemberg.

Cátedra García, Pedro M. 1994. *Sermón, sociedad y literatura en la edad media: San Vicente Ferrer en Castilla (1411-1412)*. Salamanca: Junta de Castilla y León.

Castañeda Delgado, Paulino y Hernandez Aparicio, Pilar. 1989. *La Inquisicion de Lima (1570-1634)*. Madrid: T.I. Editorial Deimos.

Cesarani, David and Gemma Romain, editors. 2006. *Jews and Port Cities 1590-1990*. London: Vallentine Mitchell & Co., Ltd.

Cesarani, David. 2006. "Introduction" in *Jews and Port Cities 1590-1990*. Edited by David Cesarani and Gemma Romain. London: Vallentine Mitchell & Co., Ltd. Pages 1-13.

Chazan, Robert. 1991. *Daggers of Faith: Thirteenth-Century Christian Missionizing and Jewish Response*. Berkeley: University of California Press.

Cohen, Jeremy. 1999. *Living Letters of the Law: Ideas of the Jew in Medieval Catholicism*. Berkeley: University of California Press.

Bibliography

Cohen, Martin A.
- 2001. *The Martyr: Luis de Carvajal, a Secret Jew in Sixteenth Century Mexico*. Albuquerque: University of New Mexico Press.
- 1977. *Consolation for the Tribulations of Israel*. Philadelphia: The Jewish Publication Society.

Croitoru Rotbaum, Itic. 1967. *De Sefarad al Neosefardismo: contribucion a la Historia de Colombia*. Tomo I. Bogota: Editorial Kelly. 1971. Tomo II. De Sefarad al Neosefardismo. Documentos Coloniales: originados en el Santo Oficio del Tribunal de la Inquisicion de Cartagena de Indias. Bogota: Tipografia Hispana.

Crow, John A. 1985. *Spain the Root and the Flower: An Interpretation of Spain and the Spanish People*. Third edition, expanded and updated. Berkeley: University of California Press.

D'Abrera, A.Y. 2008. T*he Tribunal of Zaragoza and Crypto-Judaism, 1484-1515*. Brepols Publishers.

Davis, Ruth F., editor. 2015. *Musical Exodus: Al-Andalus and Its Jewish Diasporas*. New York: Rowman & Littlefield.

Diaz del Castillo, Bernal. 2009 edition. *Historia Verdadera de la Conquista de la Nueva España*. Mexico: Editorial Porrúa.

Diaz-Mas, Paloma. 1997. *Los Sefardíes: Historia, Lengua y Cultura*. Barcelona: Rio Piedras Press.

Diaz-Mas, Paloma and George K. Zucker. 2007. *Sephardim: The Jews of Spain*. Chicago: University of Chicago Press.

Dimont, Max. 1962. *Jews, God, and History*. New York: Simon and Schuster.

Dobrinsky, Herbert C. 2002. *A Treasury of Sephardic Laws and Customs*. New York: Yeshiva University Press.

Duncan Hart, Ron
- 2016a. *Fractured Faiths: Spanish Judaism, the Inquisition, and New World Identities*. Co-editor with Roger L. Martínez and Josef Diaz. New Mexico History Museum catalogue. Albuquerque: Fresco Books.
- 2016b. "The Exile Factor." *El Palacio*. Vol. 121. No. 2. Santa Fe: Museum of New Mexico Press.
- 2016c. *Sephardic Jews: History, Religion and People*. Santa Fe Gaon Books.
- 2015. *Judaism*. Santa Fe: Gaon Books.
- 2010. "Colombia," in *Encyclopedia of Jews in the Islamic World*. Edited by Norman A. Stillman. The Hague: Brill Academic Publishers.
- 2006. "World Politics Illegal Jews and the Inquisition of Cartagena." *Halapid*. Vol. XIII. No. 3. Fall.
- 2004. "Damia al-Kahina" in *Great Lives from History: The Middle Ages and Pre-Renaissance*. Leslie Ellen Jones, editor. Pasadena: Salem Press. Pages 604-606.

- 2002. "St. Vicente Ferrer and the Anti-Semitism of Fifteenth Century Spain." *HaLapid*. Vol.IX. No. 2. Spring.

Elazar, Daniel J. 1989. *The Other Jews: the Sephardim Today.* New York: Basic Books.

Elbaz, Vanessa Paloma.
- In Press. "Intertwined Identities: Arabic, Spanish and Hebrew as Intrinsic Elements in the Language and Music of Northern Morocco's Jews," in Proceedings of the Conference on the Jews of Morocco UCL, Hilary Pomeroy, editor. Netherlands: Brill.
- 2018a "Contemporary Jewish Women's Songs from Northern Morocco: Core Role and Function of a Forgotten Repertoire." Ph.D. dissertation. Paris: National Institute for Oriental Languages and Civilization, Sorbonne. Original in French.
- 2018b. "Los Cantares de las Antiguas: Recuerdos sobre la transmission femenina en el norte de Marruecos" Actas del 18 Congreso de Estudios Sefardíes, Madrid: CSIC.
- 2017a. "Kol B'Isha Erva" eds. Doris Gray & Nadia Sonneveld, *Women and Social Change in North Africa: What Counts as Revolutionary?* Cambridge: Cambridge University Press, pp. 263-288.
- 2016. "De tu boca a los cielos: Jewish women's songs in Northern Morocco as Oracles of Communal Holiness" *Hesperis-Tamuda LI* (3), pp. 239-261.
- 2015a. "Judeo-Spanish Melodies in the Liturgy of Tangier: Feminine Imprints in a Masculine Space." *Musical Exodus: Al-Andalus and its Jewish Diasporas.* ed. Ruth Davis, Lanham: Rowman & Littlefield, pp. 25-43.
- 2015b "The Power in Transmission: Haketia as a Vector for Women's Communal Power" Judeo-Spanish and the Making of a Community. ed. Bryan Kirschen, UK: Cambridge Scholars Publishing, pp. 172-193.
- 2012. "Judeo-Spanish in Morocco: language, identity, separation or integration?" in La Bienvenue et l'adieu: Migrants juifs et musulmans au Maghreb (XVe au XXe siècle) ed. Frederique Abecassis, Karima Direche et Rita Aouad, Casablanca: La Croisée des chemins, Vol I, pp. 103-112.
- 2009a. "¡Ay Esterica! Lover, Mother, Bride, Saint or Adulteress? Gender, Language, Ritual and Power in Romances from Tangier's Jews," Tangier at the Crossroads, ed. Khalid Amine, Tangier: ICPS, pp. 53-58.
- 2009b. "Gender and Liturgy in Music: Masculine and Feminine Forms of Language and Ritual in Sephardic Secular and Sacred Music," in *Perspectives on Jewish Music: Secular and Sacred.* Jonathan L. Friedmann, editor. New York, Toronto: Lexington Books, pp.77-96.

Bibliography

Elizondo, Ricardo. 1987. *Los sefarditas en Nuevo León, Remincencias en el folklor.* Monterrey: Archive General del Estado de Nuevo León

Elkin, Judith Laikin. 1998. *The Jews of Latin America.* Revised Edition. New York: Holmes & Meier Publishers, Inc.

Elkin, Judith Laikin and Gilbert W. Merkx, editors. 1987. *The Jewish Presence in Latin America.* Boston: Allen & Unwin, Inc.

Faber, Eli. 1998. *Jews, Slaves and the Slave Trade.* New York: New York University Press.

Fawcett, Luise and Eduardo Posada Carbo. 1998. "Árabes y Judíos en el desarrollo del Caribe Colombiano, 1850-1950" in *Boletín Cultural y Bibliográfico.* Bogotá: Biblioteca Luis Ángel Arango. Vol. XXXV. No. 49. Pages 3-29.

Feitler, Bruno. 2009. "Jews and New Christians in Dutch Brazil, 1630-1654," in *Atlantic Diasporas: Jews, Conversos, and Crypto-Jews in the Age of Mercantilism, 1500-1800.* Richard L. Kagan and Philip D. Morgan, editors. Pages 123-151.

Ferry, Barbara and Debbie Nathan. 2000. "Mistaken Identity? The Case of New Mexico's 'Hidden Jews,'" in *The Atlantic.* December. Pages 85-96.

Fine, Marcia. 2017. *Hidden Ones: A veil of Memories.* L'Image Press, LLC.

Finn, James. 2012. *Sephardim: History of the Jews, Spain and Portugal.* Forgotten Books.

Foster, George. 1988. "The Validating Role of the Humoral Theory in Traditional Spanish-American Therapeutics," in *American Ethnologist.* Vol. 15, No. 1, pages 120-135.

Freeman, Charles. 2002. *The Closing of the Western Mind: Rise of Faith and the Fall of Reason.* London: William Heineman.

Garcia, Charles. 2012. "Was Columbus secretly a Jew?" Special to CNN.

Garcia-Arenal, Mercedes. 2013. "Creating Conversos: Genealogy and Identity as Historiographical Problems," in *Bulletin for Spanish and Portuguese Historical Studies.* Vol. 38, Issue 1, pp. 1-19.

Garver, Eugene. 2018. *Spinoza and the Cunning of Imagination.* Chicago: Univerity of Chicago Press.

Gerber, Jane S.
- 2016. "Communal Integrity and Sephardic Identity: Jewish Life in Spain Prior to 1391," in *Fractured Faiths: Spanish Judaism, the Inquisition and New World Identities*, edited by Roger L Martínez, Josef Diaz and Ron Duncan Hart. Albuquerque: Fresco Books.
- 1992. *The Jews of Spain: A History of the Sephardic Experience.* New York: The Free Press.

Gerber, Jane S., editor. 2014. *The Jews in the Caribbean.* Oxford: The Littman Library of Jewish Civilization.

Giles, Mary E., editor. 1999. *Women in the Inquisition: Spain and the New World.* Baltimore: The Johns Hopkins University Press.

Gitlitz, David M. 1996. *Secrecy and Deceit: the Religion of the Crypto-Jews*. Philadelphia: The Jewish Publication Society.

Gojman Goldberg de Backal, Alicia.

- 2020. *Converts in New Spain*. Mexico: Inteliprix Ediciones.
- 2016a. Personal Communication. Santa Fe, New Mexico. May 22.
- 2016b. "Diaspora: New Identities, New Opportunities, and Renewed Persecution from 1492 to 1649," in *Fractured Faiths: Spanish Judaism, the Inquisition and New World Identities*, edited by Roger L Martínez, Josef Diaz and Ron Duncan Hart. Albuquerque: Fresco Books.

Goldberg, Harvey E. editor. 1996. *Sephardi and Middle Eastern Jewries: History and Culture in the Modern Era*. Bloomington: Indiana University Press.

Goldish, Josette Capriles. 2008. *Once Jews: Stories of Caribbean Sephardim*. Princeton: Markus Wiener Publishers.

Gonzalez Maeso, David. 2001. *El Legado del Judaismo Español*. Madrid: Editorial Trotta.

Gradwohl, David Mayer, 1996. "On Vestiges and Identities: Some Thoughts on the Controversy Concerning 'Crypto-Jews' in the American Southwest," in *Jewish Folklore and Ethnology Review*. Vol. 18. Nos.1-2, pages 83-84.

Graizbord, David

- 2019. "Men and Women of the Nation: How the Inquisition's conversos defined Jewish religious and ethnic identity in ways that are still prevalent today," *Tablet Magazine*. https://www.tabletmag.com/jewish-arts-and-culture/289739/men-and-women-of-the-nation.
- 2013. "Who and What was a Jew? Some Considerations for the Historical Study of New Christians," in *Anais de História de Além-Mar*, Vol. XIV, Pages 15-44.
- 2008. "Religion and Ethnicity Among 'Men of the Nation': Toward a Realistic Interpretation," *Jewish Social Studies: History, Culture, Society*, n.s. 15 no. 1 (Fall). Pages 32-65.
- 2007."Philosemitism in Late Sixteenth-and Seventeenth-Century Iberia: Refracted Judeophobia?" in *Sixteenth Century Journal*. Vol. XXXVIII, No. 3. Pages 657-682.
- 2006. "Inquisitorial Ideology at Work in an Auto De Fe, 1680: Religion in the Context of Proto-Racism." in *Journal of Early Modern History*. Vol. 10. No. 4. Pages 331-360.
- 2003. *Souls in Dispute: Converso Identities in Iberia and the Jewish Diaspora, 1580-1700*. Philadelphia: University of Pennsylvania Press.

Greenleaf, Richard E. 1969. T*he Mexican Inquisition of the Sixteenth Century*. Albuquerque: University of New Mexico Press.

Gubbay, Lucian and Abraham Levy. 1992. *The Sephardim: Their Glorious Tradition from the Babylonian Exile to the Present Day*. London: Carnell Ltd.

Bibliography

Guibovich Perez, Pedro. 1998. *En Defensa de Dios: Estudios y documentos sobre la Inquisición en el Peru*. Lima: Ediciones del Congreso del Peru.

Halevy, Schulamith C.
- 2011. "Descendants of the Anusim (Crypto-Jews) in Contemporary Mexico." Updated version of a Thesis for the Degree of Doctor of Philosophy. Jerusalem: Hebrew University.
- 1999. "Jewish Practices Among Contemporary Anusim," *Shofar*. No. 18, pp 80-99.
- 1996. "Manifestations of Crypto-Judaism in the American Southwest," in *Jewish Folklore and Ethnology Review*. Vol. 18. Nos.1-2, pages 68-76.

Halkin, Abraham. 2009. *Epistles of Maimonides: Crisis and Leadership*. Philadelphia: Jewish Publication Society.

Hamui Sutton, Silvia.
- 2016. *Lyrical Eroticism in Judeo-Spanish Songs*. Santa Fe: Gaon Books.
- 2010. *El sentido oculto de las palabras en los testimonios inquisitoriales de las Rivera: judaizantes de la Nueva España*. Mexico City: Universidad Nacional Autónoma de México.
- 2008. *Cantos Judeo-Españoles: simbologia poética y visión del mundo*. Santa Fe: Gaon Books.

Heller, Reginaldo Jonas. 2010. "Judeus do Eldorado: reinventando uma identidade en plena Amazônia," in Rio de Janeiro: E-papers.

Herz, Cary. 2009. *New Mexico' Crypto-Jews: Image and Memory*. Albuquerque: University of New Mexico Press.

Hordes, Stanley M.
- 2016. "To the Far Northern Frontier of New Spain: Converso Settlement in New Mexico, 1598-1900," in *Fractured Faiths: Spanish Judaism, the Inquisition and New World Identities*, edited by Roger L Martínez, Josef Diaz and Ron Duncan Hart. Albuquerque: Fresco Books.
- 2005. *To the End of the Earth: A History of the Crypto-Jews of New Mexico*. New York: Columbia University Press.
- 1993. "The Sephardic Legacy in the Southwest: The Crypto-Jews of New Mexico." *Jewish Folklore and Ethnology Review*. Vol 15. pages 137-138.
- 1982. "The Inquisition as Economic and Political Agent: The Campaign of the Mexican Holy Office Against the Crypto-Jews in the Mid-Seventeenth Century." *The Americas*. Vol. 39, No. 1, pages 23-38.

Israel, Jonathan.
- 1998a. *European Jewry in the Age of Mercantilism 1550-1750*. Oxford: Littman Library of Jewish Civilization.
- 1998b. *The Dutch Republic: Its Rise, Greatness, and Fall 1477-1806*. Oxford: Oxford University Press.

- 2003. *Conflicts of Empires: Spain, the Low Countries and the Struggle for World Supremacy, 1585-1713*. New York: Bloomsbury Publishing.
- 2009. "Jews and Crypto-Jews in the Atlantic World Systems, 1500-1800," in *Atlantic Diasporas: Jews, Conversos, and Crypto-Jews in the Age of Mercantilism, 1500-1800*. Kagan, Richard L. and Morgan, Philip D. Editors. Baltimore: The Johns Hopkins University Press. Pages 3-17.

Jacobs, Janet Liebman. 2002. *Hidden Heritage: The Legacy of the Crypto-Jews*. Berkeley: University of California Press.

Kagan, Richard L. and Morgan, Philip D. Editors. 2009. *Atlantic Diasporas: Jews, Conversos, and Crypto-Jews in the Age of Mercantilism, 1500-1800*. Baltimore: The Johns Hopkins University Press.

Kamen, Henry.
- 2003. *Empire: How Spain became a World Power 1492-1763*. New York: Harper Collins Publishers.
- 1997. *The Spanish Inquisition: a Historical Revision*. New Haven: Yale University Press.

Kasteen, Josef. 1936. *History and Destiny of the Jews*. Garden City, Garden City Publishing Co., Inc.

Klein, Misha. 2016. *Kosher Feijoada and Other Paradoxes of Jewish Life in Sao Paulo*. Gainesville: University Press of Florida.

Klooster, Win. 2009. "Networks of Colonial Entrepreneurs: The Founders of the Jewish Settlements in Dutch America, 165s and 1660s," in *Atlantic Diasporas: Jews, Conversos, and Crypto-Jews in the Age of Mercantilism, 1500-1800*. Richard L. Kagan and Philip D. Morgan, editors. Pages 33-49.

Kritzler, Edward. 2008. *Jewish Pirates of the Caribbean*. New York: Doubleday.

Kunin, Seth D.
- 2016. "Fluid Identities: New Mexican Crypto-Jews in the Late Twentieth Century," in *Fractured Faiths: Spanish Judaism, the Inquisition and New World Identities*, edited by Roger L Martínez, Josef Diaz, and Ron Duncan Hart. Albuquerque: Fresco Books.
- 2009. *Juggling Identities: Identity and Authenticity among the Crypto-Jews*. New York: Columbia University Press.

Leite, Naomi. 2017. *Unorthodox Kin: Portuguese Marranos and the Global Search for Belonging*. Oakland: University of California Press.

Leon, Rabbi Stephen. 2017. *The Third Commandment and the Return of the Anusim*. Santa Fe: Gaon Books.

Levine, Frances.
- 2016a. *Doña Teresa Confronts the Spanish Inquisition: Seventeenth Century New Mexico Drama*. Norman: University of Oklahoma Press.

Bibliography

- 2016b. "Two Women and the Long Arm of the Inquisition," in *Fractured Faiths: Spanish Judaism, the Inquisition and New World Identities*, edited by Roger L Martínez, Josef Diaz, and Ron Duncan Hart. Albuquerque: Fresco Books.
- 2013. "So Dreadful a Crime: Doña Teresa Aguilera y Roche Faces the Inquisition for the Sin of Chocolate Consumption," in *El Palacio*. Winter 2012. Pages 52-59.

Levy, Rabbi Martin. 2015. Personal Communication. June 4. Santa Fe.

Lewin, Boleslao.
- 1987. *Los Criptojudios: un fenomeno religioso y social*. Buenos Aires: Editorial Mila.
- 1971. *Como Fue la Inmigración Judia a la Argentina*. Buenos Aires: Editorial Plus Ultra.
- 1971. *La Inquisición en Mexico: racismo Inquisitorial (El singular Caso de Maria de Zarate)*. Puebla: Editorial Jose M. Cajica Jr., S.A.
- 1967. *La Inquisición en Hispanoamerica: Judio, Protestantes y Patriotas*. Buenos Aires: Editorial Paidos.
- 1960. *Los Judios Bajo la Inquisición en Hispanoamerica*. Buenos Aires: Editorial Dedalo.

Liebman, Seymour B.
- 1983. "Review of New World Jewry 1493-1825: Requiem for the Forgotten." *The Jewish Times*. Vol. 9, No. 1. Jan. 14, 1983.
- 1982. *New World Jewry, 1493-1825: Requiem for the Forgotten*. New York: KTAV.
- 1970. *The Jews in New Spain*. Coral Gables: University of Miami Press.
- 1967. *The Enlightened: The Writings of Luis de Carvajal, el Mozo*. Coral Gables: University of Miami Press.
- 1964. *A Guide to Jewish References in the Mexican Colonial Era: 1521-1821*. Philadelphia: University of Pennsylvania Press.

Lopez de Mesa, Luis. 1963. *Oraciones Panegiricas*. Medellin: Editorial Bedout.

Maimonides, Moses. 1956. *The Guide for the Perplexed*. New York: Dover Books.

Marcus, Jacob Rader.
1953. *Early American Jewry: The Jews of Pennsylvania and the South*. Philadelphia: The Jewish Publication Society of America.
2012. *The Jew in the Medieval World: Source Book*. Literary Lessing.

Martínez-Dávila, Roger L. 2018. *Creating Conversos: the Carvajal-Santa Maria Family in Early Modern Spain*. South Bend: University of Notre Dame Press.

Martínez-Dávila, Roger L., Josef Diaz and Ron Duncan Hart, editors. 2016. *Fractured Faiths: Spanish Judaism, the Inquisition, and New World Identities*. Albuquerque: Fresco Books.

Mathews, Holly F. 1983. "Context-Specific Variation in Humoral Classification," in *American Anthropologist*. Vol 85, No. 4, pages 826-847.

Matt, Daniel C. 2017. *The Zohar*. 12 volumes published 2003-2017. Stanford: Stanford University Press.

Mccoby, Hyam. 1982. *Judaism on Trial: Jewish-Christian Disputations in the Middle Ages*. London: The Littman Library of Jewish Civilization.

McKay, John P., Bennett D. Hill, John Buckler. 1996. *A History of World Societies*. Boston: Houghton, Mifflin Co.

Medina Sandoval, Isabelle.
- 2012. *Hidden Shabbat: the Secret Lives of Crypto-Jews*. Santa Fe: Gaon Books.
- 2009. *Guardians of Hidden Traditions*. Santa Fe: Gaon Books.
- 1996. "Abraham's Children of the Southwest," in *Jewish Folklore and Ethnology Review*. Vol. 18. Nos.1-2, pages 77-82.

Medina, Jose Toribio. 1952. *Historia del Tribunal del Santo Oficio de la Inquisición de Mexico*. Mexico.

Mehlman, Daniel Rabbi. 2016. Personal Communication. El Paso, Texas.

Melammed, Renée Levine. 2004. *A Question of Identity: Iberian Conversos in Historical Perspective*. New York: Oxford University Press.

Mesa Bernal, Daniel. 1996. *De los judíos en la historia de Colombia: La azarosa y apasionante historia de los inmigrantes hebreos desde los tiempos de la Conquista hasta la colonización antioqueña*. Bogotá: Planeta Colombiana Editorial, S.A.

Mier, José María de. 1988. "Gobiernos del general don Tomás Cipriano de Mosquera" in *Historia de Colombia: la Nueva Granada y los Estados Unidos de Colombia I*. Bogotá: Salvat Editores Colombiana, S.A. Pages 1257-1279.

Millar C., Rene. 1996. *Inquisición y Sociedad en el Virrenato Peruano: Estudios sobre el Tribunal de la Inquisición de Lima*. Lima: Instituto Riva-Aguero, Pontificia Universedad Católica de Peru. Santiago: Instituto de Historia, Ediciones Universidad Católica de Chile.

Ministerio de Cultura. 1992. *La vida judía en sefarad*. Madrid: Dirección General de Bellas Artes y Archivos.

Mirones Lozano, Eunate. 1999. *Los judíos del reino de Navarre en la crisis del siglo XV*. Pamplona: Gobierno de Navarre.

Monter, E. William. 2003. *Frontiers of Heresy: The Spanish Inquisition from the Basque Lands to Sicily*. Cambridge: Cambridge University Press.

Moore, R.I. 1987. *The Formation of a Persecuting Society: Power and Deviance in Western Europe, 950-1250*. New York: B. Blackwell.

Moreno-Goldschmidt, Aliza. 2018. *Conversos de origen judío en la Cartagena colonial: Vida social, cultural y económico durante el siglo XVII*. Bogota: Universidad Javeriana.

Bibliography

Muñiz-Huberman, Angelina.
- 1998. *El Mercader de Tudela*. Mexico City: Fondo de Cultura Económico.
- 1997. *La lengua florida: antología sefardí*. Mexico City: Fondo de Cultura Económico.

Naar, Devin. 2016. *Jewish Salonica: Between the Ottoman Empire and Modern Greece*. Stanford: Stanford University Press.

Nadler, Steven
- 2018. *Menasseh ben Israel: Rabbi of Amsterdam*. New Haven: Yale University Press.
- 2018. *Spinoza: A Life*. 2nd edition. Cambridge: Cambridge University Press.

Navarrete Maria Cristina 2002 "Judeoconversos en la Audiencia del Nuevo Reino de Granada Siglos XVI y XVII" In *Revista Historia Crítica*. Universidad de los Andes. Pages 73-90.

Netanyahu, Benzion.
- 2001. *The Origins of the Inquisition in Fifteenth-Century Spain*. 2nd edition. New York: New York Review of Books.
- 1999. *The Marranos of Spain: From the Late 14th to the Early 16th Century, According to Contemporary Hebrew Sources*. Revised edition. Ithaca: Cornell University Press.
- 1997. *Toward the Inquisition: Essays on Jewish and Converso History in Late Medieval Spain*. Ithaca: Cornell University Press.

Neulander, Judith
- 2014. "Inventing Jewish History, Culture and Genetic Identity in Modern New Mexico," in *Who is a Jew?: Reflections on History, Religion and Culture*, edited by Leonard J. Greenspoon. West Lafayette: Purdue University Press. Pages 69-103.
- 2006. "Folk Taxonomy, Prejudice and the Human Genome: Using Disease as a Jewish Ethnic Marker," in *Patterns of Prejudice*. 40:4-5, Sept/Dec. Pages 381-398.
- 2003. "The Ecumenical Esther: Queen and Saint in Three Western Belief Systems," in *The Book of Esther in Modern Research*. Editors Sidnie White Crawford and L.J. Greenspoon. London: T & T Clark International.
- 1996. "The Crypto-Jewish Canon: Choosing to be 'Chosen' in Millennial Tradition," in *The Jewish Folklore and Ethnology Review*. 12: 1-2, Pages 19-58.

Nidel, David. 1984. "Modern Descendants of Conversos in New Mexico." *Western States Jewish Historical Quarterly*. 16:249-262.

Pacheco, Ana. 2016. *A History of Spirituality in Santa Fe: The City of Holy Faith*. Charleston: The History Press.

Patai, Rafael. 1983. *On Jewish Folklore*. Detroit: Wayne State University Press.

Perelis, Ronnie.
- 2016. *Narratives from the Sephardic Atlantic: Blood and Faith*. Bloomington: Indiana University Press.
- 2009. "'These Indians Are Jews!' Lost Tribes, Crypto-Jews, and Jewish Self-Fashioning in Antonio de Montezinos's Relacion of 1644," in *Atlantic Diasporas: Jews, Conversos, and Crypto-Jews in the Age of Mercantilism, 1500-1800*. Richard L. Kagan and Philip D. Morgan, editors. Pages 195-211.
- N.D. "The Manuscripts of Luis de Carvajal," https://www.khanacademy.org/humanities/art-americas/new-spain/viceroyalty-new-spain/a/the-manuscripts-of-luis-de-carvajal. Consulted July, 2020.

Perez Villanueva, Joaquin y Bartolome Escandell Bonet. 2000. *Historia de la Inquisición en España y America*. Madrid: Biblioteca de Autores Cristianos, Centro de Estudios Inquisitoriales.

Pike, Ruth. 2000. *Linajudos and Conversos in Seville: Greed and Prejudice in Sixteenth and Seventeenth Century Spain*. New York: Peter Lang Publishing, Inc.

Primack, Karen, editor. 1998. *Jews in Places You Never Thought Of*. Hoboken: KTAV Publishing House.

Pulido Serrano, Juan Igancio. 2016. "Assault and Fragmentation Emergent identities from 1391 to 1492," in *Fractured Faiths: Spanish Judaism, the Inquisition and New World Identities*, edited by Roger L Martínez, Josef Diaz and Ron Duncan Hart. Albuquerque: Fresco Books.

Quiros, Alfonso. 1986. "La expropiación inquisitorial de cristianos nuevos portugueses en Los Reyes, Cartagena y Mexico 1635-1649." in *Historica*, Vol. X, No. 2. Lima.

Rabkin, Orit. 2019. *Emma Lazarus: A Sephardic Woman of Letters*. Santa Fe: Institute for Tolerance Studies/Gaon Books

Ramos, Gabriela. 1988. "El Tribunal de la Inquisicion en el Peru 1605-1666: un Estudio Social", in *Cuadernos para la Historia de la Evangelización en America Latina*, No. 3. Cusco.

Ray, Jonathan. 2013. "Creating Sepharad: Expulsion, Migration, and the Limits of Diaspora," in *Journal of Levantine Studies*. Vol. 3, No. 2 Winter. pp. 9-35.

Rodrigues De Silva Tavim, Jose Alberto. 2011. "Jews in the Diaspora with Sepharad in the Mirror: Ruptures, Relations, and Forms of Identity: a Theme Examined Through Three Cases," in *Jewish History*. Vol. 25. pp. 175-205.

Roncancio Parra, Andres, editor. 2000. *Indices de Documentos de la Inaquisicion de Cartagena de Indias: Programa de Recuperación, Systematización y Divulgación de Archivos*. Bogotá: Instituto Colombiano de Cultura Hispanica. Ministerio de Cultura.

Bibliography

Roth, Cecil.
- 1964. *The Spanish Inquisition*. Re-issued 1996. New York: W.W. Norton & Co.
- 1932. *A History of the Marranos*. Philadelphia: Jewish Publication Society.

Roth, Norman.
- 1995. *Conversos, the Inquisition, and the Expulsion of Jews from Spain*. Madison: University of Wisconsin Press.

Ruderman, David B. 2011. *Early Modern Jewry: A New Cultural History.* Princeton: University of Princeton Press.

Sabloff, Paula.
- 1978a. "Second Interview with Loggie Carrasco". Albuquerque, NM. Unpublished manuscript. February 9, 1978.
- 1978b. "New Mexico Jews and Marranos: Recollections of Loggie Carrasco." Unpublished manuscript.

Sachar, Howard M. 1994. *Farewell España: The World of the Sephardim Remembered*. New York: Alfred A. Knopf.

Santos, Richard.
- 2000. Silent Heritage. San Antonio: New Sepharad Press.
- 1983. "Chicanos of Jewish Descent in Texas," *Western States Jewish Historical Quarterly*, 15, no. 4 (July). Pp 327-333.

Schama, Simon. 2013. *The Story of the Jews: Finding the Words 1000BC-1492AD.* New York: HarperCollins.

Schaposchnik, Ana E. 2015. *The Lima Inquisition: The Plight of Crypto-Jews in Seventeenth-Century Peru*. Madison: University of Wisconsin Press.

Schwarz, Samuel. 1925. *Os Cristãos-Novos em Portugal no Século XX*. Lisbon: Empresa Portuguesa de Livros.

Sharot, Stephen. 1980. "Jewish Millenarianism: A Comparison of Medieval Communities," in *Comparative Studies in Society and History*. Vol. 22, No. 3 (July, 1980) pp. 394-415.

Sloan, Dolores. 2009. *The Sephardic Jews of Spain and Portugal: Survival of an Imperiled Culture in the Fifteenth and Sixteenth Centuries*. Jefferson: McFarland & Co. Inc.

Snyder, Holly. 2009. "English Markets, Jewish Merchants, and Atlantic Endeavors: Jews and the Making of British Transatlantic Commercial Culture, 1650-1800," in *Atlantic Diasporas: Jews, Conversos, and Crypto-Jews in the Age of Mercantilism, 1500-1800*. Richard L. Kagan and Philip D. Morgan, editors. Pages 50-74.

Sorkin, David. 1999. "The Port Jew: Notes Towards a Social Type," in *Journal of Jewish Studies*, Vol. 50, No. 1. Pages 87-97.

Sourdis Nájera, Adelaida. 1998. "Los judíos sefardíes en Barranquilla: El case de Jacob y Ernesto Cortissoz" in *Boletín Cultural y Biblográfico*. Vol. XXXV, No. 49. Bogotá: Biblioteca Luis Ángel Arango. Pages 31-47.

Splendiani, Anna Maria. 1997. *Cincuenta anos de Inquisicion en el tribunal de Cartagena de Indias 1610-1660*. Bogota: Pontificia Universidad Javeriana and Instituto Colombiano de Cultura Hispanica.

Sutton, Wesley K., et.al. 2006. "Toward Resolution of the Debate regarding Purported Crypto-Jews in a Spanish-American Population: Evidence from the Y Chromosome," in *Annals of Human Biology*. 33:1. pages 100-111.

Tejado Fernandez, Manuel. 1954. *Aspectos de la Vida Social en Cartagena de Indias Durante el Seiscientos*. Sevilla: Escuela de Estudios Hispano-Americanos.

Temkin, Samuel.
- 2018a. *Luis de Carvajal de la Cueva: Los principios del Nuevo Reino de Leon*. Monterrey: Ediciones DeLaurel. ebook.
- 2018b. *Gaspar Castano de Sosa: conquistador, explorador, fundador*. Saltillo: Universidad Autonoma de Coahuila. ebook.
- 2011. *Luis de Carvajal: The Origins of Nuevo Reino de Leon*. Santa Fe: Sunstone Press.

Toribio Medina, Jose. 1978. *La Inquisición en Cartagena de Indias*. Bogota: Carlos Valencia Editores.

Toro, Alfonso. 1944. *La familia Carvajal*. 2 vols. Mexico City: Editorial Patria.

Toro, Alfonso, editor. 1993. *Los judíos en la Nueva España*. First edition 1932. Mexico: Archivo General de la Nación and Fondo de Cultura Económico.

Toro, Sandra K.
- 2012. *Secrets Behind Adobe Walls*. Santa Fe: Gaon Books.
- 2011. *Princes, Popes and Pirates*. Santa Fe: Gaon Books.
- 2010. *By Fire Possessed: Doña Gracia Nasi*. Santa Fe: Gaon Books.

Turnbull, Stephen. 1998. *The Kakure Kirishitan of Japan: A Study of their Development, Beliefs and Rituals to the Present Day*. Abingdon: Routledge.

Twinam, Ann. 1980. "From Jew to Basque: Ethnic Myths and Antioqueno Entrepreneurship" in *Journal of Interamerican Studies and World Affairs*. Vol 22, No. 1. Pages 81-107.

Vila Vilar Enriqueta. 1979 "Extranjeros en Cartagena (1593-1630)" in *Jahrbuch fur Geschichte von Staat Wietshaft und Gesellschaft Lateinamerikas* BD.

Wacks, David. 2015. *Double Diaspora in Sephardic Literature Jewish Cultural Production Before and After 1492*. Bloomington: Indiana University Press. 2005.

Wettstein, Howard, editor. 2002. *Diasporas and Exiles: Varieties of Jewish Identity*. Berkeley: University of California Press.

Whelan, Christal, editor. 1996. *The Beginning of Heaven and Earth: The Sacred book of Japan's Hidden Christians*. Honolulu: University of Hawaii Press.

Index

Dates

1391 55-57, 59, 64, 233, 240
1492 44, 46, 57, 63-65, 74, 78, 79, 86, 87, 167, 205, 225, 227, 234, 236, 240, 242

A

Abarbanel 75, 206
Aboab da Fonseca 93, 101, 102, 112, 207, 218
Abraham Senior 75, 77
Alhambra Decree 74, 221
Amsterdam 81, 93, 98-102, 107, 108, 110-112, 114, 147, 176, 177, 181, 207, 208, 218, 230, 239
Anti-clerical 119, 172
Antioquia 41, 118, 177, 183
Anti-Semitism 51, 86, 171, 203, 205, 231
Anusim Center 186
Apodaca, Maria 23, 218, 225
Aragon 46, 58, 205
Ashkenazi 92, 196, 206
Assimilation 66
Atencio, Tomas 32, 33, 203, 211, 228
Auto-de-fé 73, 132

B

Barcelona 47, 55, 58, 213, 228, 230, 231
Barros Basto, Artur Carlos 171, 174, 175
Bathing 140
Belmonte 81, 106, 169, 230
Ben Israel, Menasseh 98, 99
Black Death 45, 53, 63, 64
Bnei Menashe 169
Bourbon 143
Brazil 41, 87, 92, 99, 101, 110, 112, 163, 168, 177, 181, 182, 229, 233
Burgos 55, 58-60
Burned at the stake 25, 73, 74, 86, 114, 116, 118, 130, 132, 134

C

Camino Real 134, 140
Carrasco, Blanca Garza Enriquez 26, 225
Carrasco, Loggie 241
Carrillo, Charley 156, 157, 218
Cartagena 40, 110-116, 118, 141, 167, 183, 207, 208, 227, 231, 240-242
Carvajal, Bill 180
Carvajal el Mozo, Luis 25, 128
Carvajal family 60, 61, 127, 134
Carvajal y de la Cueva, Luis 127
Castile 46, 55-58, 60, 205
Catholicism 11, 25, 28, 45, 54, 61, 64-66, 78, 80, 83, 86, 172, 173, 176, 207, 213, 221, 230
Catholic kings 44
Chazan, Robert 203, 217
Christian intolerance 43
Cinewest 218, 225
Circumcision 145
Colombia 41, 87, 92, 94, 105, 114, 118, 125, 167, 168, 177, 183, 229, 231, 238
Colonial Crypto-Judaism 40
Columbus 46, 85, 86, 206
Community 175, 229, 230
Comunidad Sefardita de Antioquia 183
Congregation B'nai Zion 26, 185
Converso 11, 32, 58, 60, 62, 66, 79, 84, 94, 106, 125, 134, 167, 171, 181, 196, 205, 211, 221
Cortes 87
Cristiani, Pablo 47
Cromwell 99
Crusades/Crusaders 43
Crypto-Jew 11, 82, 106, 117, 131, 167, 209

Cultural Hybridity 94
Cultural Identity 225
Culture of hiding 35, 94
Curaçao 92, 110, 183

D

Death rituals 145
Diaspora 84, 86, 93, 99, 172, 217, 234, 242
Disputation 47, 58, 59, 221
Disputation of Barcelona 47, 58
Disputation of Tortosa 58, 59
DNA 169, 170, 200, 201
Dominican 45, 62, 71, 80
Drake, Sir Francis 110
Duke of Naxos 97
Dutch 41, 86, 92, 93, 95, 96, 98, 100, 101, 110-113, 117, 118, 131, 133, 147, 181, 207, 208, 233, 235, 236
Dutch West India Company 112

E

Easter 45
Edict of Expulsion 58, 74, 75, 79, 84, 213, 221
English 26, 41, 86, 92, 93, 95, 96, 99, 110, 112, 113, 118, 133, 147, 208, 241
Enlightenment 100, 206
Esther 82, 116, 145, 155, 185, 239
Ethnic Roots Movement 170
Expulsion 5, 44, 58, 64, 69, 74, 75, 78, 79, 82, 84, 85, 87, 99, 170, 206, 213, 221, 228, 240

F

Fasting 82
Fast of Esther 155
Feigned Conversions 65
Ferdinand and Isabella 46, 71, 74
Ferrán Martínez 55
Ferrer, Vicente 54-60, 203, 204, 230, 231

Forced Conversions 5
Fourth Lateran Council 43, 44, 203

G

Garcia, John 25, 218, 223, 225, 233
Gendra, Rabbi Jordi 21, 218, 225
Gerber, Jane 55, 62, 203, 204, 207, 223, 233
Gitlitz, David 76, 77, 82, 193, 205-207, 209-211, 213, 217, 233
Gojman de Backal, Alicia 125, 132, 209, 210, 234
Gold 74, 76, 114, 133
Golden age 39, 84
Gradwohl, David 195, 213, 234
Graizbord, David 66, 205, 212, 217
Grand Conspiracy 5, 111, 117, 118, 209

H

HaLapid 171, 174, 203, 219, 231
Halevi, Rabbi Solomon 58, 59, 60
Halevy, Schulamith 128
Herrera, Timothy 192
Hordes, Stanley 30, 34, 131, 145, 168, 171, 203, 208-211, 217, 223, 235

I

Ibn Shushan Synagogue 56
Inquisition 25, 30, 33, 35, 40, 41, 60, 62, 66, 69, 71- 74, 78, 80, 82-84, 86, 92-95, 97, 98, 105, 106, 108, 109, 111, 113-118, 125, 126, 128-132, 134, 135, 140-147, 155, 163, 173, 183, 184, 207-210, 219, 221, 223, 227, 228, 231, 233-237, 240, 241
Israel, Jonathan 53, 208

J

Jacobs, Janet Liebman 171, 217

Index

Jewish Emancipation Movement 99
Jewish holidays 58, 65, 108, 115, 130
Jewish law 58, 182
Job 155, 157
Judaizing 66, 73, 79, 82, 84, 86, 105, 106, 108, 126, 131, 132, 139, 142, 145, 208, 209
Judeo-Spanish 92, 160, 235
Judeus Amazonicos 182

K

Kabbalah 48, 50, 221
Kahal Zur Israel synagogue 112
Kamen 73, 77, 205, 207, 236
King Manuel 79, 80
Kosher 108, 117, 145, 173, 182, 183
Kunin, Seth 30, 31, 33, 64, 171, 193, 195, 217

L

Ladino 92, 97, 227
Latin American republics 93, 94, 170
Law of Moses 117, 118, 128, 129, 176, 230
Leon 26, 185, 212
Levine, Frances 139, 141, 210, 236
Levy, Abraham 234
Levy, Rabbi Martin 49, 203
Lighting candles 32, 41, 135, 145, 168, 176, 182, 194
Lima 40, 113, 116-118, 207, 228, 230, 234, 238, 240, 241
Limpieza de sangre 78, 127
Linajudo 78
López Mendizábal, Bernardo 113, 139
Loya, Sonya 20, 218, 225
Lumbroso, Joseph 129

M

Marranos 55
Marriage 145
Martinez Dávila, Roger L 60, 203, 204, 223, 237
Medina Sandoval, Isabelle 14, 213, 218, 238
Mejia, Rabbi Juan 17, 183, 218, 225
Mercantile 86, 95
Messiah 47, 50, 56, 83, 99, 154, 155
Messianism 50
Mexico 5, 10, 28, 30-32, 40, 41, 60, 61, 86, 87, 92, 94, 95, 105, 106, 113, 125, 126, 128, 130- 135, 137, 138, 140-142, 144-147, 154, 155, 161, 167, 168, 170, 171, 173, 184, 185, 193, 195, 208, 209, 211, 217, 219, 223, 227, 228, 230, 231, 233, 234-242
Mikveh 133
Millennial dreams 50
Minyan 115
Monterrey 185, 213, 232
Morocco 77, 81, 87, 91, 114, 147, 174, 182, 213
Moses 49, 94, 100, 117, 118, 128, 129, 145, 154, 155, 176, 230, 237
Moses de León 49
Muslim 39, 42, 43, 46, 48, 65, 74, 77, 78, 84, 86, 91, 92, 97, 108, 205, 221
Mysticism 48, 49

N

Nahmanides 47, 48, 58, 203
Nasi, Doña Gracia 91, 97, 98, 207, 230, 242
Navarre 46, 238
Neulander, Judith 195, 213, 239
New Christian 11, 61, 79, 134, 221

New Mexico 5, 10, 28, 30-32, 41, 87, 113, 125, 133-135, 137, 138, 141, 142, 144-147, 155, 161, 168, 170, 171, 193, 195, 208, 217, 219, 223, 228, 230, 231, 233-236, 239, 241
New Spain 5, 123, 125, 133, 235, 237
North Africa 219
Nuñez de Carvajal 127
Núñez Pérez, Luis 131

O

Oñate, Juan 133-135
Oral tradition 66, 160
Ottoman Empire 84, 87, 91, 93, 97, 98, 114, 211, 214, 228, 239

P

Paloma Elbaz, Vanessa 104, 169, 218, 225
Papal Bull 110
Patai 204, 212, 239
Pérez, Manuel Bautista 117
Peru 87, 92, 94, 105, 125, 167, 208, 228, 234, 238, 240, 241
Pope Benedict XIII 55, 58, 59
Pope Innocent III 43, 44, 47
Portugal 5, 11, 35, 39, 46, 79-82, 84, 87, 91, 93, 94, 96, 98, 101, 102, 106-108, 110, 130, 131, 169, 171, 175, 177, 196, 201, 205, 227, 233, 241
Protestant 31, 91, 95, 172, 181, 206
Purim 116, 155

R

Recife 101, 102, 111, 112, 181, 207
Re-Judaization 176
Retablo 154
Rio Grande 95, 134, 184, 185

S

Sabloff, Paula 211, 241
Saint Esther 155
Saint Esther's Day 155
San Benito 73
Santa Fe 4, 14, 134, 135, 137, 139, 141, 208, 219, 223, 231, 234, 235, 237, 238-240, 242
Santa Maria, Pablo de 59, 60
Santero 156
Second Vatican Council 170
Secrecy 40, 217, 233
Sepharad 9, 28, 39, 221, 228, 241
Sephardic Diaspora 86, 172
Seville 55, 78, 79, 111, 117, 240
Shabbat 58, 65, 82, 115, 116, 133, 141, 144, 195, 217, 238
Shabbetai Zvi 50
Silver 95, 110, 114, 116-118, 133
Society for Crypto-Judaic Studies 171, 219
Spain 5, 9, 11, 31, 35, 39, 42, 44, 45-47, 53-57, 60, 63-66, 71, 72, 74-82, 84, 86, 87, 91, 93, 95, 96, 98, 105, 108, 110, 111, 123, 125, 130-134, 141, 147, 167-170, 176, 177, 184, 194, 196, 200, 201, 203-208, 213, 217, 219, 221, 223, 225, 228, 231, 233, 235-237, 239-241
Spanish Crown 62, 72, 113, 117, 127, 130, 135, 221
Spanish shipping 97, 208
Spectrum of Jewishness 83
Spinoza 99, 100, 101, 207, 228, 239
Sugar 40, 81, 96, 110, 114, 181, 208
Surinam 208

T

Taxco 125, 130, 133
Teresa, Doña 139-142, 208, 236, 237
Toledo 43, 55, 56, 84
Tolerance 43

Index

Torah 47, 86, 99, 100, 221
Torquemada 71, 75
Trampas 138
Treaty of Guadalupe Hidalgo 170
Twilight of Crypto-Judaism 41

V

Váez Sevilla, Simón 130, 131
Vasco da Gama 80

Y

Yearning 25, 26, 50
Yeshivah 99
Yom Kippur 82, 106, 145, 155

Z

Zacatecas 125, 130, 133
Zacuto, Abraham 80, 86
Zohar 49, 237

The Institute for Tolerance Studies
is a not for profit organization (501-c-3) focused on
education about diversity in human life
and the importance of tolerance and co-existence
between people, going beyond religious, ethnic, racial,
and other differences.

www.ingramcontent.com/pod-product-compliance
Lightning Source LLC
Chambersburg PA
CBHW030138170426
43199CB00008B/110